3

LEARNING
•••••••••••••**services**

01209 616259

Classic Cars

THE

MASTERPIECES

Classic Cars

THE

MASTERPIECES

BROWN
BOOKS

Brown Books
255-257 Liverpool Road
London N1 1LX

Editorial and design by Brown Packaging Ltd

Copyright © 1996 Aerospace Publishing Ltd
Copyright © 1996 Orbis Publishing Ltd

Reprinted 1997

ISBN 1-897884-19-2

A copy of the British Library Cataloguing in Publication Data is available from the British Library.

Material previously published as part of the partwork *The Encyclopedia of Supercars*

Printed in Italy

CONTENTS

INTRODUCTION

The sleek lines of Chevrolet's Sting Ray, produced in the early 1960s. This car featured retractable headlights, fibreglass body and an awesome fuel-injected V8 5359 cc engine that generated 360 bhp. Built essentially for speed and reliability, the American motoring press went wild about this masterpiece when it appeared in their own backyard. The Sting Ray was an epoch-making car that ranks high in the automobile hall of fame.

The car industry was born in 1886 with the Benz Tricycle. However, 10 years later, despite the growing popularity of the horseless carriage in Europe, there were no more than six cars on the roads of Britain. The first car appeared on those roads in July 1895, when the Hon. Evelyn Ellis shipped his Panhard over from France and drove it from Southampton to his home in Datchet. At the first British Motor Show, held later that year, there were just five exhibits, including Ellis's Panhard. This was also the year in which the Fareham Police Court issued the world's first speeding ticket, 'for driving a locomotive [a Lutzmann] at 6-7 mph', the equivalent of 9.66-11.27 km/h.

By the turn of the century the French motor industry was booming, though the first master-piece was born in Britain. In 1904 Henry Royce and Charles Rolls had joined forces, and it was not long before they produced the Rolls-Royce 40/50 bhp Silver Ghost. Produced between 1907 and 1925, the Silver Ghost was powered by a six-cylinder engine. Like its contemporary, the Ford Model T, it was an Edwardian design that remained viable long after other models had become obsolete, thanks to the inherent qualities of design and the use of superior materials.

The particular car that really set the seal on this superlative model's greatness was the London-Edinburgh chassis of 1911. No other car at that time could match its performance. With the collaboration of the Royal Automobile Club it was driven from London to Edinburgh and back using only the top gear, and then, without any

alteration, was driven round the Brooklands circuit at speeds of 125 km/h (78 mph).

The Silver Ghost name was not used until the thirteenth car, however. This was chassis number 60551, ordered for use by the Belgian Royal Court. It was strenuously tested under scrutiny for 24,130km (15,000 miles), and then delivered with its bonnet heavily coated in silver plate. The model went on to set new standards of reliability, economy, speed and luxury.

Henry Ford, having established his company in 1904, broke the speed record the following year in his 999 special, which reached a speed of 147 km/h (91.37 mph) on the frozen Lake Michigan. The immortal mass-produced Model T followed, in 1907. Although it was a 15-million seller, it was utterly unlike the Silver Ghost in all but its ability to carry passengers from one place to another.

In Europe during the 1920s, motoring was still largely the preserve of the rich. As a result, it became the heyday of sports motoring, with many powerful models made for the pleasure of driving fast on open roads. These had large engines, often fitted with superchargers for that extra boost of impressive power. A few cars, such as the Duesenberg J and the Bentley, could now top 161 km/h (100 mph), and the manufacturers were beginning to exploit the publicity that was to be gained from motor racing success. Alfa-Romeo, Bugatti, Bentley, Chevrolet and Duesenberg all earned their reputations on the race track. The added bonus was that the technical experience that was gained by winning races, and the innovations made in order to do so, were quickly incorporated into the cars that were being produced for the ordinary motorist.

Mercedes-Benz masterpieces

Ford had announced the production of its quarter-millionth car in 1925, but by the dawn of the next decade America was turning out over five million cars annually (Britain's total achievement for 1930 was a little over 200,000 units).

The Benz tricycle had been a technological breakthrough. In 1899 a Benz agent, Emile Jellinek, entered and won the Nice-Magagan-Nice touring race in a Wilhelm Maybach-designed Daimler which he had entered under the pseudonym Mercedäs, the name of his daughter. Immediately upon winning he ordered 36 cars, at a cost of 550,000 gold marks, on the condition that his agency became a sole agency for Daimler and that the cars were named Mercedes. In 1901, the first of these Mercedes cars were delivered and the following year the trademark Mercedes became protected. In order to survive the post-war pressures, the two internationally known companies of Daimler and Benz entered a contractual association in 1924, and merged in 1926 to form a single company, Daimler-Benz AG.

The marque gained fame under Paul Daimler for its six- and eight-cylinder sporting models, many of which were fitted with superchargers. These models encompassed the legendary SS, SSK and SSKL models, and culminated with the 500K and 540K. In 1936, the company converted the 500K into the 540K, with an engine capacity of 5401 cc (329.5 cu in) and a supercharged output of no less than 180 bhp. This was the ultimate production Mercedes-Benz of the 1930s, easily capable of 169 km/h (105 mph), a phenomenal speed for a road car of its day.

There was neither time nor investment money available after World War II to develop new models, so slightly modified versions of pre-war models were pushed back into production. Exports of British cars rose steadily to 50 per cent of production by 1956. However, these models were frequently, and rightly, criticised for their obsolete design, poor finish, unreliability and inefficient sales and service. Jaguar was one of the earlier manufacturers to show some innovation, and in 1948 the Jaguar XK120 was the undisputed star of the Earls Court Motor Show. It was a combination of knockout looks, Jaguar's

superb 3.4-litre straight-six twin-cam XK engine and a very affordable price tag. Its lovely design featured the curved rear quarter window that was to become a company hallmark.

By 1950 the UK was the largest exporter of cars, outstripping even the USA. This yielded such benefits as the creation of the Issigonis-designed Mini, which went on to sell over five million units by 1986 and became a legend in its production lifetime of 35 years. Sadly, though, the boom had spawned too many companies. As some marques began to disappear, others merged for the sake of a long-term future. One such amalgamation was that of Austin and Morris, which led to the formation of the British Motor Corporation (BMC), and to another automotive masterpiece.

The Donald Healey Motor Company had been making sports cars when Healey obtained a number of Austin components in 1952. From them he built a two-seater sports car which he took to Belgium and tested. On returning to London, he took the car straight to the Motor Show at Earls Court and to immediate stardom. So impressed was Sir Leonard Lord, managing director of BMC, that he concluded a deal with Healey on the spot. The Austin-Healey 100 was born. The real Healey masterpiece, though, was the 3000, which was launched in 1959 with a 124 bhp three-litre engine. It sold 40,000 units in its three versions, the Mk I, Mk II and Mk III.

By 1954 most of the French luxury car makers had gone, killed off by a combination of fiscal measures and old-fashioned designs, but Facel (Forges et Ateliers de Construction d'Eure et de Loire SA) went against the trend with the Vega. This had a 4.5-litre DeSoto V8 engine, which fed its 180 bhp through a two-speed automatic transmission. In 1959, an upgrade appeared as the HK 500 with a beautifully tuned 360 bhp 6.3-litre engine, but by the end of the following year Facel was bankrupt and its limited-production masterpiece also disappeared.

The 1960s – Detroit holds centre stage

Mercedes-Benz introduced the 220 sedan in 1959; it had tail fins, but they were a pale imitation of those which had sprouted on American cars in their heyday between 1956 and 1960. Those were the years when glittering Buicks, Cadillacs, DeSotos, Dodges and Oldsmobiles drew the world's attention with their panoramic windscreens, quad headlights and towering fins.

As the 1960s dawned, Detroit, having attracted its clientele by the wild overstatement of the packaging, concerned itself more with what was under the bonnet. The fins were replaced by a sculptural style that was sustainable; after all, they could not have continued to rise indefinitely. After the fizz of the 1950s, the 1960s formed a plateau when American cars still had that essential swagger resulting from cheap petrol, straight roads and big cars with big engines. Back in 1955, Chevrolet had already introduced its small-block V8 with 4343 cc (265 cu in). Now the horsepower race was truly engaged, with the 1960 Chrysler 300F engine producing 400 bhp. By 1961 Chevvy's was 409 bhp; Plymouth and

Rolls-Royce's Silver Ghost. Powered by a six-cylinder engine, it was an Edwardian design that remained viable long after other models had faded into obscurity. Sporting a superb chassis, the Silver Ghost was speedy, reliable and luxurious.

The Maserati Ghibli, probably the most stunning of all Maserati road cars. It used the same chassis as the Mexico model, though on a shorter wheelbase. The two-seater masterpiece was designed by Giorgio Giugiaro and sold 1274 units.

Dodge raised theirs to 413 bhp in 1962. The following year all the big manufacturers were offering 426 or 427 bhp on their option sheets, the ultimate muscle car ending up with the 6982 cc (426 cu in) 426 Hemi. This was the culmination of a whole series of hemispherical-head engines produced by Chrysler, which were widely used both on and off the track.

Ford's next gamble was in transforming the lowly compact Falcon into a sporty Mustang for 1964. This created a new market, launching Barracudas, Camaros, Cougars, Challengers, Firebirds and Javelins and the public loved them, especially with big V8s.

Introduced by Chevrolet in 1953, the Corvette had acquired a 5.7-litre engine in 1958, but for 1963 the Chevrolet Corvette was called the Sting Ray. It featured not only retractable headlights and a fibreglass body, but also a highly developed fuel-injected V8 5359 cc (327 cu in) engine that produced 360 bhp.

Texan Carroll Shelby, meanwhile, had installed a Ford V8 into the British AC roadster to create the legendary racing Ford AC Cobras. Unimpressed by the Mustang's performance, he set about transforming the car, replacing the

soggy wallowing with razor-sharp reflexes and introducing a raucous 4727 cc (289 cu in) V8 Windsor engine.

In a similar scenario, TVR's racing successes in the early 1960s had so impressed American driver Jack Griffith, that from 1963 for two years he installed 4727 cc Ford V8s into imported TVR bodies. In 1990, TVR reintroduced the Griffith name on a range of cars with Rover engines and far better handling than the original Griffith 200.

The Camaro, unveiled by Chevrolet on 29 September 1966, was curvier and with cleaner styling than its Ford Mustang rival. Within a few months of its launch Chevvy really let rip with the big-block 6490 cc (396 cu in) V8 tuned to either 325 or 375 hp. The Camaro went out of production in 1970, the year of Plymouth's winged wonder, the Road Runner Superbird. Conceived by Plymouth as a limited edition to meet NASCAR homologation requirements, it was produced only for 1970.

Meanwhile, Europe was creating masterpieces such as the Lamborghini Miura, launched at the Geneva Motor Show in 1966. This was the first true exotic or supercar, an innovative masterpiece. Ferrari's response was to produce its

own mid-engined road-going supercar – the 512 Berlinetta Boxer – in 1972.

The Ghibli, perhaps the most stunning of all Maserati road cars, was launched in 1966. Beautifully styled, it used the same chassis as the Mexico model, though on a shorter wheelbase. This two-seater masterpiece was styled by Giorgio Giugiaro and sold 1274 units during its 1966-73 production run. It was Maserati's stunner, with the 4.9-litre version producing a staggering 49 kgm (354 lb/ft) torque at 4000 rpm.

Aston Martin's legendary V8s

The 365 GTB/4, Ferrari's fabulous front-engined Berlinetta concept, was developed with the careful rapidity typical of Maranello, and subsequently made its public debut at the Paris Salon in October 1968. It gained its Daytona nickname, which immediately fell into common usage, from the world's press.

Aston Martin announced its magnificent DB6 at the London Motor Show in October 1965. Immediately recognisable as having been developed from the DB4 and DB5, its new bodyshell gave the impression that the DB6 was far more deep-chested and substantial. It was fractionally longer, with more head room and a different, swept-up tail, which gave a spoiler effect. For many years Aston Martin have used 'Vantage' to designate a tuned version of a standard production engine. The DB6 had a triple Weber-carburetted Vantage version which offered 325 bhp. The DB designation was dropped after 1972; thereafter the DBS model was redesignated V8 and produced in three versions: the V8 Vantage, V8 Volante and V8 Volante Vantage.

The Ferrari Berlinetta Boxer

Models hallmarked in the 1970s were to be spectacular: the surprising Citroën SM, the competing Lamborghini Countach and Ferrari Berlinetta Boxer, the rallying Lancia Stratos and the pair of Porches launched in mid-decade, the 911 Turbo and the 928.

The Ferrari 365GT4BB Berlinetta Boxer arrived in 1973 with a new multi-tube frame in a truly beautiful Pininfarina design. Ferrari's mid-engined competition version, the 512BB, sparked off a supercar race between Ferrari and Lamborghini. Lamborghini had drawn first blood with the Countach, by dint of launching it in 1971 when the BB was just a distant dream. When the Maranello model did arrive, it was the first Ferrari road car not to have a vee engine. The flat-12 power unit was derived from the company's Formula One boxer engine, with a capacity of 4390 cc, the same as its front-engined Daytona. Meanwhile, Lamborghini was busy working on a larger engine and announced an increase from a capacity of four litres to 4754 cc for 1982, and as a result was able to reduce the 0-96.54 km/h (60 mph) time to 4.8 seconds.

By 1985, the Countach was the fastest car to have been road tested by the British specialist press, at 286 km/h (178 mph). Unfortunately it came with a price tag that also made it the most expensive car imported into the UK. Price apart, what Pininfarina had done for Ferrari, Bertone did for Lamborghini: the Countach's body design was the company's finest.

More American masterpieces

Among the most significant cars of the 1980s was the Audi Quattro. In 1980 it amply demonstrated the advantages of four-wheel drive. This gave it an advantage not only in rallies, of which it won 32 World Championship events, but also in general road use.

The 1980s were a good time, not exclusively for the established marques. The Audi begins the decade and it ends with another Ferrari, but in the middle, against all the odds, the genius of a designer won through with two models reminiscent of the pioneering years. Marcos had been founded in 1959, was forced to fold in 1971 and was reborn 10 years later. On resuming business, the company offered kits which relied on a range of Ford engines for their power. In 1984 it introduced the Mantula, a model powered by a 3.5-litre Rover V8, but was otherwise very similar to the earlier Ford-engined cars.

Towards the end of the 1980s there were rumours of the advent a whole new breed of supercars. This time Ferrari was to get there first, when in the summer of 1987 it launched its limited anniversary edition. Designed to celebrate 40 years of Ferrari cars, it was also planned to upstage the Porsche 959 as the world's fastest production car. The F40 had a very dramatic appearance, sporting a large integral rear spoiler. Mechanically it was logically evolved from GTO, with the same design of engine that produced 478 bhp at 7000 rpm and a claimed top speed of 325 km/h (201 mph).

The first new challenge for the F40's pedestal came, surprisingly, from north America: the Dodge Viper. If the no-excuses, gutsy, heart-stopping Viper was short on legs to challenge the F40's top speed, the Jaguar XJ220, with a top speed of 341 km/h (212.3 mph), was not. A limited-edition production run of 350 was put in hand, and heralded a burgeoning generation of super-expensive supercars. They offer unusable levels of power and performance, combined with a staggeringly high degree of mechanical sophistication. These cars are technological showcases, masterpieces for a price that should ensure their exclusivity.

In recent years, Jaguar has been steadily consolidating the reputation of its saloon cars, breaking export records and establishing new levels of style, reliability and smoothness of ride. A new generation of Jaguar's sleek, fast XJ-S models appeared in 1991, with extensive, though subtle, revisions to the body, ushered in by the single-year production of the XJR-S, with its brutish, supercharged 5.3-litre fuel-injected V12 engine.

McLaren's tiny team of irrepressible romantics set out to produce the ultimate supercar, in which the driver is centrally seated, with dramatic gull-wing doors and a four-cam, 48-valve 6.1-litre V12, purpose-built by BMW Motorsport. McLaren's Gordon Murray sums it up when he says: 'we are confident this McLaren production model represents the pinnacle of twentieth-century high performance sports car design.' The F1 certainly takes your breath away, being engineered to an enormous level of refinement.

The last word in this introduction must concern Ferrari, the company driven for so long by the enigmatic Enzo. In the early days of its activities, Ferrari built cars which could be used with only a few minor alterations for Formula One, sports events or every day use. When announcing the F50, by way of a celebration of the company's earlier activities, Ferrari promised that it would be the closest possible thing to a road-going Grand Prix car.

As Formula One cars had evolved, it became impossible for the average driver to take the wheel of a racing Ferrari, and so in 1995 Ferrari decided once again to give all of its clients the opportunity to experience this adrenaline rush, in the form of the F50. Only 349 road-going F50s will be produced, because Ferrari estimated that the market potential was 350 units and Enzo always advised building one less than the market demanded. Production will span a three-year period, with the bulk of the initial 100 orders being destined for north America. They will beat the tougher emission requirements to be introduced there in 1997, where drivers are currently enjoying cheap petrol. Both these factors have helped to assure the company of an eagerly waiting market.

The Porsche 928, which is powered by a superb 4474 cc fuel-injected V8 engine, with one camshaft per bank of cylinders. The Series 2 model of 1984 had a four-speed automatic gearbox, which was an engineering masterpiece ahead of all of its rivals.

Ferrari F-50

This latest offering from the workshops at Maranello is the fruit of research based exclusively on Ferrari's vast experience in producing some 45 racing models and endless gran turismo and sports models. The F50 adopts the same constructional criteria as for a Formula One car. It is a mid-engined two-seater with a grand-prix-derived V12 engine, mounted as a structural unit direct to the carbon-fibre honeycomb chassis. The engine also acts as a bearing structure for the gearbox-differential rear suspension assembly. The carbon-fibre monocoque also encloses the 105-litre (23-gal) aeronautical rubber-lined fuel tank, the pushrod suspension and separate band braking system.

The F50, the direct descendant of Alain Prost's 1990 Formula One Ferrari, has become the company's new flagship. He drove the 3.5-litre 641/2 to six Grand Prix victories in that year, including Ferrari's one hundredth, which was achieved in the French GP. The F50 combines all of these Formula One characteristics, slightly modified to form a two-seater with a larger, though less powerful, 4.7-litre engine, down from 750 bhp to 513 bhp.

The superior styling of Pininfarina

The wildly exotic shape of the F50 is deliberately without any styling indulgence, gimmickry or luxury extras, to the point of austerity in the pursuit of pure functionality. The surfaces envelop the mechanics in a single sensuous sweep, from the front air intake to the rear spoiler. Volumes, as required by the project, are kept to a minimum. Pininfarina, traditionally Ferrari's body designers, have employed their vast talents to succeed in designing shapes that recall the prototypes of the years of the World Marque Championship by adhering to the ultimate design principal of form following function.

The F50 comes as a dual coupé and roadster, with the hard top taking about 30 minutes to alter guise, the car looking right in both forms thanks to Pininfarina's ingenuity. There is a hip-level black groove decoration around the body, and altogether the F50 is far more curvaceous than its predecessors. That said, the rear light clusters and shape of the air intakes represents an element of styling continuity inherited from the F40.

Also derived from its Formula One heritage, the F50 has, at both front and rear suspension, wishbones and reaction arms that act on spring and damper by way of a pushrod system. The dampers were specially developed by Bilstein. The front track is wider than the rear to guarantee a tendency to understeer – there is no power assistance to the steering. The steering itself is by rack and pinion, using a TRW cast-aluminium steering box. Amedeo Felisa, head

The breathtaking look of the Ferrari F50, a car that adopts the same constructional criteria as for a Formula One racing car. There are some concessions to road driving, however, such as the hard top, which takes about 30 minutes to fit.

of project development at Ferrari, declared: 'We had no interest in using power-assisted steering. Not on this car.'

The spring/damper control mechanism is linked to a computer-controlled electronic damper control system, using a combination of lateral acceleration, the steering angle and longitudinal acceleration. As with racing cars, all the joints linking the suspension to the chassis are of rigid type. On the rear axle, the suspension arms are fixed to an intermediate element between the engine and the gearbox, which acts as an oil tank, as it does in Formula One. The length of the arms so obtained improves the contact between the wheels and the ground, considerably reducing sweep and improving overall road holding, a factor that Ferrari has striven to emphasise.

The new ultra-close ratio gearbox, which is set longitudinally behind the engine, has six

The austere interior of the F50 is deliberate. The designers left no space for an audio system, but then again the V12 engine utters such a scream that it would be entirely redundant. This is a car built for performance – passenger comfort takes a back seat.

DIMENSIONS AND WEIGHTS

Length	4.480 m (176.4 in)
Width	986 m (78.2 in)
Height	1.120 m (44.1 in)
Wheelbase	2.580 m (101.6 in)
Front track	1.620 m (63.8 in)
Rear track	1.602 m (63.1 in)
Unladen weight	1230 kg (2712 lb)
Tyres	Goodyear Fiorano
Rear	235/30 ZR 18
Front	245/35/ZR 18

speeds plus reverse, operated by a manual control with lever, selector fork and rod and rigid shaft fitted on sliding couplings. The differential is of the limited-slip type with a differentiated lock percentage in drive and reverse. The hydraulic-actuated clutch is of the dry twin-plate type, with self-centring thrust bearing. In addition, a water-oil heat exchanger keeps the oil temperature constant.

The braking system, necessarily impressive for such a powerful car, was sized so that it would not need servo-assistance. Cast-iron Brembo discs, 33.02 mm (1.3 in) thick, are used – 355.6 mm (14 in) at the front and 335.28 mm (13.2 in) at the rear – splinted directly on the aluminium hub. The callipers are in aluminium with four larger ground cylinders, like those used in Formula One. Disc ventilation is guaranteed by a jet of air on the hubs, and the air is then aspirated by the disc ventilation effect. Cooling is guaranteed by dynamic air intakes at both front and rear.

The 65-degree V12 engine is accommodated in the rear of the vehicle. It is cooled by large, dynamic lateral air intakes at front and rear which cool the engine bay. In addition, disc ventilation is guaranteed by jets of air on the hubs.

The F50's cast-iron engine block is, apart from increased bore and lengthened stroke, identical to Prost's 1990 Formula One engine. The 65-degree V12 displaces 4.7 litres, has five valves per cylinder (three intake and two exhaust, which means a total of 60 valves), four overhead camshafts driven by two Morse chains, and uses titanium camrods and forged aluminium pistons to permit sustained high revs. The electronics and injection are provided by Bosch's Motronic 2.7 brain, and there is dry sump lubrication. At maximum power the engine produces 513 bhp at 8000 rpm, with maximum torque of 48 kgm (347 lb/ft) at 6500 rpm. The Ferrari F50 is driven through the rear wheels with the engine positioned amidships.

In creating the F50, Ferrari did not set out to build the fastest supercar that technology would permit, although at 325 km/h (202 mph) and 0-96.54 km/h (60 mph) in 3.7 seconds, this is no slouch. The company strove to obtain excellent driveability, and has attained a considerable advance over the F40. The screaming V12 prevents the F50 from being a quiet brute, which is perhaps why Ferrari left no cockpit space for an audio system. In fact the cockpit is spartan, apart from the driving controls. All functions are carried out by the three switches on the dash, three column stalks and two air conditioning knobs which are all that bedeck the console. This is the closest street-legal thing you can get to a grand-prix car.

F50 Styling

• front bonnet, which is deeply scored by the radiator air vents, with front wings much in evidence. This is because of the size of the wheels and because of the low bonnet and windscreen base

• fixed headlights, which are much lighter and more aerodynamic than the pop-up variety

• front spoiler shape, which is rounded at the centre to aid the passage of air under the body

• strongly wrapped windscreen, like those of group C prototype racing cars

• large lateral air intakes, which cool the engine bay, enclosed by the underbody fairing

• rear spoiler, which is raised and stretches the whole width of the car to balance the slightly negative lift of the underbody. It emerges from a gentle movement of the side and completes it naturally

Aston Martin DB6

A solid British Grand Tourer underneath its Italian-styled fastback lines, the Aston Martin DB6 was a racing-inspired thoroughbred which, with up to 325 bhp, offered superb handling and super-fast acceleration to beyond 140 mph.

Above: A 1966 Aston Martin DB6 in full flight, as it was intended to be driven. Impressed with its performance, Motor reported in January 1966 that "the Aston is in a strong position to say to 99 per cent of production cars: 'Anything you can do, I can do better'".

By the time the DB6 was launched, in October 1965, it was in many respects already outdated, even anachronistic, but it was still pure Aston Martin in character, as staunchly British as any Ferrari was overtly Italian, and still one of the world's most impressively rapid Grand Tourers.

That, more than ever by 1965, was how the Aston was being offered and received. As *Road & Track* put it in April 1966: "It's a dated design, but it's a car of great character, the expression of one man's idea of what a GT car should be at the time of its inception. If it has fallen behind the times, it most definitely hasn't fallen into the rut of being a car designed to satisfy as many people as possible and edify none."

The 'one man' they referred to was David Brown, the DB of all those Aston Martins from DB1 to DBS, and the man who picked up the reins at Aston after World War II, when the company was going through one of its periodic financial crises.

Brown, machine-tool maker and tractor manufacturer, had acquired his controlling interest in Aston Martin in February 1947, and immediately set out to stamp his own philosophy onto the cars.

The pre-war Aston Martin Atom was redesigned and was soon well on its way to becoming the DB1, but it remained underpowered. The solution was to use the six-cylinder engine from Lagonda, a firm Brown had also bought. The DB2 raced well, and soon evolved into the sports-racing DB3, which finished second at Le Mans in 1955 and 1956.

Aston's next road car, the DB4, as it was in-

Above: Here DB5s race at Brands Hatch. The DB5, launched in 1963, was the direct ancestor of the longer and more spacious DB6.

evitably called, was introduced in 1958, and started the 'second generation' of post-war Aston Martins, which was developed through the DB5 and culminated in the DB6.

Its development had started when Tadek Marek joined the company in 1954, and Harold Beach (who replaced Eberhan von Eberhorst as chief engineer in 1956) worked alongside him in developing a new chassis. As well as the race-developed Marek engine, there would be Beach's new chassis and, just as important, new styling. For the DB4, Aston wanted something totally new, and they went to Touring of Milan.

The design they produced was exceptionally handsome, modern yet retaining a strong Aston Martin flavour. It also used Touring's patented *Superleggera* method of body construction, in which the light alloy body panels were fitted around a light tubular superstructure – in effect a delicate skeleton in the outline shape of the body. To do that, Touring required that Aston (who would build the bodies under licence) change from their usual perimeter-type chassis to a more modern, fabricated steel platform. Harold Beach obliged in double-quick time during the summer of 1957.

Powered by a 3.7-litre, 240-bhp version of the handsome and modern twin-cam six, the DB4

Right: This rear view of a 1967 DB6 with Webasto sunroof shows the vertical Kamm tail which, with the higher rear window, improved both the rear seat space and the aerodynamics. The boot held a useful 8.1 cubic feet of luggage.

the start of one of their finest families of car. The DB4 was produced for five years, and constantly developed through five recognisable phases before giving way to its direct descendants, the DB5 and DB6.

The DB5 was launched in July 1963, and with its more softly rounded front and the original, neatly integrated roof and tail lines, it was arguably the most attractive of the whole series. Moreover, engine size had been increased to virtually four litres by widening the bore slightly (to the size already used in the Lagonda variant of the engine), and power was increased to 282 bhp thanks to that larger displacement and three rather than two SU carburettors.

A luxurious, high-speed Grand Tourer

A five-speed ZF gearbox was offered first as an option (replacing the four-speed-plus-overdrive David Brown unit) and later as standard (with a three-speed automatic added as the other option). Girling disc brakes replaced the original Dunlops, and 15-in rather than 16-in wire wheels accommodated the latest developments in wider Avon Turbospeed or Dunlop tyres. On the comfort side, adjustable damping was offered, plus the option of power-sapping air conditioning.

The DB5 was consequently a bit heavier than the DB4, but the bigger engine was more than capable of overcoming that, with a top speed still in the region of 140 mph and a 0-60 mph time of around eight seconds. As before, more power was optional, but this time in the standard-wheelbase chassis, in the guise of the 315-bhp Vantage model.

In just over two years of production (to September 1965) almost as many DB5s were sold as the DB4 in its entire five-year run, so the formula was obviously still working. Now Aston were ready to extend it further, with the DB6 – which was intended to offer more generous passenger space, more comfort, and better road manners, all without sacrificing performance or character.

Looked at from the nose, the new DB6 was identical to the DB5 save for a split bumper and bigger oil-cooler duct, but from the side and the rear it was very different. The changes were to improve the accommodation and the high-speed handling. Now, the DB was seen more than ever as a luxurious high-speed Grand Tourer, and increasingly suitable for four people where desired, even if the rear seats still weren't quite saloon-car size or standard. To that end, the wheelbase had been increased by around four inches, and the roof line raised slightly towards the rear, to improve leg and head room. The biggest changes were visible from behind, where the DB6 had gained an almost vertical Kamm tail, surmounted by a lip spoiler. That improved the downforce and thus the high-speed stability, lowered the drag coefficient marginally, and perhaps as an incidental bonus even gave just a tiny bit more luggage space.

Whatever anyone thought of the aesthetics, the DB6 continued the family's success. Mechanically, little else but the wheelbase (and a change from *Superleggera* construction to a steel inner shell) had changed other than in detail. Basic power was still 282 bhp, with 280 lb ft of torque; the triple-Weber-carburated Vantage engine now offered 325 bhp and 290 lb ft, making the Vantage a near-150-mph motor car. A Powr-Lok limited-slip differential was standardised and power steering was offered as an option for the first time, but it was still hardly a lightweight.

Production continued for just over five years, until November 1970, by which time over 1,500 examples had been built – making the DB6 the most successful Aston up to that time, if not quite such a quick seller as the DB5. In September 1967 another new generation had arrived alongside it, in the form of the more angular DBS, but the DB6 nevertheless evolved into a 'Mk II' version late in 1969. That variant had a slightly chunkier look with the wider DBS wheels and tyres, and fuel injection was offered as an option, but the latter found few takers and never really worked adequately.

It was rather a bitty exit, but it couldn't detract from what the DB6, and the DB5 and DB4 before it, had achieved – as some of the most elegant of all post-war British Grand Tourers.

Left: An immaculate 1966 DB6, one of 1,327 coupés built between October 1965 and July 1969, followed by a further 240 DB6 Mk IIs.

was launched at the Earl's Court Motor Show in October 1958. It was more refined and more sophisticated than any of the DBs that had gone before. It was a 2+2, and with the clear role of fast, luxurious Grand Tourer it was very well received. Its prospects were improved by the fact that its cousin, the DBR1, having finished second at Le Mans in 1958, finally won the world's most prestigious race in 1959 – en route to capturing that year's World Sports Car Championship.

It was Aston's finest hour and the DB4 was

Top: An Aston DB6 Vantage could accelerate to 60 mph in 6.1 seconds and to 100 mph in 15, but fuel consumption was heavy, at around 13 mpg.

Above: A superb 1968 DB6 Volante, one of only 178 built. It offered speed, comfort and open-air motoring in the grand style.

Inset right: This Volante version of the DB6's direct predecessor, the DB5, was capable of around 140 mph. In all, 123 were built.

Driving the DB6: *masculine motoring*

Sexist or not, there is no better way to describe the DB6 than as 'a man's car'. Generously-shaped leather seats and good-quality carpet were combined with big, easy-to-read instruments and well-designed, clearly-identified switch gear. The steering (assisted or not), clutch and brakes were considered heavy even in their day, but their solidity and power showed both Aston's build quality and their racing experience of the late 1950s. The standard 282-bhp DB6 was quite fast enough for a luxurious GT, while the 325-bhp Vantage would give rivals from Ferrari and Maserati a good run for their money, with a top speed of close to 150 mph and

0-60 mph in just over six seconds.

This performance was accompanied by exceptional flexibility and a very distinctive sound and feel from the straight-six; not as exotic as a V12, perhaps, but strong and musical. The chassis, too, had that characteristic Aston feel – mechanically solid, never sacrificing handling for softness. The ride was firm, roll minimal and control excellent – and made admirably exploitable by precise if heavy steering and strong, progressive brakes. The DB6 really was capable, too, of accommodating four people, but most of all it could never be mistaken for anything other than an Aston.

PERFORMANCE & SPECIFICATION COMPARISON	Engine	Displacement	Power	Torque (lb ft)	Max speed	0-60 mph	Length (in/mm)	Wheelbase (in/mm)	Track front/rear	Weight (lb/kg)	Price
Aston Martin DB6 Vantage	Inline-six, twin-cam	3995 cc	325 bhp 5750 rpm	290 lb ft 4500 rpm	148 mph 238 km/h	6.1 sec	179.5 in 4559 mm	102.0 in 2591 mm	54.3 in 53.5 in	3360 lb 1524 kg	£4,998 (1966)
Ferrari 275 GTB/4	V12, quad-cam	3286 cc	300 bhp 8000 rpm	217 lb ft 5500 rpm	166 mph 267 km/h	6.7 sec	173.6 in 4409 mm	94.4 in 2398 mm	55.2 in 55.8 in	2425 lb 1100 kg	£7,063 (1967)
Jaguar E-type 4.2 2+2	Inline-six, twin-cam	4235 cc	265 bhp 5400 rpm	283 lb ft 4000 rpm	139 mph 224 km/h	7.4 sec	184.5 in 4686 mm	105.0 in 2667 mm	50.3 in 50.3 in	2700 lb 1225 kg	£2,033 (1966)
Lamborghini Miura	V12, quad-cam	3929 cc	350 bhp 7000 rpm	271 lb ft 5100 rpm	172 mph 277 km/h	6.7 sec	171.6 in 4359 mm	98.4 in 2499 mm	55.6 in 55.6 in	2851 lb 1293 kg	£9,165 (1966)
Maserati Ghibli	V8, quad-cam	4719 cc	340 bhp 5500 rpm	326 lb ft 4000 rpm	154 mph 248 km/h	6.6 sec	180.7 in 4590 mm	100.4 in 2550 mm	56.7 in 55.4 in	3746 lb 1699 kg	£9,500 (1968)

Aston Martin DB6 Data File

The Aston Martin DB6 was the last version of a family that started with the DB4 in 1958 and which introduced Italian styling and the lightweight *Superleggera* form of construction to Aston Martin. That was continued through the DB5 line, launched in 1963, and although the DB6 (introduced in 1965) had moved away from *Superleggera* construction, the styling still retained Touring's sure touch despite the wheelbase, and thus the whole car, being longer to give proper seating for four people. The DB6's original power output was 282 bhp, which increased to 325 bhp for the tuned Vantage version, and in addition to that outright performance model a convertible, Volante, version was added to the range; this stayed in production until 1970, when US safety legislation seemed set to outlaw convertibles.

Above: The DB6 was the culmination of a line that began with the DB4 in 1958; unlike the earlier models, the longer-wheelbase DB6 had room for four.

Styling

From its classic fluted nose and faired-in headlamps to the trailing edges of its doors, the DB6 (split bumper and revised oil-cooler duct apart) was almost identical to the DB5, which was in turn little different from the later versions of the Touring-designed DB4; behind the doors, however, in the roof line and especially in the tail, the styling had been revised to suit the car's new identity as a more spacious 2+2 Grand Tourer. The four-inch longer wheelbase was well disguised, although new quarter-lights in the door windows hinted at it, and the higher rear roof line led to a shorter and slightly less elegant rear quarter-window shape. The overall length was only two inches more than the DB5's, and the biggest visual changes were around the tail, which was higher and much squarer, sacrificing the earlier cars' delicate sweeps for a fashionable (but admittedly effective) Kamm design. Following the lessons Aston had learned in sports car racing, the near-vertical slab tail was used to cut drag while the full-width lip-type spoiler improved high-speed stability.

Below: These side views show the subtle styling evolution of three closely related models: the DB4, DB5 and (bottom) the DB6.

Aston Martin DB4

conventional front light

short wheelbase

Aston Martin DB5

three tail lights

faired-in lights

same wheelbase as DB4

Aston Martin DB6

higher roof line

abbreviated side windows

rear boot spoiler

longer wheelbase

Left: Curved glass covers over the headlights faithfully followed the contour of the wings.

Right: The cut-off Kamm tail increased rear boot space and improved aerodynamics.

Above: The distinctive vent with trim flash aided air circulation in the engine bay.

Left: The cockpit was trimmed in leather, and the fascia was well-stocked with instruments.

The DB6 variants

As well as offering individuality, Aston have traditionally offered choice, and in the DB6 that extended to variants not only in performance but also in body style. The performance option, of course, was the Vantage – the productionised successor to the DB4 GT and the ultra-rare, ultra-lightweight, racing-orientated DB4 GT Zagato. As the DB6 Vantage, it continued using the name first applied during the DB5's reign. The convertible version of the DB6 was the Volante, and although Aston had offered a soft-top variant from the earliest days of the DB4, they only gave it a name when the DB6 was launched, at the 1965 London Show. The first 37 DB6 Volantes were in fact built on the shorter-wheelbase chassis of the old DB5, but the 'real' DB6 Volante (complete with a version of the coupé's definitive Kamm-tailed styling) was introduced at the 1966 Show. The strangest DB6 variant came from coachbuilder Harold Radford. Having done a similar conversion on a dozen DB5s, he built six DB6 Shooting Brakes – which were often described as the world's fastest estate cars, and with very little fear of contradiction.

Below: The Radford DB6 estate car was bizarre, but it offered space and pace. Pictured at bottom is a late Volante.

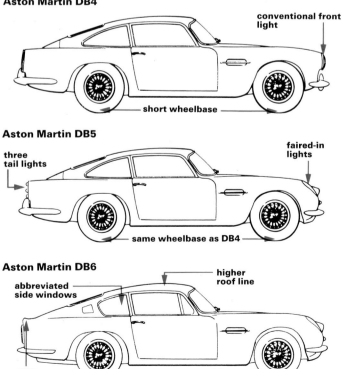

Chassis and running gear

Engine

The choice of Touring of Milan to style the DB4, and the adoption of Superleggera body construction, prompted a change from Aston's earlier perimeter frames to a simpler steel platform with box-section sills, and that carried through to the DB6, even though this car finally saw true Superleggera construction replaced by a rather more conventional structure of a fabricated steel inner shell clothed in aluminium panels. For the DB6, the wheelbase was extended by four inches over that of the DB5 (to just under 102 inches), and both the spring and damper rates were modified in sympathy with the car's improved 2 + 2 accommodation and slightly more practical image. The basic suspension layout, though, was unchanged. The front used unequal-length double wishbones, with coil springs, telescopic dampers and an anti-roll bar. The rear used a live axle, located by trailing arms and a Watt linkage and suspended like the front on coil springs, but in this case fitted with adjustable dampers; four settings were selectable from a switch on the dashboard and one setting was recommended for times when the rear seats were occupied. Steering was by rack and pinion, with assistance optional, standard-equipment brakes were Girling discs all round, amply cooled inside the knock-on wire wheels. A five-speed all-syncromesh ZF manual gearbox was usually fitted, but a Borg-Warner three-speed automatic was offered as an option, largely with an eye to the US market.

The DB6's twin-cam straight-six was a direct descendant of the engine designed by Tadek Marek for the DB4 – the first post-war engine intended specifically for Aston Martin use, as opposed to being borrowed from Lagonda. With racing in mind, it had all-alloy construction with wet cylinder liners, seven main bearings for the nitrided crankshaft, and chain-driven overhead camshafts. As launched in the DB4 in 1958, its dimensions were exactly square and a 92.0-mm bore and stroke gave a capacity of 3670 cc. This grew to 3995 cc for the DB5, with the bore increased to 96.0 mm, and those just over-square dimensions continued for the DB6. It was a handsome engine as well as a potent one; the layout of the cam covers showed the wide angle of the valves, set in hemispherical combustion chambers. Central, vertical spark plugs were fed by a distributor sited inboard of the inlet camshaft at the rear of the engine. Normal equipment was a trio of horizontal SU carburettors, and with an 8.9:1 compression ratio the DB6 engine produced 282 bhp at 5,500 rpm and 288 lb ft of torque at 3,850 rpm. With three twin-choke Webers instead of the three single-choke SUs, plus different camshafts and ignition timing and improved manifolds, the Vantage version of the engine (at no extra cost) offered 325 bhp at 5,750 rpm, but with no loss of either flexibility or reliability. At the end of the DB6's run, AE-Brico fuel injection was available, but very few buyers chose it, and most of those who did reverted to carburettors in the long run because they worked better.

Below: A rear view of the axle shows the Watt linkage, trailing arms, coil springs and adjustable lever-arm dampers.

Below: The DB6's drivetrain was conventional, with a front-engined, rear-drive layout.

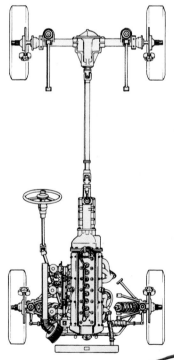

Below: An Aston Martin worker welds additional panels to produce a Volante chassis.

Below: Although the DB6's aluminium body panels were fitted to a sturdy steel shell, this longer car weighed little more than the DB5 with its far more complicated Superleggera construction of panels over a network of small tubes.

Above: The DB6's alloy block; Marek had planned on cast-iron for the original DB4 engine but Aston Martin's customary foundry, then too busy, told him Birmingham Aluminium was looking for work and thus the DB engines were produced in alloy.

Right: Knock-off wheel spinners made wheel-changing a rapid process. Behind the rear wire wheel (these were supplied either chromed or painted) can be seen the disc brake, trailing arms, coil springs and live rear axle.

Right: Girling disc brakes all round were standard, and wire wheels greatly aided their cooling. The brakes were quite heavy to use but were much-praised for their efficiency.

Left: Here is the classic twin-overhead-cam straight-six which made the DB6 a 1960s supercar. With its three single-choke SU carburettors the four-litre engine developed 282 bhp. With heavy under-bonnet insulation the car's interior was quiet up to 125 mph; on the Vantage version Weber carburettors were fitted, and under hard acceleration their intake roar tended to make the car noisier. All Aston Martin engines had to be carefully maintained.

Above: A front-sectional view of the all-alloy DB6 engine, in standard tune with SU carburettors, reveals the twin camshaft assemblies and the head's excellent flow characteristics. The spark plugs were located centrally between the valves. It was a very effective, if fuel-thirsty, design and developed tremendous torque and power.

Below: Most of the essential components were easily accessible under the aluminium bonnet.

Above: Behind the grille, below the DB6's bumper, was an engine oil cooler; oil consumption averaged 275 miles per pint.

Above: The wide grille covered a large radiator, part of a 28-pint cooling system, for the engine could run very hot when used hard and it was vital that an alloy unit did not overheat.

17

Aston Martin
V8 and Vantage

Born over 20 years ago, the Aston Martin V8 survived and flourished. By the 1980s there were Vantage and Volante Vantage versions, with over 400 bhp from quad-cam V8s and a top speed in Lamborghini Countach territory.

 s the 1960s wore on, Aston Martin realised they would lose their position as pre-eminent builders of supercars unless they could come up with more power. Rivals, notably Ferrari and Maserati, had steadily increased power outputs, and it was clear that for all its virtues the Aston twin-cam six was soon going to look pretty tame compared with the likes of the 4.4-litre V12 in the Ferrari Daytona.

Tadek Marek, Aston's gifted Polish-born engineer, who had designed the six-cylinder engine, set to work. If he ever thought of following Ferrari down the V12 route there's no evidence of it, and the appeal of a V8 layout was obvious – it was compact and smooth enough to give Aston-style levels of refinement. Marek's initial approach was to use as much of the old twin-cam six as possible, and the cylinder head layout was carried across intact. Thus the earliest V8 consisted of two four-cylinder adaptations of

the straight-six top end allied to a 90-degree V8 crankcase. A bore of 96 mm and stroke of 83 mm gave a displacement of 4.8 litres.

Unfortunately, this simple solution didn't really work, and by the time teething problems had been overcome and the engine had gone into production in 1969, displacement had risen to 5340 cc. The car it was to power, the DBS V8, was introduced in September that year, distinguished from its six-cylinder predecessor by the power bulge in the bonnet and by being no less than 21 mph faster in absolute top speed, while that massive V8 engine could power the bulky Aston to 60 mph in an amazing six seconds.

The definitive look to the V8 came in 1972, when the original fussy four-headlamp treatment was scrapped in favour of two large lights. Unfortunately, a fast, powerful and very thirsty car (you were lucky to return 15 mpg overall) like the Aston V8 was just what the world did not need during the energy crisis of the early 1970s, and

the car was lucky to survive at all. But late in the 1970s, when the world had recovered its appetite for high performance, Aston Martin set about turning the V8 into one of the world's most potent supercars.

. . . to 60 mph in a lightning six seconds

By this time the company had, in a curious reversal of the usual practice of the time, switched back from the original and troublesome Bosch fuel injection to four Weber IDF downdraught carburettors. Those carbs were just one of the things changed to form the tuned Vantage version in 1977, when the main choke size went up to 48 mm from 42 mm. The idea was to make the big V8 breathe better and the camshaft profiles were changed, larger valves fitted and

more valve overlap introduced. The changes were extremely effective; power output rocketed from 306 bhp to 360 bhp at 5,800 rpm and eventually up to 406 bhp at 6,200 rpm.

That extra power and torque required some chassis changes even to as able a car as the V8, and the rear track was widened, different Koni dampers fitted and stiffer rear springs introduced. A deep spoiler was added at the front, along with that distinctive Vantage hallmark, the blanked-off radiator grille; cooling air was now fed in through the spoiler vents.

Despite topping 4,000 lb the Vantage was extraordinarily quick; a rear brake pipe fractured on *Autocar*'s top speed test run, but by then the Vantage had already reached 167 mph, while it took a mere 5.4 seconds to reach 60 mph.

The British heavyweight was never regarded as the most sophisticated of cars; where the exotic continental opposition had mid-mounted engines, the Aston's was in the traditional place – right at the front. The car did not even have fully independent rear suspension, but supporters of its de Dion system would argue that it was just as good – the rear wheels were connected by a solid beam that curved back around the differential, which was fixed to the

chassis along with the inboard rear brake calipers. The net result was that each rear wheel stayed upright at all times and yet there wasn't the heavy penalty in unsprung weight that goes along with a live rear axle.

Keeping a truly high-performance car on the

. . . the Vantage had reached 167 mph

road is mostly down to the tyres and, in 1983, the Vantage was given flared wheel arches to allow for even larger Pirelli P7s, of 275/55 VR15 size. Everything about the Vantage was massive. In that, it followed the philosophy of the great prewar Le Mans-winning Bentleys. These may have been criticised by Ettore Bugatti as the fastest trucks in the world, but they were fast, strong and very successful. The Aston maintained that British brute-force approach; it was longer and higher than Ferrari's massive Testarossa, and just as quick, while it dwarfed Lamborghini's Countach. It went to prove that there is more than one way of building a supercar. Who's to say which is right?

Above: The Vantage model was introduced in 1977. This version, from the early 1980s, is recognisable by the blanked-off grille and bonnet scoop, and deep front spoiler.

Above: In 1983 the Vantage was improved and given larger 275/55 VR15 Pirelli P7 tyres. The switch required wider wheel arches to accommodate the extra rubber.

Above and left: Aston Martin introduced the convertible Volante model as early as 1977, but it was almost 10 years before you could buy a Volante with Vantage power. In addition to the usual Vantage features of front and rear spoilers, the Vantage Volante had skirts joining front and rear wheel arches.

Above: Astons in action. The V8 is an old design, markedly narrow and upright compared with today's supercars. Although the Aston has a virtually neutral weight distribution front to rear (despite its big front-mounted engine), its high centre of gravity does take some counteracting. The V8's de Dion axle does a good job of keeping the rear wheels as near perpendicular to the road as possible, but the Aston cannot match its more modern and exotic mid-engined rivals in terms of its ultimate grip.

Driving a Vantage: *sheer performance*

At first you might think that over 400 bhp in such an old design is a recipe for disaster, that the enormously powerful V8 is only good for straight-line speed, and that it can only be driven by a strong and courageous driver.

You would be very surprised, and pleasantly so. The Vantage may be rather tall and upright compared with exotic rivals like the Countach or Testarossa, and that does have a penalty in absolute cornering power. It leans enough to negate the grip of its massive low-profile Pirelli P7s, which like to be kept as near perpendicular to the road as possible. But if cornering limits are not quite in the mid-engined Lamborghini class the Vantage makes up for that with superb handling, courtesy of its perfect weight distribution and just the right degree of assistance to the power steering.

That, and some of the most powerful brakes fitted to any car, gives you the confidence to exploit the performance, and that's prodigious. In only 13 seconds you can be travelling at 100 mph, having passed 60 mph in a mere 5.4 seconds. The stability and ease of control even at 150 mph means the determined *autobahn* driver can go on to 170 mph!

PERFORMANCE & SPECIFICATION COMPARISON	Engine	Displacement	Power	Torque (lb ft)	Max speed	0-60 mph	Length (in/mm)	Wheelbase (in/mm)	Track front/rear	Weight total (lb/kg)	Price (1988)
Aston Martin V8 Vantage	V8, quad-cam	5340 cc	406 bhp 6200 rpm	390 lb ft 5000 rpm	170 mph 274 km/h	5.4 sec	181.3 in 4605 mm	102.8 in 2611 mm	59.3 in 59.0 in	4001 lb 1815 kg	£87,000
De Tomaso Pantera GT5S	V8, overhead-valve	5763 cc	350 bhp 5500 rpm	N/A	160 mph 257 km/h	5.4 sec	168.1 in 4269 mm	99.0 in 2514 mm	59.5 in 62.1 in	3219 lb 1460 kg	£47,621
Ferrari Testarossa	Flat-12, quad-cam, 48-valve	4942 cc	390 bhp 6300 rpm	362 lb ft 4500 rpm	171 mph 275 km/h	5.2 sec	176.6 in 4485 mm	100.4 in 2550 mm	59.8 in 65.4 in	3675 lb 1667 kg	£91,195
Lamborghini Countach Quattrovalvole	V12, quad-cam, 48-valve	5167 cc	455 bhp 7000 rpm	369 lb ft 5200 rpm	178 mph 286 km/h	4.9 sec	162.9 in 4138 mm	96.5 in 2451 mm	58.7 in 63.2 in	3188 lb 1446 kg	£86,077
Porsche 911 Turbo	Flat-six, overhead-cam, turbo	3229 cc	300 bhp 5500 rpm	317 lb ft 4000 rpm	160 mph 257 km/h	4.9 sec	168.9 in 4290 mm	89.5 in 2273 mm	56.4 in 59.1 in	3051 lb 1384 kg	£57,852

V8, Vantage and Volante Data File

Aston Martin have been producing sports cars since the company founders Lionel Martin and Robert Bamford joined forces in 1914. The first car was a modified Isotta-Fraschini, but the first Aston Martin (the 'Aston' part of the name coming from the Aston Clinton hill climb) appeared in 1919.

The company did not last long in its first incarnation. By 1925, just after the Motor Show, the company was wound up. It was then bought by £6,000 by W.S. Renwick and moved to Feltham in Middlesex.

The best and most famous early Aston Martin model was the 11.9HP International that was produced from 1926 to 1935. It was powered by a four-cylinder overhead-cam engine with dry-sump lubrication, and proved a very successful sports racer. The first post-war model was soon overtaken by events when the company was taken over by David Brown. Brown had also acquired Lagonda, and with it an engine designed by the great W.O. Bentley. The Bentley-designed 2.6-litre six-cylinder twin-cam engine powered the early DB series of cars: the DB2, DB2/4, DB3, DB3S. In 1959 Aston Martin won the Le Mans 24 Hours (with the DBR1) , after many years competing in the French classic, and the World Sports Car Championship along the way.

A totally new production model, the DB4, was introduced in 1960, and that evolved steadily, into the DB5 of James Bond *Goldfinger* fame and the 2+2 DB6. The end of that line was the differently styled DBS, which evolved into the V8 series shown here.

David Brown had sold out to Company Developments in 1972 and the DB tag was consequently dropped. Over the past few years Aston Martin has had a difficult time, but some real security was brought to the company with the Ford takeover of 1987, and the way was clear for new models like the V8 Virage.

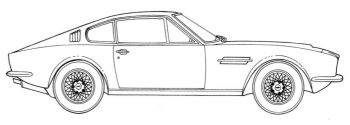

Below: The DBS V8, introduced in 1969, used the body shell of the twin-cam six-cylinder DBS.

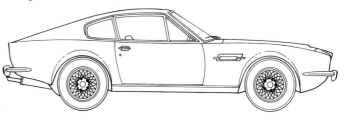

Below: A subtle restyling exercise in 1972 produced the V8, with changes to nose and tail.

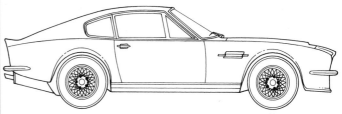

Below: The Vantage model featured spoilers front and rear.

Styling

Where the DB4 had a very sophisticated look thanks to the work of the Italian styling house, Touring of Milan, Aston Martin turned to a young British designer for the DBS in 1967. William Towns had originally been hired to design only seats, but his coupé shape was an instant success. Towns had essentially stretched the DB6's wheelbase by just one inch and widened the track front and rear by 4.5 inches. It was a more angular design than the DB6 it replaced, with more sharply defined lines to the tops of the wings and rectangular rear lights.

In retrospect, the DBS looks like an interim design between the DB6 and the V8; the redesign that changed it into the V8 improved the look considerably, making it appear far more substantial and every inch a British muscle car.

In 1977 Aston Martin followed their usual practice in building a Volante convertible version of the V8 which, top down, looked even more elegant. Although the purity of the V8 Volante's lines were spoiled somewhat by some added-on skirts and boot-lid spoiler in the Vantage version, William Towns' design was still a classic when the V8 finally went out of production in 1988 after nearly 20 years.

Above: In 1972 the DBS V8 was restyled at the front and the changed model became known simply as the Aston Martin V8.

Right: One of the main changes between the DBS V8 and the V8 that followed it was the switch from four small headlights to larger single lights on each side.

Above: The boot-lip spoiler identifies this as the rear of the tuned Vantage version rather than the ordinary V8.

Left: Aston Martin have long concentrated on their image of producing luxurious high-performance cars. The Connolly leather interiors can be ordered in a number of different colour schemes, each with the obligatory walnut dashboard and door capping.

Engine

Aston Martin engine designer Tadek Marek's original intention in designing the Aston Martin V8 was to use as much as possible of the existing six-cylinder twin-cam. It was a nice idea, but it didn't work quite as conveniently in practice. The angle between inlet and exhaust valves on the twin-cam heads had to be narrowed for space reasons, and the original block design proved to be insufficiently rigid. That problem was solved with a stiffer crankcase, longer cylinder head studs, bigger main bearing caps and an enlarged displacement, up to 5340 cc, from the original 4.8 litres.

Originally fuel was supplied via Bosch mechanical fuel injection but problems of difficult starting, poor idling and poor drive-away characteristics if the engine was not warm led to the switch to a quartet of Weber 48 IDF downdraught carburettors.

The Vantage version of the engine, with 360 bhp rather than 306 bhp, appeared in 1977, with revised cam timing, larger valves and larger, 48-mm choke Weber IDF downdraught carburettors.

In 1986 Aston returned to fuel injection, although the Vantage continued with its quartet of Weber carbs. By the time the Vantage went out of production in the late 1980s its output was 406 bhp at 6,200 rpm.

The Volante

There have been Volante, or convertible, versions of Aston Martin coupés since the DB2 of 1950. Converting coupé to convertible was in most cases simple, as the cars had separate chassis rather than being of monocoque construction, where the roof is an integral part of the car's structure.

The V8 Volante appeared in 1977 and in its case the conversion wasn't quite as simple as it should have been, given the Aston's very substantial box-section steel chassis, but in fact the first car did suffer scuttle shake until extra strengthening was welded in to secure the windscreen footings more firmly to the centre bulkhead and

Above: The ultimate development of the V8 line, the Vantage Volante, combined the performance of the most highly-tuned model with the top-down appeal of the convertible, or Volante, version.

front of the transmission tunnel.

Originally, only an 'ordinary' version of the Volante was offered, on the grounds that the extra power of the Vantage would be too much for the open car. In 1986, however, Aston Martin decided that the open car could cope with over 400 bhp, and the Vantage Volante was born.

Below: The most notable feature at the rear of the V8 is the use of a de Dion rear axle. A de Dion axle is essentially a tube that rigidly connects both wheel hubs and is curved to clear the differential unit, which is mounted to the chassis. It's an improvement over the old-fashioned live axle because it is far lighter; the springs no longer have to carry the unsprung weight of the differential and brakes, which in this case are inboard discs. Both wheels are kept upright and parallel to each other during cornering, which is not always the case with an independent system. The main drawback is that both rear wheels have to react even when only one hits a bump.

Above: The V8 Volante was introduced in 1977. It's the most attractive version of William Towns' original design, not burdened by the add-on skirts and spoilers added to the Vantage cars.

Right: There was little fundamental change to the interiors over the years, the two-spoke steering wheel being the most obvious on this left-hand-drive automatic.

Below: In 1986 extra power and convertible motoring was combined to form the Vantage Volante.

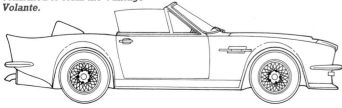

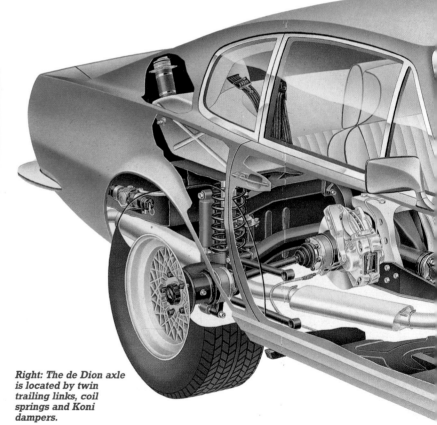

Right: The de Dion axle is located by twin trailing links, coil springs and Koni dampers.

Inside the V8 Vantage

The Aston Martin is a very traditional design, with a front-mounted engine driving the rear wheels. Engine block and heads are aluminium alloy so the car is not unduly front-heavy. In fact its weight distribution is surprisingly neutral; at 50.6 front to 49.4 rear, it would be hard to improve. The quad-cam engine requires a power bulge to accommodate it, even though the proposed angle between the inlet and exhaust valves was reduced to make

the engine lower.

Power is fed from the engine to a fixed rear limited slip differential, while rear suspension is a de Dion system and the brakes are mounted inboard.

The chassis is a very strong assembly of welded steel sections and it must account for a considerable percentage of the Aston's great weight of over 4,000 lb, as the body panels as well as the engine are alloy.

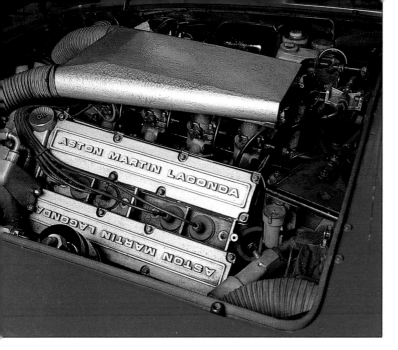

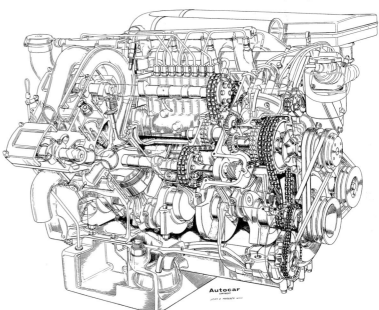

Below: The Aston's body is aluminium alloy, the car's main structural strength coming from the steel platform chassis.

Above: The Aston Martin V8 engine combines the American approach of a large displacement, in this case 5.3 litres, with the more European tradition of twin overhead camshafts for each bank of cylinders, and aluminium alloy construction. Each engine is meticulously assembled by one man.

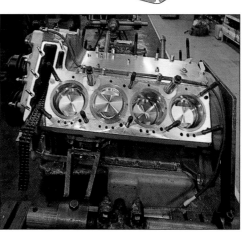

Above: The cutaway of an early Aston Martin V8 shows the chain drive to the overhead camshafts and the two valves per cylinder operating in hemispherical combustion chambers. The fuel injector pipes can be seen at the top.

Left: The V8's block is aluminium alloy and the cylinders run in so-called 'wet' liners. They are sleeves that are located in the block, to form cylinder walls. The coolant flows around the sleeves, hence 'wet' liners.

Left: Cooling air comes in through the spoiler on the Vantage.

Audi Quattro

Inspired by Volkswagen's Iltis military off-road vehicle, the Audi Quattro revolutionised the rally world in the 1980s thanks to its combination of five-cylinder turbocharged engine, four-wheel drive and 140-mph performance.

Above: The Quattro, here being driven by Stig Blomqvist on the 1988 Scottish Rally, was still a contender eight years after its motorsport introduction, although everyone concerned with the project denied that the car was developed purely as a homologation special.

The Audi Quattro was, in the opinion of many observers of the motoring scene, *the* car of the 1980s. By coupling four-wheel drive with high performance, it shifted attitudes about what makes a sports car, and changed rallying irrevocably.

The Quattro made its sensational debut at the Geneva Motor Show in March 1980. The world's press was invited to take a short, fast drive – up into the mountains and the snow, across gravel tracks, and then finally onto the motorway.

No car before could take such a challenge in its stride. But this Audi, on regular summer tyres, romped up slippery slopes and powered through hairpins and fast bends with a confidence only achieved by a two-wheel-drive car on heavily-studded tyres. And, then, out on the dry motorway it hurtled up to 140 mph.

Driving all four wheels became Audi's crusade. Ferdinand Piëch, then research and development director, now chairman of Audi, made the proposition irresistible: "It means better acceleration and faster cornering," he said.

Piëch – whose grandfather Ferdinand Porsche designed the four-wheel-drive Cisitalia racer after World War II – dismissed existing four-wheel-drive layouts with their clumsy trans-

fer boxes as "truck transmissions". Audi had in fact designed a truck of sorts for their Volkswagen parents in the form of the Iltis light military vehicle, and it was the Iltis that provided the inspiration for the Quattro.

Driving all four wheels was Audi's crusade

In 1977 – and in great secrecy – an Iltis four-wheel-drive system was installed in an Audi 80 saloon. The Quattro was on its way. As a rough-road vehicle, the Iltis did not need a differential to smooth out differences in rotational speeds of front and rear wheels. A key to the Quattro's development as a civilised road car was the centre differential, a superbly neat and compact device that could be integrated with the gearbox and would divide the engine's torque 50/50 between front and rear wheels.

Though all concerned have consistently denied that the original Quattro was intended as a 'homologation special', it is clear that from the start Audi intended to prove the car's worth in rallying. The 400 cars needed to meet the international motorsport regulations provided a con-

venient production figure to put before the sceptical Volkswagen management.

To keep costs within bounds, the Quattro used a mixture of components from other Audi models. The floorpan was from the Audi 80, the body basically that of the Coupé GT, while the turbocharged 2.1-litre five-cylinder engine and front-wheel drive were taken from the Audi 200. The rear differential came from the Iltis and was carried on a reversed front subframe with front suspension members. The spring struts, brakes and wheels were as on the contemporary 200T.

Speculation about a radical performance car from Audi increased in 1979 as enquiries were made at the governing body of motorsport about the possibility of removing the ban on four-wheel drive in the World Rally Championship. Audi's chosen driver was Hannu Mikkola, then 37 and at the height of his career. He remembers being asked to come to Audi at Ingolstadt to try a turbocharged car with four-wheel drive. He was unconvinced by the idea – "I thought it would be like a Land Rover or something" – but went anyway. Half an hour in the 80-based prototype completely changed his mind.

The Quattro's first appearance on an international rally was in October 1980 when Mikkola drove it as a course car on the Algarve Rally in

were numerous reliability problems and while the Quattro was terrific on slippery or loose surfaces, it did not have the sheer pace to win in dry Tarmac 'road races' like the Tour de Corse.

That first full season yielded no more than fifth place in the championship, but the signs were there. Coming back with a revised rally machine for 1982, Audi were to win the Constructors' Championship. Mikkola had a patchy season but his female team-mate Michele Mouton put in some heroic performances, winning three championship rounds and coming close to taking the drivers' title. In 1983 Mikkola did win the driver's crown, though Audi were narrowly beaten by Lancia in the constructors' contest. Both championships went to the Quattro in 1984.

In standard form, the Sport Quattro had 306 bhp

By then it was clear that Audi had altered the face of rallying. The rules had changed to Group B, which required a production minimum of only 200 cars, and all the top rally teams were planning four-wheel-drive, mid-engined 'specials'. For their part, Audi were not keen to depart too far from the kind of car that they offered for general sale, so a short-wheelbase version was planned, lighter and more powerful.

At first glance, the Sport Quattro, which first appeared in September 1983, looked quite normal but underneath it was a pretty exotic beast. Twelve and a half inches were taken out of the floorpan behind the front seats, the body was made of Kevlar and glassfibre, and the five-cylinder engine had an alloy block and a twin-cam, 20-valve head. In standard form, the Sport

Quattro had 306 bhp – 50 per cent more than the regular Quattro, which continued in production.

From the time of the first customer deliveries in autumn 1980 to when Audi closed what had been the pilot production line at Ingolstadt in mid-1991, 11,560 Quattros were made.

The car was usefully updated during its career. In 1984, lower, stiffer suspension, wider wheels and, most importantly, ABS were specified. The 20-valve heads first developed for the Sport Quattro found their way into the regular model to celebrate its 10th anniversary in 1990 – the resulting 2.2-litre engine developed 220 bhp.

On the rally side, the Sport Quattro was also modified – to the point where Ferdinand Piëch almost wanted to disown it. He remained sure that a 50/50 torque split was the right arrangement for four-wheel drive but accepted that for the special conditions of rallying, variations might be desirable, so a centre differential incorporating a viscous coupling was adopted.

In the quest for downforce, the competition bodywork became more and more outrageous; for obvious reasons, the last, particularly ugly S1 version, scarcely recognisable as a Quattro, became known as the 'Tonka Toy'. It was this car, with 600 bhp, that rounded off the Quattro's glorious official competition career with a third win in the annual 'Race to the Clouds' at Pike's Peak, Colorado.

The ultra-fast Group B cars were banned from the World Rally Championship after a series of accidents in 1986. Audi took that as a cue to leave the rallying scene, but by then the Quattro had made an indelible mark.

Portugal – thus having an opportunity to test it in real rally conditions without actually being entered. In fact, it was faster than all the official competitors on 24 of the 30 stages and would have won easily!

Homologation in Group 4 was confirmed on 1 January 1981. Ten days later, Franz Wittman had scored the Quattro's first victory, in the Janner Rally in Austria. In February, Mikkola led all 25 stages to win an ice-bound Swedish Rally, Audi's first success in a World Championship event. It was not to continue that easily, however. There

Top: Michele Mouton, partnered by Fabrizia Pons, put in many heroic performances with her Quattro and came close to taking the drivers' title in 1982.

Above: In the quest for greater downforce, the competition car's bodywork became more and more outrageous.

Overleaf: From 1984 onwards, the production cars included stiffer suspension, wider wheels and, most importantly, ABS; braking was the main criticism of earlier versions.

Driving the Quattro: *front-drive marvel*

In 1980, the Quattro was a revelation – it combined the best qualities of a front-wheel-drive car with the seat-of-the-pants response of a good rear-driver, although extracting the best from it did require some effort.

The short-wheelbase, Kevlar-bodied Sport is something else. Even today, when there are plenty of 150-mph cars available, this is a seriously fast car, one which can go from 0-100 mph in 12.5 seconds.

The big turbo takes some winding up, the real push coming from 4,500 rpm onwards, but thereafter it really takes off. Not surprisingly, the ultra-short 87.6-in wheelbase makes the ride fidgety on bad roads and

there is some darting around when braking heavily. The brakes, though, are magnificent (quite a contrast to the original car, where the brakes were its weakest point); the Sport Quattro's brake equipment came from the Porsche 917 racer.

Most of all, though, this is a civilised homologation special. Unlike the MG Metro 6R4 and other Group B specials of the era, the Sport Quattro was built and trimmed (by Baur in Stuttgart) to full Audi production car standards. This was a car you could take, and enjoy, on a fast trans-Continental journey. You couldn't say that for any of the others.

PERFORMANCE & SPECIFICATION COMPARISON	Engine	Displacement	Power	Torque (lb ft)	Max speed	0-60 mph	Length (in/mm)	Wheelbase (in/mm)	Track front/rear	Weight (lb/kg)	Price
Audi Sport Quattro	Inline-five, 20-valve, turbo	2133 cc	306 bhp 6700 rpm	258 lb ft 3700 rpm	154 mph 248 km/h	4.8 sec	160.0 in 4064 mm	87.6 in 2224 mm	59.7 in 58.7 in	2866 lb 1300 kg	£53,225 (1985)
Ford RS200	Inline-four, 16-valve, turbo	1803 cc	250 bhp 6500 rpm	215 lb ft 4000 rpm	140 mph 225 km/h	6.1 sec	157.5 in 4001 mm	99.6 in 2530 mm	59.1 in 59.0 in	2607 lb 1183 kg	£49,950 (1986)
Lancia Delta S4	Inline-four, 16-valve, turbo, s/c	1759 cc	250 bhp 6750 rpm	215 lb ft 4500 rpm	140 mph 225 km/h	6.0 sec	157.7 in 4005 mm	96.1 in 2440 mm	59.0 in 59.8 in	2646 lb 1200 kg	N/A
MG Metro 6R4	V6, quad-cam, 24-valve	2991 cc	250 bhp 7000 rpm	225 lb ft 6500 rpm	140 mph 225 km/h	4.5 sec	131.9 in 3350 mm	94.1 in 2390 mm	59.5 in 59.7 in	2266 lb 1028 kg	£34,784 (1986)
Peugeot 205 T16	Inline-four, 16-valve, turbo	1775 cc	200 bhp 6750 rpm	188 lb ft 4000 rpm	130 mph 209 km/h	6.0 sec	150.4 in 3820 mm	100.0 in 2540 mm	56.3 in 56.3 in	2524 lb 1145 kg	N/A

Audi Quattro Data File

Audi's distinctive four-ring badge – worn on the flanks of the original Quattro – represents the four companies that made up Auto Union back in 1932. Those were DKW, Horch, Wanderer and Audi itself, which had been formed in Zwickau in 1910 by August Horch.

Audi had sporting cars that competed with distinction in the Alpine Trials around 1912, but after the amalgamation the marque offered only small front-wheel-drive cars. Auto Union became Nazi Germany's second force in Grand Prix racing, along with Mercedes-Benz.

After World War II a new factory was set up at Düsseldorf for the production of three-cylinder front-drive Auto Union-DKWs. In 1958 Auto Union was taken over by Mercedes-Benz, who instituted more ambitious plans for bigger cars which would revive the Audi name. In 1964 Volkswagen took control and saw through the re-introduction of Audis as front-wheel-drive saloons positioned up-market of the VW range.

Though it was thought that Horch might be revived for the V8 model which was introduced in 1988, Audi has remained the only marque of the Auto Union group to survive.

Above: Car converters Treser built this striking convertible version of the Quattro.

Below: The Sport Quattro, introduced in 1983, had a shorter wheelbase than the original car.

Above: Composite plastics and glassfibre were used for the vented bonnet, helping to make the Sport a staggering 600 lb lighter.

Above: To keep costs within bounds, the original Audi Quattro used a mix of components from other models, like the Audi 80.

Styling

With the Quattro, British designer Martin Smith started a trend which has since spread from superminis to Bentleys – the extended wings with 'eyebrows' over the wheels.

Smith, a 30-year-old graduate of London's Royal College of Art, was given the job of turning the already complete, but not released, Audi Coupé (itself based on the 80 saloon) into something more aggressive which would reflect the power and performance of the turbocharged engine and four-wheel-drive transmission. Most agree that he succeeded brilliantly, and with the wider wheels and the revised front end of the later cars, the Quattro has an unmistakable stance.

Ferdinand Piëch had wanted a full four-seater Grand Touring car, rather like the Lancia Aurelia B20 of the 1950s. Though the rear-drive system takes up a good deal of space, it was incorporated without sacrificing the cabin area, so that the Quattro officially has five seats. There is not, however, room for five or even four with their

luggage; the boot is tiny, even when a space-saving mini-spare is carried.

The Quattro was criticised at first for not matching its performance, image and price with a special and luxurious interior. The first cars were effectively Audi 80s inside, with minimal instrumentation and simple cloth trim. As time went on, trim and equipment were uprated and an electronic fascia was fitted which provided more comprehensive information – though not everyone liked the way it was presented.

The styling changes that created the Sport Quattro were mostly determined by the requirements of rallying, but it was important to Audi that the family resemblance be retained. That rather tricky job fell to another British designer, Peter Birtwhistle, who succeeded well.

Below: By the time of the 1986 Monte Carlo Rally, Audi were running this, the S1, the last variation on the original Quattro theme.

Above: Heat build-up from the turbocharger led to very high cabin temperatures.

Below: Harnesses in roadgoing Sports considerably reduced rear-seat leg room.

Transmission

The heart of the Quattro system is the centre differential. A high-performance four-wheel-drive car must have some means of allowing the front and rear wheels to travel different distances (as they do when turning a corner) without the transmission 'winding up' and creating the very instability that the system is intended to eliminate.

The clever thing about the original Audi centre differential was its compactness. It fit neatly behind the gearbox, providing direct drive to the rear wheels via a two-piece propshaft. Power to the front wheels was transmitted from the centre differential by a slim shaft running inside the hollow lower shaft of the gearbox. The weight penalty – a problem with earlier four-wheel-drive systems – was calculated as only 77 lb compared with a rear-drive car.

The Audi system split the drive equally to front and rear wheels. Because a single free-spinning wheel could immobilise the car, locks were provided for the centre and rear differentials for use on soft and slippery surfaces; originally cable-operated by levers on the central tunnel, they later had a pneumatic dashboard control.

When Audi made the change to a Torsen centre differential for the 1988 model there was no longer any need for the centre lock. The Torsen automatically provides a variable torque split, so later Quattros actually depart from one of the car's original principles – that of a permanent 50/50 division of labour between front and rear wheels.

Fitting the Torsen made compatibility of four-wheel drive with ABS (anti-lock braking) easier and more efficient.

Below: Direct drive to the rear wheels was provided via a two-piece propshaft from the centre differential.

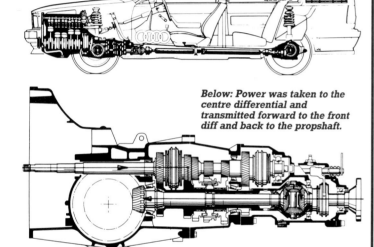

Below: Power was taken to the centre differential and transmitted forward to the front diff and back to the propshaft.

Left: The rally car's suspension was uprated compared with the standard car.

Right: Round tubes were fabricated for the lower arms and allied to Boge dampers.

Below: The rear differential carried the lock-up mechanisms, which were controlled by a dashboard switch.

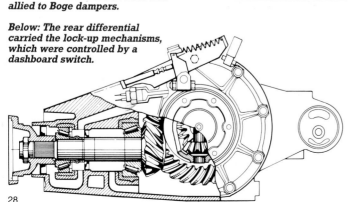

Engine

When the Quattro was being developed, Audi already had a turbocharged production car in the shape of the 200T, a version of the 'pre-aero' 100. This used a five-cylinder engine derived from the familiar VW Group 'modular' power unit; with Audi's far-forward longitudinal engine position, the five-cylinder was the longest engine they could accommodate.

In the 200T, this 2144-cc engine developed 170 bhp with the help of a single KKK turbocharger. For the Quattro it was given a charge-air intercooler and this, plus sophisticated engine electronics, allowed the output to rise to a maximum of 200 bhp. Even the first rally versions were easily uprated to produce more than 300 bhp, though it proved more difficult to give these a useful spread of torque.

When the Sport Quattro arrived, its engine was a very different proposition. It had an aluminium-alloy cylinder block and a new twin-cam head with four valves per cylinder and used a much bigger turbocharger running at higher boost. The result was a 2133-cc motor producing 306 bhp in standard form – enough to give the Sport a 154 mph maximum speed and a 0-60 mph time of under five seconds.

A mass-production, iron-block, 20-valve engine of 2226 cc, primarily intended for the new Coupé S2, found its way into the original Quattro for the 1990 model year. With the latest electronic engine management system – and a three-way catalytic converter – this produced 220 bhp, and its flat torque curve made it the sweetest of all the Quattro variants.

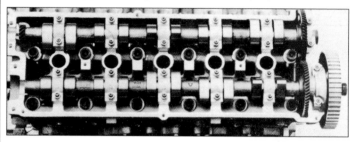

Above: The Sport's twin overhead camshafts were geared together, the lower shaft being fed power via the cogged belt from the crankshaft.

Right: Michelin developed special 235/45 VR15 tyres to cope with the Sport Quattro's top speed of over 150 mph.

Above right: The massive four-wheel ventilated disc brakes were of rally lineage and utilised four-piston calipers. The second-generation anti-lock system could be overridden by flicking a switch in the cabin. This enabled rally drivers to lock up the brakes on loose surfaces for faster cornering.

Austin-Healey 3000

If any model ever fitted the definition of the archetypal English sports car it must have been the rounded, elegantly muscular six-cylinder 'Big Healey', itself epitomised by the 148-bhp 3000 Mk III, built from 1964 to 1967.

Y ou only have to mention the 'Big Healey' today, and everyone knows what you are talking about.

The Big Healey – or to give it BMC's long-winded showroom title, the Austin-Healey 3000 Mk III – was the last, and most charismatic, of the beautiful 120-mph sports cars to be built at Abingdon in the 1960s. Other makers – rivals, naturally – looked on with despair as it continued to sell long after it should have died away. How, they asked, could a car which was designed in 1952 still be successful in the mid-1960s? How could a car the cabin of which was too narrow – and became uncomfortably hot in summer weather – and the boot of which was small, continue to sell against cars with modern style, more space, and better equipment?

The roots of the Big Healey story were planted in 1952 when Donald Healey set out to design a replacement for the Riley- and Nash-engined cars which had been produced in his small factory at Warwick since 1946. These were relatively expensive machines, sold in limited numbers.

Healey's company was busy enough, but he wanted to expand it. He wanted to make lighter, cheaper, sports cars in larger numbers, and to do

this he needed to find cheaper engines and transmissions. Early in 1952, along with his son Geoff, Barrie Bilbie (in charge of mechanical design) and Gerry Coker (designer/stylist), Healey started a new project.

The structure of the new car, which Donald Healey decided to call the Healey 100, was conventional enough – a solid box-section chassis frame was topped by a steel and light-alloy two-seater body shell. The two innovations were in its choice of running gear, and in its style.

Gerry Coker's style was an evolution of what had gone before, particularly for the Nash-Healey, but was smooth and more delicate. For running gear, Healey approached BMC for their 2.6-litre four-cylinder Austin A90 Atlantic engines, transmissions and front suspension units. The prototype was completed just before the 1952 London Motor Show.

BMC's forceful chief executive, Leonard Lord, saw the car on preview day, loved it, instantly made a deal to take over the project from Healey, renamed it Austin-Healey 100, and saw it urged into production by the spring of 1953. Healey made the first 25 cars at Warwick, but series-production began at Longbridge, near Birmingham, soon afterwards.

The original 100-Four matured well in three years (the much-modified 100S competition car was a great success), and in 1956 the car was re-launched as the 100-Six, complete with the new-generation BMC C-Series 2.6-litre six-cylinder engine, its matching gearbox and solid rear axle. At the same time the wheelbase was lengthened, the cabin made more spacious, tiny '+2' seats were installed, and the car was moved perceptibly up-market.

A car that delivered all it promised

By 1958 the cars had more power than ever before, the two-seater option had returned, and assembly was moved to Abingdon, where the cars took shape alongside the famous MGA and Austin-Healey Sprite. From mid-1959 the engine was enlarged to 2.9 litres and front-wheel disc brakes were fitted – the Austin-Healey 3000 had been born. The Mk II, with wind-up windows, followed in 1962.

The final update, creating the 3000 Mk III, came early in 1964, when the car got a new in-

It was a car that delivered all it promised. When driven gently it growled its way around the streets, lumbering its way over the bumps rather than absorbing them. At high speed, and particularly when being driven hard, its engine bellowed defiance at the elements, though its transmission needed effort and it could be hard work to steer.

Much better than the sum of its parts

The miracle was that such an integrated car, and character, could be maintained in a machine which came together in such a seemingly hotchpotch way. The chassis frames were built by John Thompson Motor Pressings, then shipped to Jensen Motors of West Bromwich, where the body was pressed, assembled, welded to the frame, painted and trimmed before it was once again shipped – this time to the MG factory at Abingdon, south of Oxford.

Above: From a 'soft' classic event to the hard competition of the real thing, with Makinen/ Wood on the 1963 Coupe des Alpes.

Engines, gearboxes and axles came from BMC (Austin actually) factories in Coventry and Birmingham, these being developments of units used in rather awful cars like the Austin A105 Westminster. Final assembly was at Abingdon.

Yet the 'Magic of MG' was unfailingly applied to this unpromising mixture when everything came together at Abingdon. The cars which were road-tested – then mostly sent to showrooms in the USA – were *much* better than the sum of their parts. When BMC came to replace the old design, by offering a six-cylinder version of the MGB called the MGC, the result was a disaster. The MGC didn't handle as well, didn't look as good, and didn't have the same character, which had died with the old car. It was no wonder that neither Donald Healey nor his son Geoffrey would have anything to do with the new machine, and a proposal to give it an Austin-Healey badge was quashed.

terior, complete with a wooden fascia, relocated instruments, a centre console which included a cubby box, and a fold-down panel ahead of the soft top which could cover up the '+2' seats and give more space for luggage stowage.

The running gear also came in for attention. The engine was boosted from 131 bhp to 148 bhp, while all but the first few cars had revised chassis side members which allowed more axle movement, and there was new radius-arm location for the back axle. This was the archetypal Big Healey, and it was built until the end of 1967.

Above: When the 3000 model superseded the 100-Six, its 2912-cc engine initially produced 124 bhp. On the 1961 Mk II, shown here, power was up to 132 bhp and then came the Mk III in 1964 with a hunky 148 bhp, still from the same capacity.

Overleaf: The quarter-windows (just visible) show this to be a late 3000, in fact a 1965 Mk III.

This Mk III has a works-type hard top and boot-lid bulge for an extra spare wheel.

Driving the 3000: *strictly for the brave*

Although the 3000 looked graceful, it was a car with a muscular character which needed a firm hand and (near the limit) a touch of bravery to extract all its 120-mph performance.

In a straight line or when cruising, the 3000 was a restrained and civilised machine with a smooth six-cylinder engine. By contrast, when pushed hard on winding roads the engine would growl, the carburettors gulp and the transmission whine. The car could bite back if the driver did not realise how bumpy the road was or that the axle would step out of line when the limits of its travel were reached.

The view along that long bonnet proved how much metal was up front, a view confirmed by understeer in most conditions. The steering was not as light as that of some of its rivals, and the gear change was firm, bordering on obstructive sometimes, but the flick-action overdrive switch was a delight to use.

In its later years the 3000 was given a large windscreen and wind-up windows to make driving a more civilised affair, while the wooden fascia and bucket seats added to the traditional Englishness of the machine which endeared it to so many. Without doubt, it was a car of great character.

PERFORMANCE & SPECIFICATION COMPARISON	Engine	Displacement	Power	Torque (lb ft)	Max speed	0-60 mph	Length (in/mm)	Wheelbase (in/mm)	Track front/rear	Weight (lb/kg)	Price
Austin-Healey 3000 Mk III	Inline-six, overhead-valve	2912 cc	148 bhp 5250 rpm	165 lb ft 3500 rpm	121 mph 195 km/h	9.8 sec	157.3 in 3995 mm	92.0 in 2337 mm	48.8 in 50.0 in	2548 lb 1156 kg	£1,106 (1964)
Daimler SP250	V8, overhead-valve	2548 cc	140 bhp 5800 rpm	155 lb ft 3600 rpm	121 mph 195 km/h	10.2 sec	160.5 in 4077 mm	92.0 in 2337 mm	50.0 in 48.0 in	2222 lb 1008 kg	£1,395 (1959)
Datsun 240Z	Inline-six, overhead-cam	2393 cc	151 bhp 5600 rpm	146 lb ft 4400 rpm	125 mph 201 km/h	8.0 sec	162.8 in 4135 mm	90.7 in 2304 mm	53.5 in 53.0 in	2400 lb 1089 kg	£2,288 (1971)
MG MGB	Inline-four, overhead-valve	1798 cc	95 bhp 5400 rpm	110 lb ft 3000 rpm	103 mph 166 km/h	12.2 sec	153.3 in 3894 mm	91.0 in 2311 mm	49.0 in 49.3 in	2030 lb 921 kg	£950 (1962)
Triumph TR5	Inline-six, overhead-valve	2498 cc	150 bhp 5500 rpm	164 lb ft 3500 rpm	120 mph 193 km/h	8.8 sec	153.6 in 3901 mm	88.0 in 2235 mm	49.3 in 48.8 in	2268 lb 1029 kg	£1,212 (1967)

Austin-Healey 3000 Data File

Donald Healey originally conceived the Healey 100 in 1952 as a simpler and cheaper-to-build car than the Riley- and Nash-engined Healey models of the late 1940s, but after BMC took it up and invented the Austin-Healey marque, its image gradually changed, becoming a civilised production sports car.

By the late 1950s the same basic car had become larger, heavier, more powerful, and altogether more completely equipped. It had a six-cylinder instead of a four-cylinder engine, wind-up windows instead of removable side screens, and was a 2 + 2 instead of a two-seater.

Along the way, though, the car's basic layout and character were preserved. It used a rugged box-section chassis frame, engines, transmissions and suspension components 'borrowed' from BMC family cars, and a smart body style with sweeping lines.

Like its stable-mate, the MGB, and its rival, the Triumph TR, the 'Big Healey' was a great success in export markets, and is now remembered as one of the last of the 'hairy-chested' British sports cars.

Above: All the traditional British sports car features are there in this 1965 3000 interior, including a wooden dash.

Above: All but the first few of the Mk III 3000s had improved rear axle location as well as a more powerful engine.

Above: This is one of the works rally cars from 1964, complete with extra lights.

Below: With its barrage of switches, the rally interior was built for business.

Styling

The shape of the first Healey 100 evolved at Warwick, as a joint effort between Donald Healey himself and Gerry Coker of his design staff, but it was further refined at the prototype stage when the first car was being built by Tickford at Newport Pagnell.

The original shape might have had vestigial rear fins, but when it was finally ready for release these had disappeared, and a very sleek two-seater style remained. In side view it had long and flowing front wings, and its waistline dipped across the top of the doors before swooping over the rear wheel arches.

The windscreen was arranged to fold, not in a conventional manner, but by the screen base sliding forward on a simple linkage if required. There was a slight but elegant styling 'crease' on the flanks, a lift-off optional hard top was proposed, while the fascia saw all instruments grouped on an oval panel behind the steering wheel, ahead of the driver's eyes.

Except that the headlamps were slightly raised, this was the graceful shape that went into production in 1953, the only real criticism being of the tail, which was rather too close to the ground when the car was heavily loaded, endangering the exhaust.

Although the same basic style was retained for the next 15 years, there were many detail changes in that time. When the six-cylinder 100-Six arrived in 1956, it featured a two-inch-longer wheelbase, an enlarged cockpit, and 2 + 2 seating, though in 1958 this was further complicated when a two-seater version was re-introduced. The early 3000s looked almost exactly like the first, small-engined, 100-Six types.

In a two-stage process – started in 1962 and finished off in 1964 – the 3000 was given a very effective facelift without destroying its lines, being transformed from a roadster to a true convertible. Instead of a fold-flat windscreen there was a larger curved screen which was fixed in place, and instead of sliding side screens there were wind-up windows. The old 'build-it-yourself' soft top was abandoned in favour of a neat, padded foldaway top. The fascia style was changed last of all, for the Mk III in 1964.

Some cars were fitted with the optional lift-off 'bubble-top' hard top and, although disc wheels were available, most cars were equipped with centre-lock wire-spokes instead.

Below: Neither a 100-Six nor a 3000, this is a modern reproduction – the Rover V8-engined Healey Mk IV.

Below: Left-routed tailpipes point to this being a left-hand-drive car; nearly 90 per cent of Big Healeys were exported.

Engine

Big Healeys in motorsport

These cars had a long and distinguished record in motorsport. Early four-cylinder-engined cars competed with honour at Le Mans and Sebring, as well as taking innumerable long-distance endurance records at the Bonneville Salt Flats.

The six-cylinder cars were more suited to rallying than to racing. Although works cars performed well, particularly at Le Mans and Sebring, it was the red Abingdon-built works rally cars which made most headlines.

As a rally car the Austin-Healey 3000 was excellent on tarmac, and ruggedly reliable on gravel surfaces. Pat Moss won the Liège-Rome-Liège rally in a 3000 in 1960, a result matched by Rauno Aaltonen in a Mk III in 1964. The Morley twins won the French Alpine in 1961 and again in 1962, while Paddy Hopkirk won the Austrian Alpine in 1964.

The fiercest of all works cars were painted red, with white tops, had bodies clothed in aluminium panels, hard tops and 210-bhp engines with aluminium cylinder heads.

Above: The 3000 was a great rally car; Rauno Aaltonen and Tony Ambrose won the 1964 Spa-Sofia-Liège Rally in this example.

Chassis and running gear

When work started on the new Healey 100 project in 1951-52, Donald Healey saw it as a car that could be assembled at Warwick, in his small but relatively modern factory.

The car would need a new chassis layout, so Healey drew up a solid but simple box-section frame, while the idea was that the two-seater body shell could be produced by one of Britain's specialist suppliers. There was no question of designing new engines and transmissions; as with the old models, these would have to be 'off-the-shelf' items from a major manufacturer. Experience with the original Healeys also convinced Healey that proprietary front suspension parts should be found 'off the shelf' too.

The basic design of the frame survived for 15 years but, because the side rails ran below the line of the rear axle, the amount of rear suspension movement was always compromised. From 1964 to 1967 cars had a revised side-rail shape, but the general design was unaffected.

Over the years almost every 'building block' in the running gear changed completely – for the 100-Six/3000 models there was a six-cylinder engine instead of a 'four', a C-Series gearbox instead of the original A90 type, and a C-Series back axle instead of the A90 variety.

Below: The Big Healey's construction was typical for its time, with a cross-braced ladder frame and steel upper structure.

For the 100-Six and later models, BMC imposed the new six-cylinder C-Series unit, which had an iron cylinder block and head, and a four-bearing crankshaft. It was originally intended for use in large, staid family cars like the Austin A90 Westminster and the Morris Isis, so a great deal of development work (especially to the cylinder head breathing and the camshaft profiles) was needed to make it suitable for the Austin-Healey.

The definitive 3000 engine had a bore and stroke of 83.36 mm × 88.9 mm, and a displacement of 2912 cc. In five years its power was gradually improved, from 124 bhp for the original type, to no less than 148 bhp for the final Mk III variety.

All Big Healeys except the early versions of the 3000 Mk II, which had three SUs, were fitted with twin SU carburettors, and every one was better when driven in the mid-ranges than when revved hard. In 1962 an aluminium head was developed for use in works competition cars. Not only did this reduce the all-up weight of the engine but, with the aid of three twin-choke Weber carburettors, it also allowed the peak power to be raised from about 180 bhp to 210 bhp.

Below: Big Healeys from the 100-Six onward used uprated versions of BMC's C-Series pushrod straight-six.

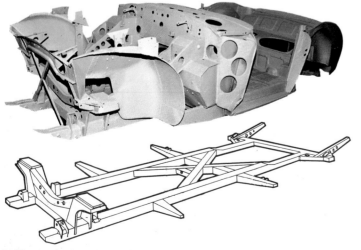

Below: Big Healeys were mostly 2+2s, but the rear seats were only child-sized.

Above: The 'underslung' chassis, with rails running below the rear springs, limited suspension travel; this was improved a little on cars from 1964 onward.

Above: Wind-up side windows and a proper foldaway soft top were 1962 improvements. Incorporating wind-up windows made the doors wider and made the cabin feel even more restricted, but that was a small price to pay.

Above: Austin-Healey 100s were drum-braked; front discs came with the 3000 in 1959. Grilles changed several times; with a big, vertically-slatted elliptical pattern, the car shown here is a 3000 Mk III.

Right: Initially of 2639-cc capacity in the 100-Six, then increased to 2912 cc for the 3000, the C-Series engine was originally intended for (and indeed served in) staid BMC saloons like the A90/A110 series. The long-stroke overhead-valve six-cylinder unit produced 102 bhp in its first Austin-Healey application; this rose to 124 bhp in the first 3000, then 132 bhp in the Mk II (which at first used three SU carburettors instead of the usual two), and finally a thumping 148 bhp in the 1964-on 3000 Mk III. Aluminium-headed competition versions put out as much as 210 bhp.

Chevrolet Camaro

It was created as GM's riposte to the Ford Mustang, but since its launch in the mid-1960s the Camaro has forged its own character and proved itself a true American muscle car – tough, popular and dependable on both road and track.

Above: Lean, squat and muscular, the 1982 third-generation Camaro was more compact than its predecessors. The Z28 model was always intended to prove its worth in competition and could be tuned to be very fast, even if the live rear axle belonged to another age of motoring.

When the Ford Mustang took the American car market by storm in the early 1960s, it was clear that General Motors would have to respond. It took the giant corporation a little while to swing into action but when they did it was a two-pronged attack, with two divisions being given the task of rivalling the Mustang with the same basic platform – the 'F' body, in GM terminology. Chevrolet's effort was the Camaro, while Pontiac built the Trans Am.

Unlike the Mustang, which was not initially designed to take a V8 engine, Chevrolet intended the Camaro to use a wide variety of engines, from the base inline six-cylinder to various permutations of their famous small-block V8 and, of course, the Mk IV big-block which, in Camaro tune, displaced 396 cu in (6.5 litres). In basic format the Camaro was the same as the Mustang: both used unitary construction (although the Camaro had a front subframe); both had independent front suspension and a live rear axle with leaf springs. Standard brakes were drums all round while steering was a rather slow recirculating-ball system. It was all very basic, and typical of American car design of the era.

Besides the usual stripes and graphics, the higher-performance SS Camaros were equipped with stiffer springs and dampers,

along with quicker-ratio steering and, most important of all, larger and more powerful engines. The SS stood for Super Sport and the car was available with either the 350- or 396-cu in V8 which in its highest tune gave 375 bhp. That guaranteed high performance, albeit in a straight line, but the car was still lacking in crucial areas like cornering and braking.

Built to compete with the Ford Mustang

The 1965 and 1966 Shelby Mustangs had shown that there was a niche in the market for a more balanced package – a car that could handle, hold the road and stop properly. Although Chevrolet did not really think it was a large enough sector to bother with, they went along with the idea and made a Camaro to suit – not to produce an outstanding road car, but to homologate the Camaro for the SCCA Trans-Am series which was in its infancy in 1966. If Ford Mustangs raced in the series there had to be a Camaro to compete with, and hopefully beat, them. The result was the Z28.

With a total of 220,906 Camaros sold in 1967, the 602 Z28s built were real rarities. That soon

changed; the Camaro's back-to-back wins in the Trans-Am in 1968 and 1969, along with favourable media coverage, enabled Chevrolet to sell 20,302 Z28s in 1969, a high point that would not be bettered until 1978. By that time, however, the Z28 wasn't much of a performance car and Chevrolet even dropped the Z28 option in 1975-76. In the 1970s the Pontiac Trans Am had clearly taken the Z28's mantle; bigger engines, better handling and a sportier image made the Pontiac far more popular.

By this stage it was time to develop the next-generation Camaro and Trans Am. There was no doubt that they would have to remain sporty cars with high-performance options but was it time to switch to front-wheel drive, which GM was finally adopting with some fervour? By 1978 the decision had been made; the cars would continue with the traditional rear-wheel drive and live rear axle. There were various good reasons for that; as Camaro volumes were relatively low, the model would not affect GM's CAFE (Corporate Average Fuel Economy) calculations so there was no need to turn it into a smaller-engined, more economical, design. Rear drive would also allow more flexibility in engine choice, from the tried and trusted small-block V8 to GM's new four-cylinder and V6 engines.

The result was the 1982 Camaro. In some respects it was little different from the original 1967

ducing a meagre 165 bhp; even that was 20 bhp more than the standard carburettor-equipped Z28 model. Neither output was sufficient for a car with any sporting pretensions, and through the decade power increased, just as it did in the Ford Mustang GT, which was still the Camaro's main rival. By 1985 the 305-cu in engine had been given a tuned port-injection system (TPI) which increased output to 205 bhp, but more significant was the addition of that injection to the 350-cu in V8 in 1987, and by 1992 that engine was rated at a respectable 245 bhp.

The ideal car – tough and predictable

During the 1980s the Camaro's profile had been raised by its being the car used in the well-publicised IROC series. IROC stood for the International Race of Champions, a series in which the top US drivers from USAC and Indy racing competed against outsiders from the world of Formula 1 or endurance racing, all in identical cars with identical power outputs. The tough and predictable Camaro proved the ideal car and gave a good few seasons of close combat from the assembled stars. Not surprisingly, Chevrolet cashed in with a special IROC model which mechanically was in Z28 specification, and by 1985 that meant 215 bhp and 130 mph.

In essence there was little difference between the first Camaros and those of the early 1990s when maximum power had risen to 245

Above: As well as IROC races, in which identical Camaros were driven by famous drivers, the IROC-Z model featured in a Firestone-sponsored series.

bhp, and in many ways that was to Chevrolet's advantage. While other manufacturers (like Mazda with their MX-5, designed to recapture the spirit of the original Lotus Elan) went for the nostalgia market, Chevrolet already had their entrant. The Z28 offered the same muscle car messages as the cars of the 1960s, and a good deal of the same performance.

By this stage it also offered open-air motoring too, as a convertible Camaro had returned to the sales list by 1987. That was a conversion sanctioned by Chevrolet and built for them by an outside company, ASC (Automotive Specialty Company). As the current-generation car was never intended to be built as a soft-top, the conversion entailed the usual problems of replacing the chassis stiffness lost in cutting off the roof. That problem was never fully resolved and was made worse by one of the Z28's main features, its extremely hard suspension. Chevrolet had managed to make the Camaro into a fine-handling car by the twin process of greatly improving the rear axle location and stiffening the suspension to the point where progress over poor surfaces rivalled the Morgan Plus 8 for the jolting that fed back into the car. But just as Morgan buyers were happy to put up with that, there was still a dedicated hard core of Camaro customers who wanted nothing more than the sounds, sensations and sheer performance offered by a small-block V8.

model. The Camaro had remained true to its roots; it had just been updated. The wheelbase had shrunk, and considerably so by seven inches, following the contemporary trend to down-sizing new models. It was when the car was compared with the Camaros of the 1970-81 era that the differences became really noticeable, with a weight-saving of over 500 lb and far trimmer, tauter lines.

In 1982 the largest engine available was a twin-throttle-body fuel-injected 305-cu in V8 pro-

Top: The 1985 Camaro IROC-Z was marketed with the same 190/215-bhp power options as the Z28, and had a top speed of 130 mph.

Above: A 1987 Camaro IROC-Z coupé, named after the cars supplied for the celebrity races and with a Z28 power output of 215 bhp from the 305-cu in V8.

Overleaf: This Camaro convertible dates from 1992. The model was attractive but the loss of the roof reduced torsional stiffness, highlighted by the hard suspension.

Driving the Camaro Z28: *refined muscle*

Above all else, the Camaro Z28 is a driver's car – it loves being driven hard and the treatment never produces any mechanical complaint. Of course it's easy to see that the car's roots lie back in the 1960s simply because of the large, rumbling V8 under the bonnet, but its road manners are anything but 1960s; the current Z28s are surprisingly nimble with sharp, accurate and well-weighted steering, and they hold on tenaciously along a twisty road. That's a remarkable achievement in many respects as, despite having been significantly down-sized compared with early Camaros, it's still a big and heavy car.

The Chevy small-block engine in Z28 tune is an absolute delight, with an instantaneous response to the accelerator. Floor the throttle and you'll be rewarded with tyre squeal and a gratifyingly hard shove in the back as the car rockets to 60 mph in 6.6 seconds and on to its maximum speed a fraction short of 150 mph. Only one change is needed from the Borg-Warner five-speed to reach 60 mph and the smooth-shifting gear change makes the performance easy to extract. It's true the firm suspension could use a little more travel on bumpy roads (which also upset the rear axle), but that's a small fault to live with.

PERFORMANCE & SPECIFICATION COMPARISON	Engine	Displacement	Power	Torque (lb ft)	Max speed	0-60 mph	Length (in/mm)	Wheelbase (in/mm)	Track front/rear	Weight (lb/kg)	Price
Chevrolet Camaro Z28	V8, overhead-valve	5735 cc	245 bhp 4400 rpm	345 lb ft 3200 rpm	150 mph 241 km/h	6.6 sec	192.6 in 4892 mm	101.0 in 2565 mm	60.0 in 60.9 in	3485 lb 1581 kg	$18,768 (1992)
Chevrolet Corvette ZR-1	V8, quad-cam, 32-valve	5727 cc	375 bhp 5800 rpm	370 lb ft 4800 rpm	171 mph 275 km/h	5.6 sec	178.5 in 4534 mm	96.2 in 2443 mm	60.0 in 62.0 in	3519 lb 1596 kg	$64,138 (1991)
Ford Mustang GT	V8, overhead-valve	4849 cc	225 bhp 4000 rpm	300 lb ft 3200 rpm	148 mph 238 km/h	7.3 sec	179.6 in 4562 mm	100.5 in 2553 mm	56.6 in 57.0 in	3445 lb 1563 kg	$16,610 (1992)
Jaguar XJR-S	V12, overhead-cam	5993 cc	333 bhp 5250 rpm	365 lb ft 3650 rpm	158 mph 254 km/h	6.5 sec	189.7 in 4818 mm	102.0 in 2591 mm	58.6 in 59.2 in	4023 lb 1825 kg	£49,950 (1992)
TVR 450 SEAC	V8, overhead-valve	4441 cc	320 bhp 5700 rpm	310 lb ft 4000 rpm	165 mph 266 km/h	4.7 sec	158.0 in 4013 mm	94.0 in 2388 mm	57.1 in 58.3 in	2315 lb 1050 kg	£37,499 (1991)

Chevrolet Camaro Data File

The Camaro and its mechanically-similar brother the Pontiac Trans Am were introduced back in the mid-1960s to offer GM customers an alternative to the Ford Mustang. The Camaro appeared in both coupé and convertible formats with a range of engine options and power outputs, from the basic 3.8-litre overhead-valve inline six-cylinder engine, coupled to a three-speed automatic transmission, to the might of the 6.5-litre V8 with a four-speed manual. There has been a Camaro in the Chevrolet line-up ever since but, like the Corvette, the car has progressed through various generations. The first restyle was in 1969; the shape changed radically in 1970, was facelifted in 1974 and 1978, and in 1982 the currrent generation of smaller and lighter Camaros was introduced with engine options ranging from four through six to eight cylinders.

Above: The 1985 Camaro Z28 IROC-Z coupé of the third styling generation. It had particularly clean and enduring sporting lines.

Styling

Although the basic form of the current-generation Camaro has been around since 1982, it still looks effective in the early 1990s. The stylist's job was made easier by the fact that there was no requirement for the shape to be space-efficient, and although the present cars are smaller than earlier Camaros they are still large enough to allow the pronounced rake (62 degrees) of the windscreen, complemented by an equally sloping back light. It's no mistake that the Camaros bear a family resemblance to the current Corvette but in fact the Camaro predates the 'Vette; there are other similarities in that the Camaro was also introduced in coupé form

only before the convertible was added in 1987. The latest Camaro's styling, apart from standing the test of time extremely well, was surprisingly versatile in that although it looked quite different from the same-generation Pontiac Trans Am, the two cars shared the same doors as well as the floorpan.

Several styling themes, principally the lower body extensions, were used to make the Z28 distinctive in 1982 and they have been continued to 1992; the current side panels are painted to match the body and feature scoops in front of the rear wheel openings. A rear deck spoiler has always been part of the package.

Above: Rear light clusters are distinctive, with acute angles echoing the windscreen rake.

Left: The long Camaro bonnet features raised panels with ventilation scoops.

Below: Stylish, race-inspired scoops in front of the rear-wheel valences are merely cosmetic.

Below: Influenced by European car interiors, the Camaro's trim and fascia were designed to reflect comfort and sophistication.

The Camaro Z28

The high-performance Z28 first appeared as a prototype in 1966, introduced as a Camaro with RPO (Regular Production Option) Z28. The Z28 name stuck but was not used on the car itself until 1968; in 1967 Z28s could only be identified by their boot and rear deck stripes. Besides its firmer suspension, 15-in rally wheels and four-speed manual transmission, the Z28 had a highly modified small-block 302-cu in (five-litre) V8 engine producing 290 bhp. Chevrolet actually deleted the Z28 from the line in 1975, only to reintroduce it in mid-1977 as a

separate model rather than an options package. By this time, however, power had dropped to a lowly 185 bhp, which was poor in a car weighing the best part of 4,000 lb.

Chevrolet started with a clean sheet of paper in 1982 and considerable emphasis was laid on improving the Z28's handling, with features like far better rear axle location. From 1982 to the early 1990s the Z28 has recovered some of its original power, the 1992 model having an optional 5.7-litre V8 with 245 bhp, enough to put it into the 150-mph bracket.

Above: A smooth muscle car, the 1992 Z28 convertible offered performance, comfort and style.

Below: The 1967 Camaro Z28, with rear stripes, was fitted with a five-litre, 290-bhp small-block V8.

Above: A 1969 Z28 fastback coupé. The first Camaros had sleek, Italian-inspired styling.

Below: A 1976 375-bhp Super Sport; the restyled body had an 'egg-crate' grille and flared arches.

Above: The revamped front styling of this 1981 Z28 was truly decadent, but underneath it the power was falling in the battle against American emissions laws.

Chassis and running gear

The down-sized platform introduced in 1982 is still used on the 1992 models; it is of welded construction with boxed side rails onto which is welded the two-door coupé or convertible body shell. In one respect it's significantly different from previous chassis, in that the front subframe has been discarded in favour of a front cross-member (attached by six bolts) which supports the engine as well as the front suspension. The mechanical make-up is just as straightforward, MacPherson struts being used at the front in conjunction with an anti-roll bar, and the Camaro shares the distinction with the Ford Mustang of being among the last high-performance cars in the world to feature a live rear axle. Considerable attention has been paid to axle location, though, with two robust

trailing arms complementing a single central torque arm connected to the differential carrier, coil springs (rather than the semi-elliptics of old), telescopic dampers and a Panhard rod.

The standard braking system consists of 10.5-in diameter ventilated discs at the front with drums at the rear, but larger (11.9-in diameter) ventilated discs can be specified for the front with 11.7-in diameter ones at the back. Chevrolet have, however, stayed faithful to the old-fashioned system of recirculating-ball steering, power-assisted of course. The V8 engine is mated to a five-speed Borg-Warner manual transmission as standard in the five-litre Z28 option, but its inability to handle more than 300 lb ft of torque means the larger, more powerful 5.7-litre V8 can only be ordered with automatic transmission.

Below: Simple and effective, the front cross-member supports the engine and the sprung lower control arms, with MacPherson struts above them.

Below: The live rear axle, with coil springs, dampers and differential, has a restraining torque arm fixed to it, plus a Panhard rod behind, to limit lateral axle movement.

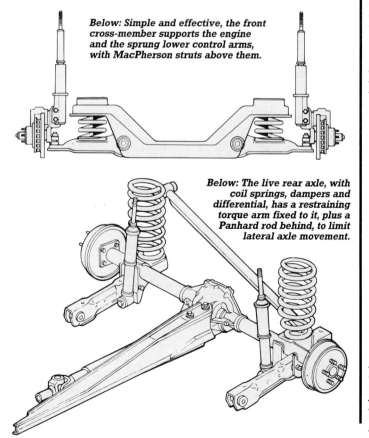

Engine

The 1992 Camaro Z28 is still powered by Chevrolet's small-block V8, which in larger, 5.7-litre, form is over-bored compared with the standard Z28 five-litre unit, having over-square bore and stroke dimensions of 101.6 mm × 88.4 mm. It's very similar to the engine used in the Corvette but, in contrast to the Corvette, the Camaro unit has retained cast-iron, instead of aluminium, cylinder heads and has soldiered on with cast-iron, rather than stainless-steel, exhaust manifolds.

In most respects both the five- and 5.7-litre versions are traditional iron American V8s with a single central camshaft and pushrod overhead-valve gear. Indeed in some ways they are more traditional than the first Z28 engine, which was a highly stressed, high-revving unit; the current versions are under-stressed and low-revving with the emphasis on producing huge low-range torque. Their cam timing, intake and exhaust systems are designed to be at their most effective at 4,400 rpm. The valve gear, however, features hydraulic roller tappets to reduce friction, and, when equipped with electronic fuel injection, power for both the five- and 5.7-litre engine is excellent at 205 and 245 bhp respectively, with torque outputs of 285 and 345 lb ft.

Below: The five-litre V8 of a 1992 Camaro with Single Point Injection gave 173 bhp at 4,000 rpm and 255 lb ft of torque at 2,400 rpm.

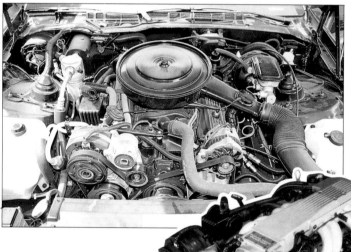

Right: The High Output V8 of 1992 was fitted with a full Rochester petrol injection system, rather than the simpler single-point system which fed fuel through a carburettor-like device (above). Power outputs rose to 213 bhp at 4,200 rpm and 285 lb ft at 3,200 rpm.

Below: The Camaro's long bonnet leaves plenty of space for the radiator and compact V8.

Above: Steering is by power-assisted recirculating-ball. Note the link to the front suspension, plus the disc brake, MacPherson strut and front cross-member, which supports the V8 and suspension coil springs.

Above: In 1992 Chevrolet decided to fit the LT1 version of the Corvette's small-block V8 engine in the Camaro. It differed from the 5.7-litre used in the 1992 cars chiefly in having four rather than two valves per cylinder, although they were still operated by pushrods and rockers from a single camshaft mounted in the centre of the 'V' in the traditional manner. The more efficient cylinder-head design helped the LT1 produce as much as 300 bhp, enough to ensure the competitiveness of the fastest Camaros.

Below: The steeply-raked windscreen is a strong style feature on the third-generation, down-sized Camaro, and the coupé roof an important structural element; the convertibles are noticeably less stiff. The interior is trimmed to a high standard and bears European influences.

Below: Rear-seat accommodation is sufficient for adults, and the long doors facilitate easy access. Broad rear pillars reduce driver visibility. Note the large rear screen and capacious boot.

Above: This special-bodied 1982 Z28 Camaro pace car was used at the Indianapolis Motor Speedway. Such a venue was very beneficial for product promotion.

Above: Shown is a five-speed manual gearbox; as with the automatic, top gear gives a comfortable 38.5 mph per 1,000 rpm. Note the torque arm which extends from the gearbox to the differential.

Above: The rear suspension features coil springs and dampers, trailing arms, a torque arm and differential, and, in front of the exhaust, a Panhard rod, joined to the chassis on the right-hand side of the car.

Above: The KKK K27 turbocharger on the Sport Quattro had its own oil feed and the benefit of water-cooled bearings.

Above: The Sport's 2133-cc engine had four valves per cylinder and a larger turbo to produce 306 bhp in standard form. Competition versions featured anything between 400 and 600 bhp.

Right: The cutaway reveals the four-valve layout of the Sport Quattro's five-cylinder twin-cam. The turbo is shown near the centre of the engine and the intercooler (sectioned) is on the right.

Above: Exclusivity was assured when Audi gave each of the initial 200 initial Sports a numbered dashboard plaque.

Chevrolet Corvette Sting Ray

Brilliantly styled by Bill Mitchell, the glassfibre-bodied Sting Ray became America's favourite sports car: it also went as fast as it looked, thanks to V8s of up to seven litres.

Above: One of only five, the competition Corvette Grand Sport was designed by Chevrolet in 1963 to beat Shelby's AC Cobras, but had to be raced by privateers because of the company's 'no-race' pledge.

Zora Arkus-Duntov always had great hopes for the Corvette. His tag as the father of the Corvette was a fairer one than many; he really did have enormous influence on how the car looked and, more importantly, how it went.

After the short-lived first-generation Corvette, which merely proved that it was possible to get a sports car built within the GM empire, the second-generation car (which ran from 1955 to 1962) showed what could be achieved with some fairly simple engineering. Duntov wanted more; he wanted to make the Corvette as sophisticated as some of its European rivals. He knew how to do it, knew that Chevrolet were capable of doing it, and outlined what was required. The car had to

be smaller and more nimble, have better handling, better use of interior space and, finally, the great advantage of independent rear suspension for the first time. The third-generation Corvette, the Sting Ray, appeared in 1963, named after chief stylist Bill Mitchell's one-off Stingray racer (confusingly, one word rather than the two of the production car), and it owed its look very much to the dominant Mitchell. Whereas the second-generation car had elements of very traditional roadster design, the Sting Ray radiated the aggressive personality of Mitchell himself. Above all, Mitchell wanted the car to have absolutely distinctive styling. He felt that the pick of the European sports cars looked too much the same – elegant, yes, but too similar and too

understated; there would be no such chance of anyone mistaking the Sting Ray for any other model... Also, by the end of the second-generation of Corvettes, the car had become heavy and looked clumsy. The Sting Ray reversed that trend in all respects. The wheelbase was reduced by four inches, and that allowed the track to be reduced front and rear while still giving the car a wide stance. The centre of gravity was also reduced, by 1½ inches, and the weight distribution was improved from 45/55 per cent to a more nearly neutral 48/52. Those chassis changes alone would have made a significant difference to the car's behaviour. They were enough that Duntov's desire for a more sophisticated form of chassis frame was overcome, and the new car retained the perimeter chassis, which was simple and strong and, as far as GM were concerned, more than adequate. There was one aspect that Duntov could not bring himself to compromise on, however, and that was the rear suspension. The old heavy live axle on semi-elliptic leaf springs was always going to affect handling and roadholding, and it had to go. The new system started a trend which the Corvette kept on into the 1990s – the use of a transverse leaf spring, in this case mounted below the differential. Even that wasn't ideal, but it was a great improvement.

The rest of the car's make-up was much as before, and although the body looked radically different and far more modern, it was made in glassfibre, like all Corvettes before and since.

Left: A front view of the rather brutally styled Grand Sport. These cars, which had smaller than standard bodies, were based on a ladder-frame chassis and fitted with hand-made suspension and transmission; power units included the 550-bhp 377-cu in V8, and the 560-bhp 427-cu in V8. Performance was phenomenal.

Right: The classic look of a 1963 Sting Ray with split rear windscreen, the model most sought-after today by collectors. Power came from a 327-cu in V8, through four-speed manual or three-speed automatic transmissions. Chevrolet offered a host of power, suspension, axle and trim options.

There was never any question about what would power the Sting Ray; it had to be Chevrolet's small-block V8, the 327-cu in powerplant introduced on the last of the previous-generation cars in 1962. It was the same with transmissions – the choice was either the four-speed manual or three-speed automatic, and the brakes were no more effective than they had been on the previous car. Duntov obviously realised that the Corvette needed disc brakes, but the first Sting Ray soldiered on with large but not very effective drums until 1965.

That was a shame if you wanted to use all the car's tremendous performance. Make no mistake, the Sting Ray was a very fast car indeed. Of course it depended on which of the huge range of options you selected, but even the base model had 250 bhp. In the first year of production you could have the 327-cu in pushrod V8 with 250, 300, 340 or 360 bhp, and the higher states of tune would power the Corvette to 60 mph from a standstill in around 6.5 seconds, and on to a top speed in the 140-mph region, while their huge torque outputs made overtaking manoeuvres ridiculously simple almost regardless of what gear you chose.

Top speed was taken over the 150-mph mark

From the beginning, Sting Rays were built in both coupé and convertible form and the 1963-model coupé had a feature dear to Bill Mitchell's heart: the split rear screen. In this instance his styling instinct was exactly right, although others disagreed. The feature did not survive, however, as it went a good way towards ruining rearward visibility, and was replaced by an unimpeded window. In other respects Chevrolet tinkered around with the Corvette from year to year, in the best American tradition. Very little indeed (by American standards) was done to the styling, the main change being the almost immediate deletion of the divided rear screen on the coupé. Two years after its introduction a larger, 396-cu in (6.5-litre), V8 was added to the range and there were as many as five levels of output for the 327 engine to supplement the incredible 425 bhp of the bigger engine. That surely was enough power for anyone, particularly in that chassis, but there was always room for more power in the mid-1960s and that was duly added in 1966 in the form of Chevy's 427-cu in (7.0-litre) big-block engine. That produced as much as 425 bhp (but, with 460 lb ft, more torque than the 396 motor). Not surprisingly, that took top speed over the 150-mph mark, dropped the 0-60 mph time down to comfortably below six seconds and meant that the standing quarter-mile was over and done with by the time 13 seconds had elapsed, and that

was important in a country where straight-line speed was valued far higher than handling. That was just as well in the case of the 427, as the greater weight of the big engine had, not surprisingly, altered the near-neutral weight distribution of the smaller-engined cars, and handling and roadholding suffered accordingly. But, because you bought a 427 for its power and acceleration, that was acceptable. Luckily, by this time disc brakes with four-pot calipers had finally made their appearance (and on all four wheels, too), and the committed 427 driver had a chance of stopping his Corvette in an acceptable distance – he certainly wouldn't have done that with the drum brakes, even the optional larger sintered metal type.

The big sintered metal brakes were really intended for competition use, but although the previous generation of Corvettes had enjoyed great success in domestic SCCA (Sports Car Club of America) race action (and shown well at Le Mans occasionally), the superior Sting Ray was overshadowed by an older, cruder, design in the shape of Carroll Shelby's AC Cobra. The Cobra was much lighter and had less front area (making up for the Sting Ray's impressive drag coefficient of 0.37). Although Dick Thomson won the SCCA Class A with a 1963 327 model, thereafter the Cobras reigned supreme.

The Cobra challenge led Duntov to create the ultimate Sting Ray (ignoring the similar-styled pure racing Grand Sport models). That was the L88 version of the 427-cu in-engined 'Vette. That sported alloy cylinder heads, a very high 12.5:1 compression ratio, an 850-cfm Holley four-barrel carburettor, and a staggering output of 560 bhp. To tame that power, the L88 came with stiffer-handling suspension, a Positraction limited-slip differential and bigger brakes. Twenty cars were built, but even they were overshadowed by Shelby's simple expedient of dropping a 427-cu in V8 into the Cobra. Nevertheless, as the Corvette has lived on after the Cobra died, America's sports car had the last laugh.

Top: In private hands, the Corvette Sting Rays, such as this 1966 coupé, won many races, even if they were no match for the AC Cobras.

Above: The Grand Sports were built to run at Le Mans in 1963, and expected to reach 180 mph on the Mulsanne straight, but in March the project was cancelled.

Overleaf: The Sting Ray convertible was very popular, and was priced in 1966 at $4,084, some $200 less than the coupé, which it outsold by two to one.

Driving the Sting Ray: *for the brave*

Once you have accustomed yourself to an interior that looks garish to European eyes, with bright-metal complemented by bright colours, the Corvette comes across as a serious performance car, particularly in, say, manual and small-block form with the Rochester fuel injection and as much as 375 bhp. That guarantees performance in any gear and, for the brave, a top speed of just over 145 mph. Very fast acceleration is easily achieved too; the clutch may be initially heavy but the four-speed Borg-Warner gear change used in the 1963 model has a short throw and is smooth and light, surprisingly so in view of how much torque it was designed to stand.

What isn't surprising is the ease with which the wheels can be spun in first and second gear, even on a dry surface, while considerable care and skill is required in the wet if the car is fitted with its original-equipment tyres rather than more modern radials. It's easy to get the back out of line using too much throttle, but thankfully the recirculating-ball steering is high-geared and precise, and the Sting Ray is basically an understeerer. Despite its incredible performance, the Corvette's independent suspension gives a comfortable ride by sports car standards.

PERFORMANCE & SPECIFICATION COMPARISON	Engine	Displacement	Power	Torque (lb ft)	Max speed	0-60 mph	Length (in/mm)	Wheelbase (in/mm)	Track front/rear	Weight (lb/kg)	Price
Chevrolet Corvette Sting Ray	V8, overhead-valve	5363 cc	350 bhp 5800 rpm	360 lb ft 3000 rpm	147 mph 237 km/h	6.5 sec	175.3 in 4453 mm	98.0 in 2489 mm	56.3 in 57.0 in	3248 lb 1473 kg	$4,252 (1964)
Aston Martin DB4 GT Zagato	Inline-six, twin-cam	3670 cc	314 bhp 6000 rpm	278 lb ft 5400 rpm	152 mph 245 km/h	6.1 sec	168.0 in 4267 mm	93.0 in 2362 mm	54.4 in 54.5 in	2765 lb 1254 kg	£5,470 (1962)
Jaguar E-type 4.2 Coupé	Inline-six, twin-cam	4235 cc	265 bhp 5400 rpm	283 lb ft 4000 rpm	150 mph 241 km/h	7.0 sec	175.3 in 4453 mm	96.0 in 2438 mm	50.0 in 50.0 in	2640 lb 1198 kg	£2,060 (1964)
Jensen CV8	V8, overhead-valve	5916 cc	305 bhp 4800 rpm	395 lb ft 3000 rpm	131 mph 211 km/h	8.4 sec	184.5 in 4686 mm	107.0 in 2718 mm	56.0 in 57.0 in	3514 lb 1594 kg	£3,392 (1963)
Maserati GTi Sebring	Inline-six, twin-cam	3485 cc	235 bhp 5800 rpm	232 lb ft 4000 rpm	135 mph 217 km/h	8.4 sec	176.0 in 4470 mm	98.4 in 2500 mm	54.7 in 53.5 in	3329 lb 1510 kg	N/A

Corvette Sting Ray Data File

The Sting Ray was the third-generation Corvette. The first appeared in the early 1950s, initially with only a six-cylinder pushrod engine and automatic transmission. It was not a huge success but was quickly changed into the second-generation Corvette, which by this time had a V8 engine, a choice of manual and automatic transmission and, depending on engine choice and tune, quite staggering performance. It was a simple design with a live rear axle, a separate chassis and a glassfibre body, but was an effective combination that even enjoyed racing success. By 1963 a change was overdue, however, and although the Sting Ray preserved the traditional separate chassis and glassfibre body, the style was radically different and independent rear suspension had been introduced.

Above: Superbly styled by Bill Mitchell, the Corvette coupé looked fast whether being driven or simply standing still. This is a 1964 model.

Styling

The Sting Ray was very much the creation of Bill Mitchell, and its descent from his one-off Stingray model was very clear. The Stingray was an open car with a D-type Jaguar-like fairing running back from the driver's position. That balanced the car, which would otherwise have looked quite flat. It clearly had to go, however, for the production car which was, in fact, designed as a coupé first and foremost (making it the first Corvette coupé). The designers' rationale was that it was far easier to start with a coupé and 'convert' that to a convertible than the other way round.

The most distinctive feature of the first year's coupé (from 1963) was the split rear window. According to Mitchell, that dividing line down the screen integrated the rear to the roof and to the central raised section on the bonnet. It only lasted one season, however, on practical grounds; the way it spoiled rear vision was very irritating. Apart from the dividing screen, the Corvette's most noteworthy styling points were the

foldaway headlights, which gave Mitchell one way of hiding the quad light set-up which seemed to be a marketing requirement in those days, and of preserving the sharp crease of the body line around the front.

The tops of the doors broke into the roof line; it was a device that had been seen before (on the ill-fated Tucker Torpedo, for example). That had the merit of allowing easier entry, at the cost of having water drip on you when the door was opened in the rain.

Although the basic shape of the car stayed the same throughout its life, there were the inevitable styling changes each season. First the two fake air vents on the bonnet were removed for the 1964 models, then for 1965 an egg-crate-type grille replaced the horizontal chrome bars and three vertical louvres were set into the front wings. The most stylish car of all, by common consent, appeared in the last year of the Sting Ray generation. The 1967 model was given five wing louvres and the sill panels were redesigned to give the car a fresher, slimmer profile.

Above: The first Stingray was a race-car and design exercise by Mitchell, started in 1958.

Below: A 1965 drop-head; the clean styling by Mitchell looked very fresh in the early 1960s.

Above: The 1963 Corvette was the first American production car to have retractable foldaway headlamps since the 1942 DeSoto.

Below: The centre console of the 1966 model held a clock, various switches and a vertical radio.

Below: From 1965 on, three open side vents ducted air from the engine bay and front wheels.

Below: Among the 1966 options offered was the Side Mount Exhaust System, for $131.65. The chromed, race-like pipes hung on both sides of the car; that year some 3,600 buyers chose them.

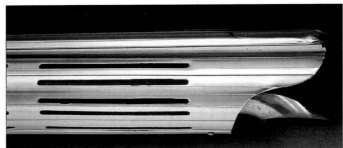

Above: Bill Mitchell had first introduced chromed, recessed tail lamps on his 1961 Corvette.

Below: The fascia incorporated a speedometer, rev-counter and many other gauges.

Below: The cross-flags badge hid the fuel filler at the rear of the body; there was no boot lid.

Chassis and running gear

Although Zora Arkus-Duntov had produced very sophisticated Corvette variants, such as his spaceframed SS model in 1958, complete with de Dion rear suspension, the practicalities of volume-production meant that the Sting Ray would be fairly conventional. The chassis was a box-section perimeter frame which kicked up at the rear to clear the rear suspension and which narrowed at the front to hold the engine and front suspension. There were cross-members behind the gearbox and under the nose of the differential, while the differential itself was bolted to another cross-member (via rubber bushes for noise and vibration insulation). The final cross-member was right at the back of the car. Front suspension was by conventional pressed-steel wishbones and coil springs, but the rear was a true novelty, featuring (for space reasons) a set of transverse leaf springs fixed to the bottom of the differential housing and acting as the lower link in an independent system in which the driveshafts were the upper links. Deep-section trailing arms were used along with small angled control rods running from the sides of the differential housing to the bottom of the hub-carriers. It was unusual, but it worked. It was revised for the 1964 model when different-thickness leaves were used in the transverse spring to give variable-rate springing and an initial softer ride without compromising handling. Gas-pressurised dampers were also introduced.

Above: The glassfibre body of the 1963 Sting Ray had much more steel built into it than earlier models, but still weighed less.

Right: Front suspension was by wishbones and coil springs. Drum brakes were fitted, and steering was the recirculating-ball type.

Below: Two views of the fully-independent rear suspension, with trailing radius arms, control arms and open driveshafts. The lower transverse leaf spring was used because the body left insufficient space for coil springs.

Engine

Apart from the very first models, which had the Blue Flame straight-six engine, all Corvettes have been powered by V8s. Until the current cars with their multiple valves per cylinder and double overhead cams, they have all been of the classic American V8 design, namely a cast-iron block and heads, a crankshaft supported on five main bearings, and pushrod actuation of two valves per cylinder by a single camshaft mounted in the centre of the 'V'.

The first Sting Rays were powered by a development of the original small-block V8 designed by Ed Cole and used in the 1955 Corvette in 265-cu in, 195-bhp, form. It was an engine capable of considerable stretching and it was the 327 version that was used in the Sting Ray, with a 4-in bore and a 3.25-in stroke, maintaining the over-square dimensions of the original design. The 327 was available in tunes of from 250 bhp to 375 bhp with various carburation arrangements from Carter to Holley carburettors and Rochester fuel injection.

During its career the Sting Ray was given the big-block V8. That was also an iron pushrod design, but the valves were angled to produce a more efficient combustion-chamber shape. That in turn meant the pushrods were set at odd angles, giving rise to the big-block's nickname, 'Porcupine'. The inlet valves were angled at 26 degrees from the cylinder axis, and the exhausts at 17 degrees. In other respects it was a conventional over-square V8, but a very powerful one in both 396-cu in and 427-cu in forms. Apart from the alloy-headed L88 version, the most powerful big-block option was the L72 with an 11.0:1 compression ratio, solid valve-lifters and 425 bhp at 6,400 rpm, showing that a pushrod V8 could rev with the best of them.

Below: Valve size was increased to the limits of the combustion chamber; the larger inlet valve is to the right of the chamber.

Below: The front of the body had a sharply creased leading edge with recessed twin headlamps.

Right: Under the glassfibre bodywork there was a sturdy perimeter-frame chassis and front assembly supporting the V8 engine and double-wishbone suspension. Note the front anti-roll bar, which improved the car's stability on corners.

Above right: The engine was set well back in the chassis, which gave nearly 50/50 front/rear weight distribution and excellent handling.

Below: The stock cast-iron Chevrolet V8 was an overhead-valve, pushrod unit with a single Holley four-barrel carburettor. The Sting Ray was offered with V8s of 327 cu in (5.4 litres), 396 cu in (6.5 litres) and 427 cu in (7.0 litres). This is the optional L79 327-cu in engine which, with its high 11.25:1 compression ratio, produced 350 bhp at 5,800 rpm.

Above: The 327-cu in (5.4-litre) engine was offered with optional Rochester mechanical fuel injection from 1963 to 1965; with an 11.25:1 compression ratio, it produced 375 bhp at 6,200 rpm. In standard carburettor form, output was a mere 250 bhp.

Below: 1963 Sting Rays had a split rear window. The fuel tank was mounted on the perimeter frame, and luggage space was behind the two seats; with no boot lid, luggage had to be taken in and out through the doors.

Left: The 1963 model had knock-off wheel spinners with two or three prongs.

Right: With its tail out, a club-racing Sting Ray leaves a Mustang behind. Although they were hard put to outpace AC Cobras, Mercedes-Benz 300 SLs and Porsches, Sting Rays won many SCCA events during the late 1960s and early 1970s.

Citroën SM

When the masters of French innovation teamed up with the makers of Italian thoroughbreds, the result was a unique blend of performance, comfort and distinctive grand touring in the Continental style – the V6 Citroën SM.

Citroën and Maserati... an odd alliance, this, between a quirky (and at times eccentric) French volume-manufacturer, and an old-fashioned Italian producer of highly expensive, exotic and very limited-production supercars.

It all started from a Citroën project to see just how much power could be fed through front-wheel drive. André Lefebvre, the man behind the *Traction Avant* Citroën, placed engineer Jacques Né in charge of testing cars with performance levels far above that of the DS saloon. Né decided to build a front-drive sports car.

A number of short-chassis DS cars were built in the late 1950s, fitted with a variety of engines, among them a V6 and a twin-overhead-camshaft 2.1-litre four-cylinder unit. Eventually Né's work was put on a more formal footing, and given a project name: S-vehicle, later formalised to SER.

S-vehicle 1 was a short-chassis DS platform fitted with a convertible body and powered by a tuned DS engine. Number 2 was another convertible, but this time fitted with the 2.1-litre twin-cam engine.

Eventually, Citroën's manager, Pierre Bercot, acquired Maserati as part of his expansion programme, and mooted a Maserati-powered GT. In early 1965 Bercot had started talking to Maserati's owners, the Orsi family. By September of 1966, they had come to terms on a joint project whereby Citroën would build a GT car powered by a Maserati engine. In March 1968, Citroën bought a controlling interest (60 per cent) in Maserati, taking full ownership during 1969.

Unconventional outside and under the skin

Citroën's own twin-cam engine, although regarded as a possibility for a lower-priced SER, was going to be too expensive to produce. By 1967, Né had a couple of Maserati V6 engines fitted into DS hacks. These vehicles were not good enough to form the basis of the SER, though: Citroën wanted to show the world how to build what they considered a proper GT.

The result, the SM, was a superb-looking car, with its sleek fastback tail, full-width glass nose-piece, faired-in rear wheels and long, low lines. If it looked unconventional from the outside, it certainly carried that through under the skin.

The engine was a 2.7-litre V6 which had four chain-driven overhead camshafts, two per bank of three cylinders. Constructed from aluminium alloy, with dry cylinder liners, the Maserati-designed engine produced 170 bhp in Weber-carburettor form, and 178 bhp when fitted with Bosch fuel injection. In 3.0-litre form, for the American market, it gave 180 bhp. At hardly more than a foot long, it was so small as to allow longitudinal mounting behind the transmission, for excellent weight distribution.

Complex and compact it may have been, but the SM's engine was relatively conventional. Not so the chassis, which was front-wheel-driven. Today, plenty of manufacturers produce truly high-performance front-drive cars – Lotus has the Elan, Lancia the Thema 8.32 and Alfa the 164, for example – but Citroën was certainly bucking the trend in 1970.

Being a Citroën, the SM was of course fitted with the company's self-levelling hydro-pneumatic suspension, which relied on gas-filled, fluid-pressurised spheres in place of conventional mechanical springs and dampers. The driver was, as with the DS, able to select one of three ride heights from a lever inside the cockpit, the most useful function being to raise the car

Above: With its faired-in rear wheels, fastback roof and long bonnet with a glass nose, only Citroën could have styled the distinctive SM.

Right: SM performance was proved in events such as the 1972 Portuguese TAP Rally, at Figueira da Foz, with drivers Bjorn Waldegaard and Hank Thorselius.

to clear obstacles or travel over rough ground.

Another novelty was the Vari-Power speed-sensitive power steering, on which the degree of assistance diminished with increasing speed. Its powered self-centring also aided parking manoeuvres. The four-wheel disc brakes were power-assisted, too, requiring only the gentlest of touches. The SM had one further novelty: inner main-beam driving lights that moved to point in the same direction as the front wheels were steered.

Between 1970 and 1975 Citroën built 12,920 of these amazing machines, before a number of circumstances – including the 1973 'energy crisis' – conspired to bury the car. Other reasons for its

demise were political. Just when the SM was going through its gestation period, Citroën wasn't only Citroën any more, but also the leading company in an automotive group that included Berliet, Panhard, Comotor (a Wankel engine project, shared with NSU) and Maserati. All through this time, Citroën was losing money – big money. So when Fiat started taking an interest in Citroën, the French carmaker's major shareholder, Michelin, saw an opportunity to rid itself of what was becoming a liability.

By January 1969, Fiat owned around 20 per cent of Citroën in a joint deal with the tyre company, but the liaison didn't last long.

The last year to see serious SM production was 1973. While just 868 SMs were completed in 1970, 4,988 rolled off the lines in 1971, and 4,036 in 1972. In 1973, 2,619 were built, but the energy crisis had killed the car and mainstream production was discontinued.

In 1974, a number were built up from existing parts stock, before production was transferred to Ligier, near Vichy, a small race-car manufacturer in which Citroën had taken a financial stake. The final SMs were built there in 1975. Of the total production run, 5,509 SMs were sold in France. Near-equal numbers were registered in Italy (2,070) and the USA (2,037). Some 971 went to West Germany, 327 to Britain, 396 to Canada, 220 to Switzerland and 338 to the Benelux countries.

Any chance of a reprieve died with the final act in Citroën's crisis management. Peugeot and Citroën merged in December 1974; Panhard was integrated within the new company, Berliet was sold to Renault, and Maserati was put into liquidation, from which it was rescued by Alejandro De Tomaso and the Italian government.

Early in the SM's career, Citroën assessed the car's motorsport potential. In 1970, four basically standard cars were entered for the Morocco Rally, where they finished first, third and fourth. For 1972, a new car was developed around the 270-bhp engine; using a short-wheelbase, chopped Kamm-tailed body, close-ratio gearing and lightweight panels, it was known as the SM Rallye. One finished third in the 1972 Portuguese TAP Rally, and another sixth in the 1973 Ivory Coast Rally.

Plans were made to race a 340-bhp 'breadvan' SM, but it never happened, and the SM rarely competed. One failed to qualify for Le Mans in 1971, another ran as high as third in the 1971 Spa 24 Hours, and one ran second in the same race in 1974, failing to finish.

In truth, though, the SM was never really a competition car, and any attempts to turn it into one were wasting money that Citroën could ill afford to squander. It's best regarded as a brave attempt to produce the ultimate GT, and some adherents reckon that Citroën succeeded . . .

Above: The SM looked right as a convertible, too, and nine were created by the famous firm of coachbuilders, Henri Chapron. The result was a luxury tourer ideal for the warmer climes of the Continent.

Overleaf: The convertible's rear end treatment looks angular compared with the flowing lines at the front, owing to the removal of the rear window, but Citroën was noted for eccentric design features. The company is more conservative today.

Driving the Citroën SM: *easy does it*

It takes a little time to get used to a Citroën SM. The powered steering is so sensitive that at first you invariably use too much force, both at high and low speeds, which causes the car to lurch in an undignified fashion. Once you have come to terms with it, however, you are quite likely to become a convert.

The brakes, too, need delicacy: apply the normal amount of pressure to the mushroom-like button and the car will stand on its nose – a gentle hint is all the SM needs to haul it down from high speed.

It's hard to believe that a true GT car can ride so well. The SM absorbs bumps with supreme ease and is

uncannily stable. The only drawback to the hydro-pneumatic suspension system's suppleness is the degree of roll in hard cornering.

The Maserati V6 initially feels out of character with the car. It pulls well from low rpm but really needs to be revved hard to produce the best performance. That's hardly surprising really, as although the SM's top speed shows some aerodynamic efficiency, it is a heavier car than its rivals and the engine's torque output is lower. Nevertheless in injected form the engine will push the SM to 137 mph, but its raciness seems at odds with the car's serene cruising ability.

PERFORMANCE & SPECIFICATION COMPARISON	Engine	Displacement	Power	Torque (lb ft)	Max speed	0-60 mph	Length (in/mm)	Wheelbase (in/mm)	Track front/rear	Weight (lb/kg)	Price
Citroën SM	V6, quad-cam	2670 cc	178 bhp 5500 rpm	171 lb ft 4000 rpm	142 mph 229 km/h	8.3 sec	192.5 in 4890 mm	116.1 in 2949 mm	60.1 in 52.5 in	3197 lb 1450 kg	£6,154 (1973)
Alfa Romeo Montreal	V8, quad-cam	2593 cc	200 bhp 6500 rpm	173 lb ft 4750 rpm	137 mph 220 km/h	8.1 sec	166.0 in 4216 mm	92.5 in 2350 mm	54.3 in 52.5 in	2811 lb 1275 kg	£4,999 (1973)
BMW 3.0 CSL	Inline-six, overhead-cam	3003 cc	200 bhp 5500 rpm	199 lb ft 4300 rpm	133 mph 214 km/h	7.3 sec	183.4 in 4658 mm	103.3 in 2624 mm	56.9 in 55.1 in	2888 lb 1310 kg	£7,469 (1973)
Ferrari 308 GTB	V8, quad-cam	2927 cc	255 bhp 7700 rpm	210 lb ft 5000 rpm	154 mph 248 km/h	6.5 sec	166.5 in 4229 mm	94.1 in 2390 mm	57.9 in 57.5 in	2870 lb 1302 kg	£11,997 (1976)
Maserati Merak	V6, quad-cam	2965 cc	208 bhp 5800 rpm	188 lb ft 4500 rpm	143 mph 230 km/h	7.7 sec	170.4 in 4328 mm	102.2 in 2596 mm	57.8 in 57.0 in	3062 lb 1389 kg	£7,821 (1974)

Citroën SM Data File

There was no precedent for the SM in Citroën's past. The Paris-based company made its fortune with simple, keenly-priced cars in the 1920s, before shocking the automotive world in 1934 with the front-wheel-drive *Traction Avant*. This was the world's first practical front-drive car, but it bankrupted the company. From this time on, however, Citroën was committed to front-wheel drive. Its next revolutionary product, the DS of 1955, was also front-driven, with the addition of the ingenious hydro-pneumatic suspension concept. This used gas-filled spheres at each wheel in place of metal springs (compression of the gas provided inherently progressive springing), linked by a hydraulic system pressurised by an engine-driven pump, which provided damping, self-levelling and ride height control. A further sphere accumulated pressurised fluid to act as a reservoir for instant response, and both brakes and steering were power-assisted from the same source.

When Citroën linked up with Maserati to produce the SM (S-vehicle Maserati), it was inevitable that this, too, would be front-wheel-driven, but no-one quite thought that it would look so sensational, and no-one could have foreseen the technical ingenuity under the skin.

Above: With the top up, the convertible SM looks even more curious – note the redesigned, deeper, rear window shape.

Above: The ultimate SM?: Henri Chapron's Presidential four-door convertible. Two were built.

Below: Chapron built nine four-door limousines, and the results were very harmonious.

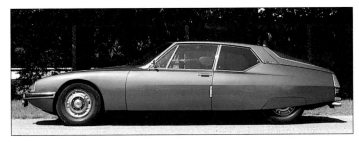

Above: Robert Opron's design looks very aerodynamic, but the measured Cd figure of 0.39 is not particularly low today.

Styling

By the time the SM project was under way, Citroën's chief stylist, Flamingo Bertoni, creator of the Traction Avant and DS, was dead. In his place came Robert Opron, a 32-year-old who had begun his career as an architect. Under his management, in 1968, the exterior and interior studios were separated, and one of the first products of this approach was the SM.

The car that emerged was stunning. With its sleek, pointed nose, faired-in rear wheels and long fastback, it also provided the starting point for both the CX and GS models which followed. The SM looked even better when riding on Michelin's optional carbonfibre road wheels. It appeared incredibly sleek, yet despite aerodynamic studies made early on, the SM didn't have a particularly outstanding drag coefficient, at 0.39; the science of aerodynamics has progressed far since its creation.

Various proposals were made for the interior, the oddest being one which featured an oval steering wheel and strip-type speedometer. Big circular dials gained management approval, but it was found in

prototypes that there just wasn't room for them. So Henri Dargent's studio produced a dash with ellipsoidal instruments, matched by a slightly oval, typically Citroën, single-spoke steering wheel.

Several special SMs were made. Citroën actually built a full-scale mock-up of a four-door SM. This was vetoed by management but coachbuilders Chapron and Heuliez carried out a number of conversions. First of these was the Heuliez-built Espace, a 'T'-roofed semi-convertible with a type of sunroof on both sides of the central 'T'-bar, shown at the Paris Salon in 1971. In 1972, Chapron built the Opéra, a four-door formal notchback limousine produced for Queen Elizabeth's visit to Paris, with 20 inches added to the wheelbase. The same firm was responsible for two other SM variants. There was the Presidential, a long-wheelbase four-door convertible with a removable hard-top cover for the front seats. Best of the lot was Chapron's Mylord, a gorgeous-looking two-door convertible. Like the four-door, it never made it into production.

Right: The SM boasted fuel injection and unusually-shaped stainless-steel brightwork.

Below: The innermost of the faired-in headlights turn with the wheels, as with the DS.

Right: In the multi-function cluster of information lights, the centre light is for the primary pump.

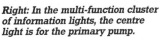

Below: Note the oval instruments and wheel, and, just visible, the button brake control, which was very sensitive to pressure.

Below: From any angle, no other car looks like an SM – which must be one of the attractions of owning one.

Chassis and suspension

The SM was a novelty in the early 1970s high-performance firmament, in that it used a front-engine/front-wheel-drive configuration, as opposed to the more conventional front-engine/rear-wheel-drive approach or the then-fashionable mid-engine/rear-drive layout pioneered by Lamborghini. The platform-type chassis was conventional enough, sharing as much as was practical with the DS to lower costs. The suspension was radical, though, as it was adapted from the Citroën DS. Whereas the DS had leading arms at the front, the SM was given a twin-trailing-arm arrangement with parallelogram geometry. An anti-roll bar was also fitted. At the back there were DS-type trailing arms, linked by an anti-roll bar.

Like the DS, the SM used Citroën's hydro-pneumatic system, which provided superbly supple progressive-rate springing with inherent damping and self-levelling. Engineer Jacques Né investigated active suspension for the SM, developing hydro-mechanical control of the car's roll angles. But although Citroën had an active suspension system operational in 1975, it was too expensive to put into production and was put on the shelf until suitable electronic sensors and micro-processors became available.

Perhaps the most novel piece of chassis engineering on the SM was its Vari-Power steering. A very fast 9.4:1 rack was fitted, giving just two turns lock-to-lock, controlled by variable power assistance. The amount of assistance varied with vehicle speed and steering position, so that full power was available at low (parking) speeds, and virtually none at high speeds. This was added to power-assisted self-centring, which came into play when there was no driver-applied force on the steering wheel.

The brakes were powered by the same engine-pressurised hydraulic system as the suspension – another carry-over from the DS. The front discs were mounted inboard, with the rear discs outboard. Braking effort to the rear wheels was modulated by the rear suspension: with weight off the wheels, rear braking effort was decreased. The brake control had an unusually short travel, and the button, used in place of a conventional pedal, was extraordinarily sensitive.

The gearbox was mounted in front of the engine. It was a five-speed-and-reverse unit, with fourth and fifth both overdrive ratios. For the US market, a three-speed Borg-Warner automatic transmission was available.

Above: The Vari-Power steering system provided speed-related assistance, and self-centring; note the pump, driven from the engine, and the large fluid reservoir to the right. The SM's steering geometry was superb.

Left: This is the heart of the hydro-pneumatic self-levelling suspension: no springs, but four of these spheres filled with nitrogen (blue) under very high pressure, sitting on columns of oil (red) supplied from the central pump.

Below: The very powerfully-assisted disc brakes all round were operated by a button which responded to foot pressure rather than actual movement.

Engine

The SM engine was designed and built by Maserati for its French owner in very short order – six months, in fact. In order to fulfil Citroën's brief, Maserati engineer Giulio Alfieri simply modified a 3.0-litre V8 design he had on the stocks, chopping off one cylinder from each bank, since Citroën had requested a V6 (more for packaging reasons than anything else). One major drawback with the modification was that the V8's 90-degree-included angle between cylinder banks was less than ideal. In terms of balance, the optimum for a V6 is 60 degrees. By heavily counterweighting the crankshaft, though, Alfieri got away with it.

With an 87-mm bore and 75-mm stroke, the original type 114/1 engine displaced 2670 cc, although it was enlarged later to 2965 cc by the simple expedient of increasing the bore to 91.6 mm. The engine used four overhead camshafts to actuate two inclined valves per cylinder, and the heads had hemispherical combustion chambers. The cam drive was quite complicated, with a duplex timing chain taking drive from the nose of the crankshaft to an intermediate shaft placed in the centre of the 'V'. This, in turn, powered two sets of duplex chains, each providing the drive for the twin cams per cylinder bank. The intermediate shaft also drove the water pump, high-pressure suspension/braking hydraulic pump, alternator, and air-conditioning pump.

All the major elements of the engine – crankcase, cylinder heads and cylinder block – were cast in aluminium alloy. The dry cylinder liners were spin-cast from nitrided cast-iron. The crankshaft had four main bearings, and the compression ratio was 9:1. Fuel supply was by triple Weber 42DCN F/2 twin-choke carburettors, although these were replaced in the summer of 1972 by Bosch D-Jetronic fuel injection for the European market. In standard carburetted 2.7-litre form, the engine gave 170 bhp at 5,500 rpm, with 172 lb ft of torque at 4,000 rpm. The US-specification 2965-cc engine yielded 180 bhp and 181 lb ft, while the Bosch-injected unit gave 178 bhp and 171 lb ft.

Although the engine needed careful maintenance – the cam chains needed renewing every 50,000 miles, otherwise valves touched pistons – it later found a home in Maserati's Merak, in 2.0-, 2.7- and 3.0-litre forms. The Merak SS version gave 208 bhp.

Below right: At the rear, the suspension spheres and trailing arms appear compact and effective.

Below: The close-up of the engine bay shows one suspension sphere, the main hydraulic pump and, to the right, the engine-driven pump pulley.

Above: The SM's engine bay was crowded, with the inlet manifolds of the very short Maserati V6 visible behind the air filter boxes, tubes and pipes. The engine's rearward location aided weight distribution.

Below: Maserati created the SM's V6 by cutting two cylinders off the Indy's 4.1-litre V8. The result was impressively powerful and compact, and the main alloy block was very rigid. Here it can be seen connected to Citroën's five-speed all-indirect gearbox.

Below: Note the large reservoir from which the pump drew oil, sending it under high pressure to the four suspension cylinders.

Below: The engine was mounted with the gearbox in front, and with the pumps and ancillary equipment on top of it.

Right: The four-bar steering linkage on the front wheel resulted in zero camber, castor and kingpin inclination.

Dodge Viper

Power and performance personified, with no modern comforts, yet the brutal Viper is a huge success even in the environmentally-conscious 1990s. The attraction of Dodge's uncompromising sports car lies in its sheer wickedness.

Until it actually happened, the notion that a car like the Dodge Viper could be touted by one of America's 'big three' manufacturers for the socially-sensitive 1990s would have sounded very far-fetched indeed. From financially beleaguered Chrysler it would probably have sounded most unlikely of all. Yet as soon as it first appeared in public, at the Detroit Auto Show in January 1989, the unique Viper caused a sensation.

At that stage it was described as a 'concept car', but Chrysler were already having trouble convincing the public that that was all the dramatic two-seater was meant to be, and they soon found themselves swamped by prospective customers. Enthusiasts who had been starved of no-compromise sports cars like the Viper for far too long were literally queuing up to offer deposits, and all of a sudden the Chrysler Corporation was forced to start regarding the astonishing, bright red, V10-engined prototype as a real production prospect. As such, it would follow an honourable tradition. If it was to be built at all, it certainly couldn't be built (or sold) in serious volumes and, on that basis, profit on sales alone couldn't be the prime motive for producing such a car.

There were other considerations, though. Chrysler, having been on the verge of bankruptcy, needed to display self-confidence – outwardly to customers, inwardly among its own engineers and other employees. A car like the Viper could serve as a flagship, as a statement of philosophy and proof of the company's ability to get the job done; even if relatively few people would ever buy it, its image would attract enthusiasts into Chrysler showrooms where they might at least buy something less exotic from the Viper-makers.

Lots of power in a straightforward chassis

It was a ploy that had worked before – not least in the 1960s for arch-rival Ford, with a car called the Cobra. And it was the legendary Cobra, not contemporary US opposition like General Motors' ultra-rapid but really rather re-

Left: Conceived as a latter-day Cobra, the Viper is designed to look as arresting as it is exciting to drive. The front of the car is styled with the added target of aerodynamic efficiency, although with the huge output generated by its V10 engine that's hardly necessary . . .

Shelby, creator of the Cobra itself, prime mover in Ford's World Championship-winning GT40 programme of the 1960s and the man whose name summed up Ford's sporty image in those golden years. In 1978, Lee Iacocca, the man who had created Ford's 'Total Performance' programme but finally become frustrated by their softer image of the mid-1970s, had walked into the hot seat at Chrysler, as chairman. The company was in big trouble, and by no means certain even to survive, but performance-fan Iacocca helped turn it round. And in 1982 he brought Shelby on to the team with his own research and development role, to inject more sporting life into Chrysler's generally rather dull range.

From a low-key, low-budget starting point, Shelby had progressed quickly, from largely cosmetic upgrades to some very sporty cars for the Dodge division – and soon the Shelby nameplate was on all manner of product, from small, sporty front-drive cars to the fast Shelby Dakota pick-up. When the Viper prototype appeared at the Detroit Show, Shelby's name was prominent there too, in linking the Viper philosophy to the Cobra, as well as for early engineering and testing input, but the Viper had more than one father.

The Viper project cost only $75 million

Alongside Shelby were Chrysler styling chief Tom Gale, engineering boss François Castaing (the former Renault Grand Prix racing manager) and, most important of all, Bob Lutz, formerly executive vice-president of Ford, now Chrysler president. Lutz was also a serious car enthusiast. And, according to Chrysler, he was the real father of the Viper. But there was another vital element in the Viper's creation. Engineers dream constantly, but in the modern motor industry turning dreams into production reality is an expensive business, with development and tooling costs often running into billions of dollars spread over years of work. Thus, big manufacturers don't normally build small-production-run cars and, at very best, that was all the Viper would ever become.

Chrysler, fortunately, were evolving a new

design philosophy (largely at the instigation of Castaing) which made the Viper possible. It involved a relatively small team working on all aspects of development (such as design, engineering, manufacturing, and procurement and supply) in parallel, rather than one after the other, which is the normal industry way. Chrysler call the method their 'platform team' system and in refined form they now apply it to all their new-product design.

The platform system involved no more than 85 people, all working together to a very rigid overall budget but otherwise with almost complete freedom to spend how they thought most efficient, and with a great deal of autonomy from the usual corporate bureaucracy. According to Chrysler, the whole Viper project, from concept to production-readiness, cost only $75 million.

When it first appeared, of course, the Viper wasn't a production prospect at all, but that was about to change. In May 1990, at the end of an 'image-boosting' tour, Chrysler chairman Lee Iacocca, the man who had given the go-ahead to the Cobra some 28 years before, announced that the Viper would go into production and would be on sale by the beginning of 1992 – with very little 'taming' from the form in which it had initially appeared as a show car. In the meantime further show appearances and other glimpses of the Viper kept the order book growing. In May 1991, for instance, Carroll Shelby (recently recovered from a heart transplant) drove the Viper as pace car for the Indianapolis 500, and later in the year a handful of journalists were allowed to drive the first pair of Viper prototypes, in something close to production specification.

That meant a 400-bhp eight-litre V10 engine, designed by Chrysler and refined by Chrysler subsidiary Lamborghini, in a fabricated chassis with all-round independent suspension and clothed in a spectacular, plastic composite body, styled by the Chrysler studio under Tom Gale. Frills were to be kept to a minimum – not so much as a proper roof option or even side windows; the Viper was all about uncomplicated power in a good old-fashioned sports car, and at a reasonable price by 1990s standards. Chrysler played up the Cobra analogy and had no reservations about claiming a top speed of 165 mph, 0-60 mph in 4.5 seconds, and 0-100 mph in 11.5 – figures which would worry a Ferrari F40, and which magazine road-testers could nearly match.

Everybody who tried the Viper loved it. It was exactly what it had set out to be – an awesomely quick, incredible-looking, no-frills sports car of the old school, with an image that really did evoke the legendary Cobra.

fined Corvette ZR-1, which the Viper would most allude to. Like the Cobra it would be a simple car, with lots of power in a straightforward chassis, with few high-tech frills and little by way of luxury or weighty comfort equipment, and it would look the part. It was a real enthusiast's car and the men behind it were real enthusiasts, with backgrounds in engineering and racing, not in bean-counting and marketing.

Significantly, one of them was Carroll

Above: Huge 17-in wheels with tyres to suit give superb grip at high speed. The powerful Viper is no wild animal to drive; it feels stable, and mild understeer is its only noticeable handling foible.

Inset above: With peak torque of 450 lb ft at just 3,200 rpm, the Viper accelerates fast in any gear.

Overleaf: With a 400-bhp V10 overhead-valve engine, the Viper can reach 60 mph in 4.6 seconds and go on to a top speed of 159 mph.

Driving the Viper: *slow-burning rocket*

Any doubt about the Viper's character disappears immediately the V10 starts. It advertises its 400 bhp with a thunder you can feel. Six gears are largely an irrelevance; the car's power and torque are so awesome that you could leave it in, say, fourth gear and drive it as an automatic, but you wouldn't. Peak torque is 450 lb ft at only 3,200 rpm but by 1,600 rpm it is already delivering an incredible 400 lb ft. In any gear the Viper accelerates like a slow-burning rocket, hard enough to be on the edge of unsettling even for a driver used to very fast cars – because, aside from everything else, this is an open car to put wind in the hair. Up to a point it is

easy to drive, with instant throttle response, a slick gear change and only a touch of sharpness in the clutch. The brakes are superb (100 mph to rest in less than five seconds) and the grip from the 275/40 front and 335/35 × 17-in rear rubber is so massive that few drivers would approach its limits. For those who do, intentionally or otherwise, it isn't the disaster you might fear. Weight distribution is nearly 50/50 and the handling balance almost neutral. A heavy right foot will make the car oversteer practically anywhere, but fewer than 2.5 turns between locks help catch it, so long as you are quick and accurate and the road is dry.

PERFORMANCE & SPECIFICATION COMPARISON	Engine	Displacement	Power	Torque (lb ft)	Max speed	0-60 mph	Length (in/mm)	Wheelbase (in/mm)	Track front/rear	Weight (lb/kg)	Price
Dodge Viper	V10, overhead-valve	7997 cc	400 bhp 4600 rpm	450 lb ft 3200 rpm	159 mph 256 km/h	4.6 sec	175.1 in 4448 mm	96.2 in 2443 mm	59.6 in 60.6 in	3200 lb 1452 kg	$54,640 (1993)
Chevrolet Corvette ZR-1	V8, quad-cam, 32-valve	5727 cc	375 bhp 5800 rpm	370 lb ft 4800 rpm	171 mph 275 km/h	5.6 sec	178.5 in 4534 mm	96.2 in 2443 mm	60.0 in 62.0 in	3519 lb 1596 kg	$65,318 (1993)
Jaguar XJR-S	V12, overhead-cam	5993 cc	333 bhp 5250 rpm	365 lb ft 3650 rpm	158 mph 254 km/h	6.5 sec	189.7 in 4818 mm	102.0 in 2591 mm	58.6 in 59.2 in	4023 lb 1825 kg	£49,950 (1992)
Lamborghini Diablo	V12, quad-cam, 48-valve	5729 cc	492 bhp 7000 rpm	428 lb ft 5200 rpm	205 mph 330 km/h	4.2 sec	175.6 in 4460 mm	104.3 in 2650 mm	60.6 in 64.6 in	3474 lb 1576 kg	£143,937 (1992)
TVR Griffith	V8, overhead-valve	4280 cc	280 bhp 5500 rpm	305 lb ft 4000 rpm	161 mph 259 km/h	4.7 sec	156.1 in 3965 mm	90.0 in 2286 mm	58.0 in 58.4 in	2304 lb 1045 kg	£27,206 (1993)

Dodge Viper Data File

With the Viper, Dodge returned to its performance roots which were sown back in the 1950s with the advent of the Red Ram V8 engine. Dodge's performance reputation was really made in the late 1960s, however, with the Charger and the limited-edition Charger Daytona (the Plymouth Road Runner Superbird lookalike). Cars like the Challenger of the early 1970s, with up to 425 bhp, continued the trend but by the late 1970s Dodge's parent company, Chrysler, was in grave financial trouble and there was no place for performance cars. As the company recovered, Dodge did move back towards producing sportier cars, in the form of models like the Daytona Coupe of the early 1980s with its 144-bhp turbocharged overhead-cam four. That was a world away from the big, early V8s and Dodge customers had to wait until the 1990s for real performance and the Viper.

Above: Although the Viper is designed to have absolutely no frills, a basic soft-top cover is a tiny concession to the possibility of rain.

Styling

The Viper isn't modest about its spectacular mechanical specification, and few sports cars have ever looked more dramatic. It was designed by an in-house Chrysler team led by chief stylist Tom Gale – who also had considerable input on Lamborghini's Diablo. The outer shell is of low-pressure-moulded plastic composite panels, which are delivered to the assembly plant in full-body sets, ready-painted in any colour you like so long as it's red. With great emphasis on checking for accurate alignment, the panels are mainly rivetted to the bonded-on inner shell. There are actually very few pieces; the bonnet is one very large panel, the tail moulding incorporates most of the Targa-hoop, and then there are the doors, the sills and the nose-dam moulding. The distinctive cutaway sweeps ahead of the doors are

functional, in allowing hot air out from under the bonnet and around the massive V10. It is a soft, sculpted look, hinting at the car's power in the same way that the Cobra's styling did, but brought up to date with details like the ellipsoidal headlights, integrated body-coloured bumpers and the steeply-raked windscreen. There are minimal creature comforts, with no side windows, no roof option other than a rudimentary and rather ugly soft top, nor even any external door handles. For America, the drainpipe-sized exhausts exit from below the doors, in the moulded sills; but for Europe, regulations require them to be conventionally routed to the back of the car. But with its hugely long, broad nose and small, set-back cockpit, the Viper's proportions are what really give it its aggressive, muscular presence, in any spec.

Above: The body is made of pressure-moulded plastic composite panels.

Below: The Detroit-built Dodge Viper is available in just one dramatic colour – red.

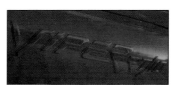

Above: The Viper name was chosen as a deliberate echo of the original AC Cobra.

Right: Sculpted rear lights mirror the style set by the elongated front units.

Above: Extra lights are integrated into the substantial colour-co-ordinated bumpers.

Left: The ellipsoidal headlights contain a spirit level for precise alignment.

Left: Distinctive side scoops allow hot air out of the V10's cramped engine bay.

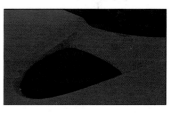

Above: The bonnet is one huge panel with outlets for hot air in front of the windscreen.

Left: Large, 17-in diameter, three-spoke wheels reveal enormous disc brakes beneath.

Below: In US spec, the twin exhaust pipes exit from the sills at the side. UK regulations dictate conventional routing to the rear.

Below: The functional cockpit has minimal creature comforts. The door locks and handles are on the inside, and instruments are a stark white.

Chassis and running gear

See a Viper chassis before the outer bodywork is grafted on, and there is no mistaking the sheer strength of the chassis engineering. It is a conventional car only in so far as it has a longitudinally-mounted front engine and rear drive, but little about its actual construction is standard practice. The chassis structure starts with a massive inner frame, fabricated from mainly rectangular-section steel tubes and boxes, with all the mounting and pick-up points attached. The fully-fitted dashboard assembly is then added, the inner body panels are bonded on and the roll-hoop structure is rivetted and bolted into place, to be followed by all the running gear. The six-speed gearbox has both fifth and sixth as overdrive ratios, sixth having an extremely high ratio of 0.50:1. Front

suspension is by double wishbones, coil springs with gas-filled dampers, and an anti-roll bar. At the rear the layout is essentially the same but with a separate toe-link. And at 3,200 lb the Viper is no lightweight, but ventilated discs of no less than 13-in diameter all round (and mounted conventionally outboard) are more than capable of stopping it – although anti-lock isn't even offered as an option. The enormous (10-in × 17-in front, 13-in × 17-in rear) three-spoke cast-alloy wheels further enhance the braking performance by providing excellent cooling even for repeated heavy stops. Also reflecting both the Viper's weight and its exceptionally generous tyre footprints, power assistance is specified as standard for the quickly-geared rack-and-pinion steering.

Below: Suspension is by double wishbones, coil springs and gas-filled dampers, with an anti-roll bar front and rear. At the rear there's also a separate toe-link.

Above: The Viper has a tubular spaceframe with a central spine. The tubular outriggers support the body panels, and front rails are incorporated into the body structure.

Below: An all-new six-speed manual transmission, developed by Borg-Warner, is designed to deal with the Viper's huge torque output; top gear is immensely high, giving nearly 50 mph per 1,000 rpm.

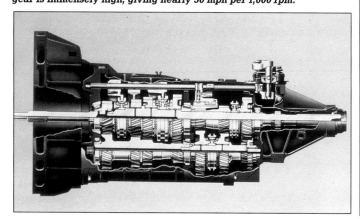

Engine

The popular notion that the Viper's V10 was derived from a truck engine falls rather wide of the mark. The all-alloy Viper engine came first, and an iron-blocked truck engine did follow, but in reality the two had little more in common than their number of cylinders. The Viper's 90-degree 'V' engine was designed by Chrysler and refined by Lamborghini, which Chrysler owns. It isn't particularly sophisticated (with only two valves per cylinder, operated by pushrods and rocker arms from a single central camshaft) but it is finely developed and very potent. Size, of course, is on its side; bore and stroke of 101.6 mm × 98.6 mm give a capacity of 7997 cc, and eight litres is big even by American 'muscle car' standards of

the golden days of the 1960s and 1970s. The powerplant uses electronic ignition and sequential multi-point fuel injection. An impressive nest of cross-over inlet tracts sits in the centre of the 'V', cast in aluminium and finished in red-crackle paint. Each bank of inlets is fed from a ribbed plenum chamber running the full length of the engine, inboard of the opposite rocker cover. Each plenum has a large throttle body at its front end, fed from a single, filtered air intake above the radiator. The exhaust manifolds are a complex tangle of tuned-length steel pipes, and most of the engine ancillaries are front-mounted and belt-driven. With a compression ratio of 9.1:1, this mighty unit produces 400 bhp at 4,600 rpm and 450 lb ft of torque.

Above: The potent V10 was developed by Chrysler and refined by their subsidiary Lamborghini.

Right: A large oil cooler is mounted below and in front of the radiator. Moulding the bonnet and bumper in one piece was both a weight- and cost-saving exercise.

Left: The V10 is set well back in the engine bay, to improve weight distribution. The first sight that presents itself under the bonnet is the array of inlet tracts. Each bank of cylinders is fed by a plenum chamber (joined to a common air intake and filter) mounted on the opposing bank, thus allowing long inlets to give more effective breathing.

Right: The Dodge V10 is a compact, shallow, unit thanks to the use of a dry sump. As the block and heads are alloy, it's also light. It is a relatively simple design with a single block-mounted camshaft operating two valves per cylinder via pushrods, rockers and hydraulic tappets. With a V10 design there is little option but to have a five-into-one exhaust manifold, which is hardly ideal.

Below: The Viper's windscreen frame has a foam-wrapped steel centre with RTM composites forming the outer surface. The frame provides a complete surround for the windscreen. It is a unique process which Chrysler has patented.

Below: Additional strength is given to the Viper's chassis by incorporating a steel roll-over hoop behind the cockpit. Moulded panels help it blend seamlessly into the rounded bodywork.

Above: Each rear concentric coil spring/ damper unit is mounted at an angle on the front arm of the lower wishbone, to provide clearance for the driveshafts. There was no space to mount the damper units above the top wishbones.

Above: The side-mounted exhaust pipes run alongside the massive main chassis outer rails before exiting just ahead of the rear wheels. The chassis uprights holding the door hinges are equally robust.

Above left: The Viper's front axle line is ahead of the engine, indicating just how far back the Dodge engineers were able to locate the V10 in the engine bay.

Facel Vega

The combination of French styling with Chrysler V8 power produced France's foremost luxury models of the 1950s and 1960s – the Facel Vegas, elegant yet capable of 140 mph.

Above: Although Facel Vega was not a long-established marque, the company knew the value of creating an image, and the distinctive triple front grille was retained on all models.

Fearsomely expensive and rare even in its day, the French-built Facel Vega HK500 was rightly claimed in the late 1950s to be the world's fastest saloon, and remains a classic because of its matchless combination of sheer power (courtesy of a large Chrysler V8 engine) and Parisian coachbuilt luxury in a large two-door coupé form. The result was a Grand Tourer capable of effortless acceleration and a top speed of 140 mph, produced by a small company whose founder, Jean Daninos, was evidently unafraid of taking on the likes of Rolls-Royce, Ferrari and Maserati. Clients included royalty, aristocracy and the heads of French industry, and had the firm not tried to expand down-market with the 1600-cc Facellia, motoring history might have been different . . .

Facel Vega's founder, Jean Daninos, worked for Citroën during the 1930s, then left to register the Facel Metallon company in 1939. War soon interrupted business, but Daninos had many contacts in the motor industry, and after the war his company made coachbuilt bodies for Panhard and Simca. From 1950 Facel began exhibiting its own car designs at the Paris Salon, and Daninos then began to plan and build cars with American V8 power, the formula which would evolve into the HK500. The first Facel Vega was shown at the 1954 Salon, and what was in effect the first French post-war luxury car created great interest.

The cars were hand-built at the factory at Colombes, a system which allowed changes to be continuously introduced; the engine became a 4.8-litre V8, then 5.4 litres. In 1956 Facel launched a larger model, a limousine called the Excellence, 17 feet long and fitted first with a 6.4-litre and later a 5.9-litre V8. As comfortable as any Rolls-Royce, it was capable of 125 mph in near-silence. The price was astronomical but sales were sufficient to indicate that if the coupé was given similarly improved performance, more buyers would be attracted.

60 mph reached in less than nine seconds

The Facel Vega was redesigned during 1957 and 1958, with the tubular steel chassis stretched and widened and fitted with the high-compression 5.9-litre V8. There was independent suspension at the front, a live rear axle, and the body styling was further refined and balanced. The result, launched in 1958, was a coupé just over 15 feet long with good looks, luxury and tremendous performance; the new HK500 was capable of 0-60 mph in less than nine seconds and a maximum speed of around 140 mph. Racing tyres were recommended for

Left: Moderately hard cornering would naturally induce the heavy Facel Vega to lean, but the car was never intended as an out-and-out sports model.

1600-cc twin-cam four and a car which would emerge in 1960 as the Facellia. It looked like a scaled-down HK500 and was available in convertible, four-seat and 2 + 2 guises. Unfortunately the 115-bhp engine, which had been expensive to develop, gave problems, costing the firm even more money.

Against this backdrop, in 1960 the company launched the most powerful version of the HK500, the Facel Vega II, fitted with Chrysler's 6.3-litre V8. It produced 360 bhp, which, in real terms, was equivalent to the output of the original Ferrari Testa Rossa. But whereas the Ferrari had around 250 lb ft of torque, the high-compression V8 gave no less than 425 lb ft, and without having to rev very high to do so. Performance in the manual four-speed version was phenomenal, and for drivers interested in both effortless cruising and fierce acceleration, an automatic model with a three-speed TorqueFlite gearbox was offered, with the engine detuned to 355 bhp. The cast-iron V8, with a 10.0:1 compression ratio, was fed by twin four-choke Carter carburettors and would rev to 5,200 rpm. In the manual version, 100 mph – reached in 21 seconds – represented a lazy 3,700 rpm, with maximum bhp at 5,200 rpm. It was thirsty, of course, giving around 12 mpg, but that hardly worried Facel Vega customers.

Goods looks, luxury and tremendous performance

In 1960 *The Motor* drove a new Facel Vaga 2,000 miles across Europe and discovered why the company's clients had not been deterred by high taxation and prices: "In the world of motoring, some few cars come to deserve the adjective 'great' because, although they have faults like everything else in this imperfect world, they provide such a highly desirable combination of virtues . . . we found it hard to keep superlatives out of the conversation. It is not merely one of the world's very, very fast cars but it is also extremely comfortable and well finished, is highly controllable in every sense and consequently safe when handled intelligently." High praise for a car which in the UK cost £4,739 17s 6d – more than a large detached house.

The Facel was softly-sprung rather like an American car, but the handling received high praise, the car deemed "capable of being cornered with all the effortless verve of a first-rate sports two-seater". That was something of an exaggeration, but the HK500 could leave most sports cars in the distance and did behave well on its independent front suspension, with wishbones and an anti-roll bar. As with the earlier model, racing tyres were recommended for

Above: The rear-end treatment was rather heavy-handed but one neat touch saw the twin exhausts routed through holes in the bumper.

high-speed cruising, when the car really came into its own. At low speeds the only drawbacks were the heavy steering, with 4½ turns lock-to-lock, and the clutch, which had a helper-spring to avoid clutch spin and tiring the driver's leg. *The Motor's* tester noted that the long steering column did vibrate occasionally "to an extent sufficient to shake the ash off a driver's cigar".

Inside, there was traditional luxury in the form of leather seats, folding arm rests, pile carpets and full instrumentation including oil pressure and temperature gauges, an ammeter, rev-counter and water temperature gauge, plus a clock, radio and electric windows. Optional extras included power steering, fitted luggage, an opening roof and a Powr-lok limited-slip differential.

The car looked right and drove superbly, and the people with the means to buy it did not ignore such road reports, despite the fact that other manufacturers, such as Jaguar and Maserati, were also producing fast saloons. But sales did begin to tail off and the company's main product, the Facellia, had financial problems. It was renamed the Facel III, to show its links with the Facel Vega II, still selling in small numbers, but the decline continued, despite its being fitted with Volvo's 1800-cc engine. In 1962 the receiver was called in and Facel was subsequently taken over by SFERMA. The Facellia, then fitted with a BMC six-cylinder, was relabelled as the Facel 6, but sales gradually waned until by the autumn of 1964 there was no point in going on. Efforts to find a buyer for the marque failed.

Had Jean Daninos continued to build luxury cars in small numbers the company might have survived, but it was probably a mistake to diminish Facel's reputation for luxury performance and limousines with a cheaper model, especially one that had so many engine problems. As it is, the Facel Vega HK500s remain rare examples of true Grand Tourers – extraordinarily fast, and with the kind of individual appeal for which French coachbuilders were so famous.

drivers keen to venture beyond 120 mph with any regularity. Stopping was achieved by finned alloy drum brakes until discs became standard in 1960. Over 200 HK500s were sold that year, most of them for export, as sales in France were much depressed by the engine-size-related car taxation, which had severely hurt other luxury car-makers like Delahaye and Bugatti. But, despite the price, the Facel Vega was a desirable product which established the company's reputation.

However, Jean Daninos also wanted to produce a smaller car with an engine that would escape the high taxation. Work began on a

Top: The pillarless side-window treatment added to the HK500's elegance. Despite the car's size, it was only a two-door model; consequently the doors were massive.

Above: Behind the imposing radiator grille was, from 1958 onwards, a mighty 5.9-litre Chrysler V8 engine.

Overleaf: Once under way the Facel Vega was a very quick car, capable of cruising far beyond 100 mph with great ease.

Driving the HK500: *power and luxury*

In its day very few cars offered the combination of power, luxury and solidity of the Facel Vega. This expensive blend results in tremendous performance even today, as well as very effective insulation against engine and road noise. The HK500's weight also ensures that its momentum and relatively soft springing soak up the sensation of most pot-holes and other road irregularities. The cockpit is spacious for the two front-seat occupants, with excellent visibility all round. The leather seats are comfortable, although they offer little in the way of sideways support.

The gear lever has a wide arc of movement compared with modern systems, but is usefully angled towards the driver. At idling speed the big V8 gives a barely discernible rumble, and the noise hardly rises as the car accelerates effortlessly. When pushed harder there is a roar from the engine, but not much penetrates the cockpit. It is a big car, low and wide, and the near-even weight distribution means there is little tendency to body roll except under hard cornering; when the rear wheels do begin to slide they can easily be controlled through the smoothly progressive throttle. In the wet as well as the dry, the Facel Vega's handling adequately matches the power that is so readily available.

PERFORMANCE & SPECIFICATION COMPARISON	Engine	Displacement	Power	Torque (lb ft)	Max speed	0-60 mph	Length (in/mm)	Wheelbase (in/mm)	Track front/rear	Weight (lb/kg)	Price
Facel Vega HK500	V8, overhead-valve	6286 cc	360 bhp 5200 rpm	425 lb ft 3000 rpm	140 mph 225 km/h	8.4 sec	181.0 in 4597 mm	105.0 in 2667 mm	55.5 in 57.5 in	4032 lb 1829 kg	£4,739 (1960)
Bentley Continental	V8, overhead-valve	6230 cc	N/A	N/A	112 mph 180 km/h	12.1 sec	212.0 in 5385 mm	123.0 in 3124 mm	58.5 in 60.0 in	4460 lb 2023 kg	£8,713 (1960)
Jensen CV8	V8, overhead-valve	5916 cc	305 bhp 4800 rpm	395 lb ft 3000 rpm	131 mph 211 km/h	8.4 sec	184.5 in 4686 mm	107.0 in 2718 mm	56.0 in 57.0 in	3514 lb 1594 kg	£3,392 (1963)
Lincoln Continental	V8, overhead-valve	7049 cc	300 bhp 4100 rpm	465 lb ft 2000 rpm	125 mph 201 km/h	12.9 sec	212.4 in 5395 mm	123.0 in 3124 mm	62.1 in 61.0 in	4927 lb 2235 kg	$6,067 (1961)
Maserati Quattroporte	V8, quad-cam	4136 cc	260 bhp 5000 rpm	N/A	143 mph 230 km/h	9.7 sec	196.9 in 5001 mm	108.3 in 2750 mm	54.7 in 55.0 in	3854 lb 1748 kg	N/A

Facel Vega Data File

T he Facel company, founded in 1939, first built special bodies for other carmakers before, in 1950, exhibiting its own designs. In 1954 the first Facel Vega appeared, a two-door coachbuilt coupé with a 4.5-litre Chrysler V8. Production of these hand-built cars began in 1955; in 1956 the engine grew to 4.8 litres and 200 bhp, and to 5.4 litres in 1957. The HK500 was launched in 1958 – longer, wider and restyled, and with the 5.9-litre Chrysler V8 offering very high performance. In 1960 the restyled HK500 Facel Vega II appeared; with the 6.3-litre Chrysler V8 giving phenomenal performance and a top speed of around 140 mph, it was said to be the world's fastest saloon. At the same time the company was venturing down-market with the Facellia – a small version of the HK500 fitted with Facel's own 1600-cc twin-cam engine – but high development costs and continuing engine problems caused the company's downfall, with sales diminishing until the factory closed in 1964.

Above: Although the bodywork was very deep, the combination of a low roof and the sloping rear lines of the wheel arches suggested speed.

Styling

There was a strong family resemblance between all the Facel Vega models – the HKs, the Excellence and the Facellia – and in each case the styling, which was done in-house, very successfully embodied elegance, speed and status. The HK500 was a large two-door coupé with a relatively high waistline, which gave an impression of strength and solidity, and a flowing pillarless roof line, which evinced a counter-balancing delicacy. Some models had wrap-around windscreens with reversed quarter-lights.

The front-end treatment was centred on a central vertical grille with twin horizontal grilles at the side flanked by vertical light clusters in the leading edges of the wings. The long bonnet had a smoothly raised central section which hinted at the power below. Trim was restrained, with brightwork along the lower edges of the body and along the doors, effectively joining front and rear chromed bumpers. There was broad brightwork around the windows but this was blended in functionally rather than appearing decorative. At the rear the tail-lights were smoothly faired into the tops of the wings – an elegant solution, as was the passing of the twin exhaust pipes through discreet outlets integrated into the bumpers.

A variety of wheels was fitted – alloy designs with large knock-off spinners, which were in keeping with the cars' sporting performance.

In styling terms alone the restraint and balance of the Facel Vegas would have earned them classic status. Inside, the HK500 embodied a formula which was as right in its day as it is decades later: leather upholstery, thick pile carpets and a wood fascia.

Above: Facel Vega had the justified confidence to do all its styling in-house.

Below: The Elegance was a stretched four-door version of the car, introduced in 1956.

Above: The twin enclosed light treatment replaced the separate stacked arrangement.

Above: At one stage the rear and brake lights were incorporated into the ends of the wings.

Right: Instruments included oil temperature and pressure gauges in addition to the usual dials.

Above: For what was essentially a 1950s design, the grille appears very modern.

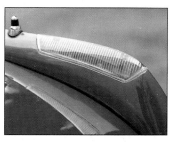

Above: Some models had the distinctive feature of rear indicators mounted on the wings.

Above: The ventilated wheels were a knock-off design with a large three-eared spinner.

Left: Small rear stop lights and reflector units were placed next to the bumper overriders.

Left and below: Inside was leather-clad luxury, but the stylish interior was not designed with ergonomics in mind, apart from the cranked gear lever.

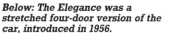

63

Chassis and running gear

The Facel Vega HK500 was built on a very solid tubular steel chassis with an all-steel welded body mounted on the chassis members and outriggers. The chassis was designed to cope with tremendous torque from the V8 and the considerable weight of the pillarless coupé body, the roof of which, not surprisingly, gave little structural strength.

Front suspension was by coil springs allied to conventional wishbones, de Carbon telescopic dampers and an anti-roll bar. Steering, through the Gemmer cam and roller, was also available with power assistance. At the rear there was a traditional rigid rear axle supporting the car through semi-elliptic leaf springs. Adjustable rear dampers were optional, as was a

limited-slip differential, the latter being advisable with so much power available. Early models of the HK500 were fitted with finned alloy drum brakes, but by 1960 all-round servo-assisted Dunlop disc brakes (12-in diameter front, 11.5-in rear) were standard. Various styles of tall (15-in) alloy wheels were offered, with knock-off spinners to speed wheel-changing. Owners intent on high performance could opt for racing tyres designed for sustained speeds of over 120 mph.

Power was transmitted through either an all-synchromesh four-speed manual or a three-speed automatic gearbox; the former necessitated a spring-assisted clutch to cope with the torque and to avoid an excessively heavy clutch operation.

Engine

Chrysler V8s were used in all Facel Vegas (except the small twin-cam Facellia) with capacities of between 4.5 and 6.3 litres, and in the USA such power units were fitted in models like the big Chrysler New Yorker.

The 6.3-litre V8 fitted to the HK500 Facel Vega II from 1960 was a typical unit, with a cast-iron, water-cooled block, a single central camshaft, pushrods and hydraulic, self-adjusting tappets. Bore was 107.95 mm, stroke 85.85 mm, and the only unusual feature was the high compression ratio of 10.0:1. The cylinders were fed through twin four-choke Carter carburettors, with 48-mm bores, on which the eight throttles opened progressively in pairs as the accelerator was pushed. The result was 360 bhp at 5,200 rpm and, from much lower revs, up to 425 lb ft of torque; the latter figure was especially the key to the two-ton car's

astonishing performance.

Ancillaries included a mechanical fuel pump on the engine and an electric pump near the tank, and the engine required little maintenance other than oil (10 pints) and water – no less than 44 pints in the large radiator and block. One limiting factor to performance was the water pump and dynamo fan belt, which was liable to leave its pulleys at over 5,000 rpm (an engine speed which equated to a road speed of 133 mph in top).

The thirsty engine delivered only 11 mpg at 110 mph (4,100 rpm) or up to 25.5 mpg at 40 mph (1,500 rpm in top gear). A large, unstressed engine like this offered brute power, reliability and surprisingly little noise except under hard acceleration, and the torque available meant that the car could be driven easily in top gear at very low speeds.

Above: One cylinder head from the Facel Vega's Chrysler V8 engine. Like the block, it was cast-iron and had an uncomplicated arrangement of two valves per cylinder.

Below right: The robust chassis rails kicked up at the rear to clear the live axle, held on long semi-elliptic leaf springs.

Below: Front suspension was by double wishbones on each side, with coil springs and telescopic dampers. A high-mounted anti-roll bar was used, with links to connect it to the bottom wishbones.

Above: As this chassis drawing shows, the Facel Vega's layout was a simple front-engined, rear-drive design.

Below: One advantage of Chrysler's V8 engines was their quiet running, thanks to the cast-iron construction and pushrod overhead valve gear, coupled with hydraulic tappets and low engine speeds.

Right: When Facel Vega did branch into engine production it was with a small, 1.6-litre, twin-cam design which produced 115 bhp at 6,400 rpm. The unit was used in the small Facellia model, but its reliability was poor.

Above: Few Facel Vega owners would be expected to lift the bonnet, which was just as well, since all the engines were standard Chrysler V8s designed for mass-production rather than aesthetic appreciation. With V8 reliability, however, under-bonnet excursions were few and far between.

Below: With a large iron V8 under the bonnet the Facel Vega was front-heavy, but having the battery next to the scuttle improved weight distribution fractionally.

Left: Despite their large displacements, the V8 Chrysler engines used by Facel Vega over the years were all very compact designs with the water pump directly behind the fan. The right-hand pulley is for the power-steering pump.

Above: The main silencer boxes on each side for the twin exhaust system were located outside the large square-section main chassis rails.

Left: Being designed for high speeds, the Facel Vega was well equipped with lights for fast night travel.

Left: For a car fitted with so much chrome trim, the bumpers on the Facel Vega were surprisingly rudimentary affairs offering little protection.

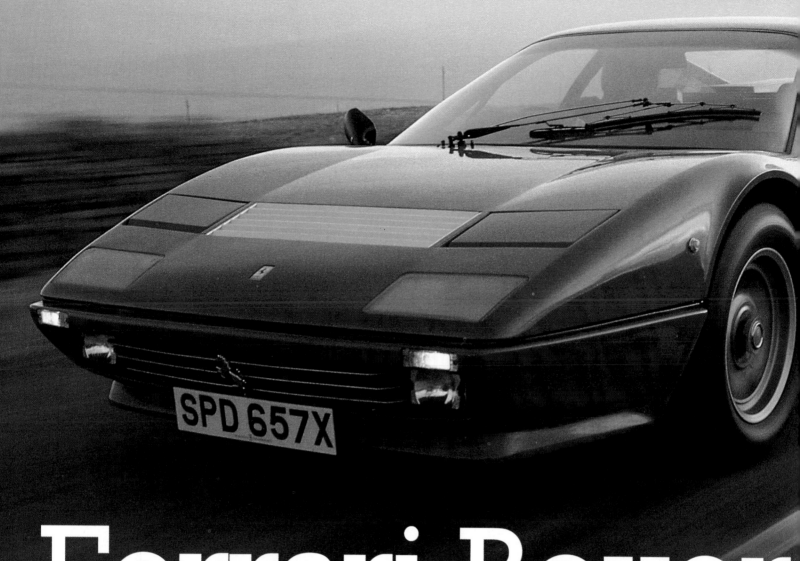

SPD 657X

Ferrari Boxer

Engineered to go one step beyond any rival by using the world's first roadgoing horizontally-opposed 12-cylinder engine, the strikingly-styled Berlinetta Boxer was among the fastest and most exciting of 1970s supercars.

Above and inset: Hitherto when departing from his favoured V12 engine configuration Enzo Ferrari had declined to use his name, but he certainly had no qualms about the flat-12 'boxer', so the BB bore the traditional prancing horse insignia, making it technically the first Ferrari mid-engined road car . . .

When the Ferrari Boxer was unveiled at the 1971 Turin Motor Show the public jumped to the obvious conclusion that this was the ultimate Ferrari, a street racer beyond compare. A vast flat-12 engine dominated a huge engine bay which left relatively little room for the two-seat passenger compartment, and those two occupants would have to travel light as there was no real boot space . . .

Production did not begin until 1973 after a lengthy development programme, and it soon became obvious that Ferrari's first mid-engined supercar was actually less of a track car than its predecessors. Its supple suspension ironed out road irregularities with a surer touch than Ferrari's previous big front-engined V12s. It had lighter steering (thanks to the weight having been taken off the front wheels) and in general was a lot easier to drive, with an easy gear change and tractable engine.

Many people thought Ferrari had been dilatory with the Boxer, given the company's almost decade-long experience of building mid-engined cars. Ferrari's reputation had suffered a huge dent when Lamborghini introduced their stunning mid-engined Miura in 1966. Not only did that have a 12-cylinder engine mounted between the cockpit and rear axle line, but it was a four-cam transverse engine to boot . . .

Ferrari's reply to the Miura

Some observers predicted that Ferrari might indeed follow Lamborghini's lead in the 1960s when the time came to replace the 275, but they were wrong, as Ferrari's answer was the front-engined Daytona. Now the Daytona has a sky-high reputation and value, but in its day it seemed an unadventurous response and Ferrari had to bow to the inevitable and come up with a mid-engined rival to the Miura.

As Ferrari's Formula 1 cars then used flat-12 engines, the choice of powerplant was easy, particularly as the flat, or 'boxer', engine has a very low centre of gravity with all the cylinders and valve gear no higher than the crankcase.

Unlike Lamborghini, Ferrari decided to use their flat-12 longitudinally, rather than across the car, and that posed certain problems. To keep the drivetrain as compact as possible, which was an absolute necessity to allow the twin requirements of a short wheelbase with reasonable cabin room, the five-speed transmission had to be mounted under the engine rather than on the end. This was not the ideal solution in many respects, as it lifted the engine higher and immediately overcame the flat-12's advantage of a low centre of gravity. That made the Boxer unsuitable as a really serious racing car (although modified Boxers were raced with some success). Even with the transmission tucked under the engine, the powerplant was still mounted further back than was ideal (although, to be fair, only 1½ sets of cylinders were actually behind the rear axle line).

The 4.4-litre 360-bhp flat-12 was mounted in a subframe held within a traditional Ferrari square-tube steel chassis clothed by a very clean Pininfarina body. Pininfarina's creation was sur-

Right: In both aesthetic and engineering senses, the Boxer was a tail-heavy design, but the Pininfarina stylists did a fine job of lessening the impact of the high engine compartment deck, giving the car softly rounded shoulders and delicately blended cabin 'buttresses'.

prisingly practical for a mid-engined design in that the rear-view mirror actually gave a reasonable view of what was going on behind, rather than simply enabling the driver to check whether all his carburettor intakes were there – which was pretty well all the Miura's achieved.

Turning the Boxer into a car that handled as well as it looked was another matter entirely. Thanks to its inherent tail-heaviness it required far more work than its predecessors, needing months of fine-tuning. Thousands and thousands of testing-miles were covered, both around Ferrari's own Fiorano track and on the surrounding

roads. Chief test-driver Giorgio Enrico's normal test-route was a mixture of mountain roads south of Maranello and long stretches of autostrada, with the Boxer on full throttle as long as possible. The first prototype logged over 30,000 miles in its first year, proving that its mechanical components were even stronger than Ferrari had expected.

The Boxer sold for three years in its original form before it became obvious that a larger powerplant would be necessary if the Boxer were not to lose its edge in satisfying the growing emission controls (not that Ferrari had bothered much with the US market, as Enzo Ferrari disdained to add large unsightly bumpers to satisfy the tougher US low-speed crash regulations). The result was the 512 BB, with a bored and stroked version of the flat-12 to give five litres. Surprisingly, what it didn't give was more power – output actually dropped from 360 bhp down to 340 bhp at lower rpm (6,200 rather than 7,000 rpm). That didn't affect the car's usable performance, however, as the larger displacement (as usual) brought an increase in torque, which went up from 311 lb ft to 331 lb ft and was available over a wider engine range, too.

0-60 mph in just over six seconds

The extra displacement of the 512 BB made little real difference to performance. Ferrari claimed that the original 4.4-litre car was good for 188 mph and that the 512 BB could manage 'just' 176 mph – the explanation for this unlikely scenario was that both figures were wrong! By the time of the 512 BB, however, Ferrari felt they could exaggerate less than before ... The truth of the matter was that both models could approach 170 mph and achieve the sprint to 60 mph in just over six seconds.

The change to the 512 BB was not the end of the Boxer's development; the 'i' that was added in 1981 signified a change away from Ferrari's traditional allegiance to Weber carburettors (in the

Boxer's case, four of them) to Bosch K-Jetronic fuel injection. Apart from cleaner, smoother running, the injection helped increase torque output below 4,000 rpm, contributing to the car's driveability. By this time there had been developments in tyre technology, too, and the 512i BB was equipped with low-profile Michelins, the French company's metric TRXs being fitted in 180TR × 415 form at the front, with wider 210TR × 415 rears. The characteristics of the wide, low-profile Michelins meant that the rear suspension was changed to suit.

Although all Boxers had a reputation for being able to pull cleanly from below 2,000 rpm, the injected engine mixed its low-speed brawn with a wonderful sweetness and was safe up to 6,600 rpm on a regular basis.

All was not sweetness inside the car, however, as drivers over six feet tall found a distinct lack of head room, and encroaching front wheel arches stole large chunks of the cockpit space, making the driver's footwell particularly cramped. Most drivers would forgive that in return for the excellent performance and handling – despite the theoretical criticisms aimed at that high-mounted engine over the transmission, it did not prove a handling problem on the ordinary road, where the car was more manageable than previous big Ferraris and, thanks to its softer suspension, more comfortable too.

In 1984 the 512i BB came to the end of its long road, to be replaced by a more aerodynamic design. That was not too hard to achieve, as the Boxer's Cd was an unremarkable 0.38. The new car was better in that respect; it was also infinitely more striking, and the Testarossa (as it was named, in an echo of one of Ferrari's most famous sports-racers) still looks striking seven years after its introduction. It was also lighter and more powerful than the 512i BB thanks to its four-valve technology. Nevertheless, even the new Testarossa couldn't diminish the Boxer's huge impact as one of the greatest supercars of the 1970s.

Below: The first Boxer was the 365 GT4 BB, which had a 4390-cc version of the flat-12 engine with four Weber carburettors.

Above and inset: The second Boxer series was the 512, introduced in 1976 with an engine enlarged to 4942 cc to cope with emission controls, losing a little top-end power but gaining torque in the process. In 1981 fuel injection was added, further improving driveability. The 512 series had various external modifications, including a chin spoiler to reduce front-end lift, and NACA-type ducts to provide extra rear brake cooling. Bonnet-top slats on all BBs provided through-flow for the front-mounted radiator.

Driving the Boxer: *staggering thrust*

One road-test of the Boxer spoke of "one long superlative staggering thrust forward; so incredibly fast and undramatic, too", but there was more to the Boxer than that. It was designed for speed allied to comfort, for travelling long distances at high speed without stress. Despite the Boxer's rearward weight bias, it was set up for understeer under normal road conditions. That was just as well, as the driver was always conscious of the sheer bulk of the car at speed, of the feeling that at one stage it could all get away from you. That feeling was strengthened by the Boxer's unfortunate tendency to lift at high speed.

That was recognised by Ferrari and cured with the addition of a front spoiler.

One thing Ferrari could not overcome, however, was the basic configuration of that high-mounted engine towards the rear. That meant – for anyone lucky enough to compare a Boxer with its chief rival, the Lamborghini Countach, on the track – the Countach had the handling and roadholding edge. But, in the car's proper elements, the Boxer driver had only such minor gripes as a heavy clutch, an awkward gear change, and steering which didn't lighten up until the car was travelling at respectable speeds.

PERFORMANCE & SPECIFICATION COMPARISON	Engine	Displacement	Power	Torque (lb ft)	Max speed	0-60 mph	Length (in/mm)	Wheelbase (in/mm)	Track front/rear	Weight (lb/kg)	Price
Ferrari Boxer 512 BB	Flat-12, quad-cam	4942 cc	340 bhp 6200 rpm	331 lb ft 4600 rpm	163 mph 262 km/h	6.2 sec	173.3 in 4401 mm	98.5 in 2502 mm	57.0 in 61.5 in	3426 lb 1554 kg	£26,000 (1978)
BMW M1	Inline-six, twin-cam	3453 cc	277 bhp 6500 rpm	239 lb ft 5000 rpm	162 mph 261 km/h	5.5 sec	171.7 in 4361 mm	100.8 in 2560 mm	61.0 in 62.0 in	3122 lb 1416 kg	£37,570 (1980)
Lamborghini Countach	V12, quad-cam	3929 cc	375 bhp 8000 rpm	268 lb ft 5000 rpm	170 mph 274 km/h	6.4 sec	162.9 in 4138 mm	96.5 in 2451 mm	58.7 in 63.2 in	2912 lb 1321 kg	£25,960 (1978)
Maserati Bora	V8, quad-cam	4719 cc	310 bhp 6000 rpm	339 lb ft 4200 rpm	160 mph 257 km/h	6.5 sec	171.0 in 4343 mm	102.5 in 2604 mm	57.8 in 57.0 in	3342 lb 1516 kg	£22,991 (1978)
Maserati Khamsin	V8, quad-cam	4930 cc	320 bhp 5500 rpm	354 lb ft 4000 rpm	160 mph 257 km/h	6.5 sec	173.2 in 4399 mm	100.4 in 2550 mm	56.7 in 57.9 in	3724 lb 1689 kg	£23,974 (1978)

Ferrari Boxer Data File

Ferrari had built mid-engined cars before the Boxer; indeed their experience went back further than most, as their first such car had been the 250 LM, the replacement for the immortal front-engined 250 GTO. There were a few roadgoing 250 LMs and there was another famous mid-engined Ferrari road car after the LM, the V6 Dino. The Dino was almost a sideshow in Enzo Ferrari's view, however (indeed he wanted Dino to be considered as a separate marque rather than a Ferrari – real Ferraris had more than six cylinders . . .). In many respects Enzo Ferrari was deeply conservative and he persisted in keeping his mainstream supercars front-engined. Had it not been for the success of the incredible mid-engined Miura which prompted the Boxer's creation in the early 1970s, that policy might well have continued even longer.

Above: Replacing the now-classic but then-outmoded front-engined Daytona, the BB came in belated response to Lamborghini's Miura.

Styling

The styling of the Boxer still looks 'right' over 20 years after it was unveiled at the Turin Motor Show. That's because elements of it were still in use years later. Look at the curve of the bodywork above and in front of the rear wheel arches; add the sort of scoop found on the 328 GTB and the 288 GTO, and it would look even more familiar. Curiously enough, such scoops were a feature of Pininfarina's 'P6' styling exercise of the 1960s which was the inspiration for the Boxer. That had an even longer, sharper, nose and a clumsy rear-three-quarter treatment as Pininfarina grappled with the problems of packaging a mid-engined car. By the time the definitive Boxer design emerged, Pininfarina had solved that problem with some style; the rear side windows helped the line, while the 'flying buttresses' on each side of the engine compartment were just the right size. That was a clever piece of styling, in fact, as it would have been all too easy to make the rear of the car

high and clumsy, particularly given that the rear bodywork had to be deep to cover the engine-on-transmission layout. Curving the rear bodywork in towards the centre was the key.

It was a practical design, too, as the whole rear bodywork section lifted from the back to give access to the flat-12 engine. Pininfarina later realised, however, that hingeing the engine cover from the front (as on the later Ferrari F40 design) was an even better arrangement, as it allowed a mechanic to work at the back. That goes to show that even designers as good as Pininfarina are constantly learning.

Below: The Boxer's rear end incorporated several changes with the introduction of the 512 BB: there were new louvres in the tail panel and extra ones in the engine cover, fewer rear lamps, and subtly different coachwork contours.

Above: The BB's cabin was well-trimmed, with large, clear instruments and very comfortable leather-covered seats.

Right: The 512 only had two pairs of circular rear lights, compared with the 365's three.

Below: Flip-up covers revealed a four-lamp headlight system.

Right: As a styling feature, the BB's rear-quarter 'flying buttresses' worked better than those on Jaguar's XJ-S.

Above: Engine compartment ventilation was improved by the 512's additional slats.

Below: This nose was used on 1979 Le Mans BBs, but the side vents presaged the Testarossa.

Engine

Chassis and suspension

The Boxer was never intended (like many previous Ferraris) to be a road and racing car, and as such there was no need to make weight-saving a priority in the design. No thought was given to making the rear-mounted engine a stressed member, as had been pioneered on the Formula 1 Lotus 49 a few years before, and in fact the engine and transmission sat in a separate subframe within the very substantial steel tube chassis. That contributed to the car's rearward weight bias of 42/58 front/rear and all-up weight in excess of 3,400 lb. The chassis itself was of deep boxed steel members running on each side of and behind the cabin with two longitudinal members running back from the cabin on each side of the engine. Attached to this substantial frame was a classic suspension system of twin wishbones at the front with a single concentric coil spring/damper unit. A similar wishbone arrangement was found at

the rear, although it differed in one crucial aspect: twin coil spring/ damper units were used on each side. This was mostly out of necessity, in that with a driveshaft to accommodate while also maintaining the lowest rear deck line possible, there was insufficient space to run an adequately-sized single spring/ damper unit. The twin set-up helped give better wheel location and control. This was even more important when the unsprung mass of the rear wheel, ventilated disc brake and tyre grew when the wider wheels and bigger Michelin TRX tyres were fitted in 1981.

Below: Seen here on a 1975 NART (North American Racing Team) sports-racer, the Boxer's front suspension consisted of unequal-length upper and lower wishbones with single, concentric coil spring/damper units on each side.

The flat-12 'boxer' engine was designed by a team of 12, under engineer Giuliano de Angelis, who broadly followed the layout of Ferrari's current flat-12 Formula 1 engine. Previous Ferrari road-car engine development was not discarded, however, as it was decided to use as many of the Daytona's V12 engine components as possible, and in fact the same pistons and connecting rods were used along with many other parts. Not surprisingly, the flat-12's displacement was the same 4.4 litres as the Daytona.

The actual displacement was 4390 cc, achieved with over-square dimensions of 81 mm × 71 mm. Its construction was familiar Ferrari; the block and heads were cast in silumin

alloy with cast-iron cylinder liners shrunk into place, and the crankshaft, machined from a solid billet of steel, ran in seven main bearings. The considerable quantities of fuel the flat-12 required were pumped into the combustion chambers via one large inlet valve per cylinder from a quartet of triple-choke Weber downdraught carburettors. It may have been too early for four-valves-per-cylinder technology for Ferrari, but the switch from the old-fashioned chain-cam drive to the quieter and more refined belt system was one sign of progress, as was the rationalisation of the ignition from traditional Ferrari practice of twin distributors to a single unit mounted on the end of one camshaft.

Above: In 1981 the fitting of Bosch K-Jetronic fuel injection in place of the traditional Weber carburation improved the engine's torque spread, and its refinement.

Left: The suspension engineers had to allow for driveshafts at the rear, as well as deal with the rearward weight bias and high centre of mass inherent in the Boxer's engine and transmission layout, so they used two coil-over-damper assemblies per side, again with double wishbones.

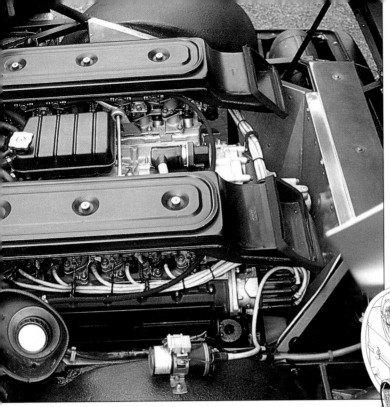

Above: The Maranello engineers opted to mount the Boxer's wide but flat, horizontally-opposed four-cam 12-cylinder engine on top of the transmission, but siting so much mass so high was not a wise decision in terms of its effect on the car's handling. On the 1976-81 512, as seen here, induction was through four triple-choke downdraught Weber 40IC3Cs (under the big 'tea-tray' filter casings). Note the spark plugs entering the cylinder heads at the side, rather than centrally between the camshafts.

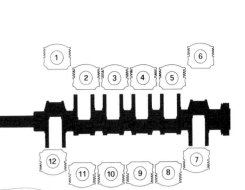

Below and right: The BB's flat-12 was developed as a result of Ferrari's success with 'boxer' engines in Formula 1, notably in the 312B series. The road version used toothed belts rather than chains to drive its four camshafts.

Below: Six exhaust tailpipes indicate that this car is a 365; as with the tail lamps, the 512 BB had only two on each side.

Above: One advantage of the gearbox being under the engine was a relatively roomy cabin (at least for a mid-engined two-seater), with no central tunnel to dominate the space.

Above: Twin fuel tanks were fitted just aft of the bulkhead. The 365's 215/70 VR15 rear tyres on 7.5-in rims grew to 225/70s on 9-in wheels on the 512.

Ferrari Daytona

Conceived by Enzo Ferrari to replace the much-loved 275, the Daytona marked the end of an era. It was the last big front-engined V12 supercar, and the fastest. Shattering performance was matched by perfect Pininfarina styling.

Above: When it was launched in 1968, the Daytona could exceed the 70-mph British national speed limit in second gear and go on to reach a top speed of 174 mph. That made the big V12-engined Ferrari the fastest car on the road, ahead of the Lamborghini Miura.

I t's a supreme irony that one of the most famous Ferraris ever built was already obsolescent when the first car left the Maranello plant in 1969.

The 365 GTB/4, more commonly known as the Daytona, was the supreme example of evolution rather than revolution and that's what has damned it in some critics' eyes while making it all the more desirable in others'. When it first appeared at the Paris Motor Show in 1968, the way forward in supercar design had already been mapped out by the staggering Lamborghini Miura, with its transverse V12 proving that it was possible to translate racing-car design into road-car production and make a mid-engined supercar. In total contrast, the Daytona carried on with a front-mounted engine driving the rear wheels in the time-honoured fashion. There was no single good reason for this; it was due to several factors which combined to make it virtually inevitable. There was Enzo Ferrari's well-known innate conservatism and a belief that there was nothing fundamentally wrong with the Daytona's predecessor, the 275 GTB/4, that demanded anything as drastic as a complete re-engineering. It wasn't felt that the US market required a change in what had been a very successful format, and finally at this stage Ferrari did

not view Lamborghini as serious rivals – a view which later changed. . .

Nevertheless the new car had to be faster overall and have better acceleration but, just as important, its engine had to be suitable for the increasingly stringent US emissions standards. Fitting the crude emissions systems of the early 1970s with their power-sapping air pumps meant that there had to be a change from the highly tuned, relatively small, 3.3-litre V12 used in the 275. Ferrari already had a four-litre variant in the form of the 330 engine used in big saloons like the 400 Superamerica and that was given a bigger bore of 81 mm rather than 77 mm to go with the 71-mm stroke to give an over-square 4390 cc and form the 365 engine (4390 cc divided by 12 cylinders).

The first 365 engines were single-overhead-cam-per-cylinder-bank affairs, but that arrangement was discarded for the Daytona. The move to quad cams, in conjunction with a reasonably high compression ratio, might suggest a search for more outright power, but although the new engine was obviously more powerful than the 3.3-litre V12 (with over a litre more displacement, that was almost inevitable) the difference was not remarkable. The Daytona had 353 bhp compared with the 300 bhp of the 275 GT B/4, but its

valve timing had been set to give far greater torque, more than just the extra one litre would have given, and at 319 lb ft at 5,500 rpm the Daytona was guaranteed fierce acceleration from an engine that could pass emissions regulations.

Guaranteed fierce acceleration

Such a large engine, even an alloy one like the Daytona's V12, mounted at the front could hamper weight distribution but Ferrari addressed that in two ways, by mounting it well back in the usual Ferrari tubular steel chassis, with all the cylinders behind the front axle line, and by locating the five-speed gearbox at the rear with the final drive unit, engine and transmission being connected by a rigid torque tube. That configuration gave the desired 50/50 front/rear weight distribution. The engine was also mounted low down in the frame to keep the centre of gravity as low as possible; this was achieved by using a motor-racing style dry-sump system, whereby no deep sump pan was needed as the oil was pumped around the engine from a separate tank.

GTB. Those brakes were also ventilated, which meant that they could work longer and harder before generating the heat that would make them fade, and they proved very effective indeed considering they were required to stop what was a surprisingly heavy car from speeds as high as 170 mph. According to the factory the Daytona weighed in at an excellent 2,825 lb, but when *Autocar* weighed their road-test example it was a substantial 3,530 lb while *Road & Track's* test car recorded a weight of 3,885 lb, despite the fact that the bonnet, door and boot panels were alloy rather than steel.

Reached 60 mph in under six seconds

In view of that, its performance was nothing short of incredible. Even though it wasn't the easiest of cars to get off the line, in the fierce standing-start treatment used to take performance figures it could still reach 60 mph in under six seconds and once into its stride it rocketed forward, past the quarter-mile post in under 14 seconds, by which time it was well past the 100-mph mark, and still only in third gear. With two more gears to go, clearly the Daytona's top speed was very fast indeed. If you calculated it from its gearing in top (in which it did 24.8 mph per 1,000 rpm) and its maximum-power rpm (7,500 rpm), then its theoretical top speed was as high as 180 mph. In fact no tester ever achieved that magical figure, but the top speeds that *were* recorded (176 mph from *Road & Track*, and from racing driver/motoring journalist Paul Frere, and 174 mph from *Autocar*) were untouched by anything else then on the road (although the Lamborghini Miura could reach 172 mph).

Purists might have complained that the Daytona broke no new ground, was far too heavy,

Above: Even non-enthusiasts would recognise the Daytona's shape from the rear. Sadly, although its lines were perfect, the curved bodywork was, like many Italian exotics of the era, rust-prone.

and required too much strength to drive, but Enzo Ferrari was vindicated by the marketplace. From the time it first went on sale in 1969 to the end of production in 1973, Ferrari sold nearly 1,400 Daytonas, showing just how desirable a car it was. Even more desirable was the factory convertible model, of which only around 100 were built. As time has passed, the convertible has become so sought-after that a good number of coupés have been converted into open cars, and passed off as genuine factory models. It was a relatively easy switch to do, as the Daytona's tubular steel structure did not rely heavily on the roof for its overall stiffness. It was truly a very robust car, and that strength was well-shown during its competition career.

Ferrari built more than a dozen competition models for his concessionaires to enter in races such as the Le Mans and Daytona 24-hour events. These were not just tuned models; they were significantly lightened (which was just as well...) with alloy bodies, and even some glassfibre panels on some cars. Power output was increased to a fraction over 400 bhp at higher revs (8,300 rpm rather than 7,500 rpm). The extra power, combined with less weight and taller gearing for Le Mans, meant that top speed down the long Mulsanne straight, for example, was a genuine 180 mph. In just a few years, however, racing design had passed it by, with mid-engined layouts having become universal, and the last and greatest of the front-engined supercars could be seen as a glorious anachronism, one for which a price of around £175,000 would be expected these days. Who says Ferrari was wrong to stick to his guns?

The dry-sump system also of course had the merit of avoiding oil surge in high-speed cornering – and corner at high speed the Daytona certainly could. It was equipped with double unequal-length wishbones front and rear with anti-roll bars at each end and large, for the time, 215/70 15-in tyres, usually Michelin XVRs. The Daytona used 15-in-diameter wheels partly because the newly-introduced low-profile tyres (and to begin with, 70 was considered a low profile. . .) meant larger wheels could be fitted without the whole assembly being too big. Bigger wheels meant more space for the brakes, and the Daytona was equipped with disc brakes large enough to cope with its performance – something that could not be said for its predecessor, the 275

Top: The rear suspension was set up with discernible negative camber, so that under high cornering loads the outside rear wheel stayed nearly upright.

Above: The Pininfarina-designed near-horizontal nose and concave tail panel ensured aerodynamic cleanliness and minimal lift.

Overleaf: Many accident-damaged Daytonas have been converted into Spyders as part of their repair because Spyder values are so high. This is the genuine article, though.

Driving the Daytona: *muscular agility*

These days the Daytona has the reputation of being a crude car to drive, all power and no finesse, a car requiring a strong driver to get the best out of it.

Some elements of the Daytona do take some mastering: the steering is very heavy at slow speeds, the clutch requires effort, and even the gear change needs a firm, deliberate hand to operate, but these aspects shouldn't be confused with crudeness. Once at operating temperature and under way, the gear change eases and the steering lightens considerably.

One of the first people to road-test the Daytona was respected racing driver and journalist Paul Frere, who found that "the Ferrari could be flung around the corners . . . it did not feel very big, and its agility belied its weight. The general cornering attitude is that of a slightly understeering car with a small tendency to tuck into bends when the throttle is closed. . ." He found the brakes excellent and the ride "surprisingly comfortable", but the sensation that lingered was of the sheer performance, which left Frere amazed at how many miles he had covered on an open road at up to 175 mph, and had another road-tester talking of the "neck-cracking tug of acceleration that leaves the stomach behind" past 4,000 rpm.

PERFORMANCE & SPECIFICATION COMPARISON	Engine	Displacement	Power	Torque (lb ft)	Max speed	0-60 mph	Length (in/mm)	Wheelbase (in/mm)	Track front/rear	Weight (lb/kg)	Price
Ferrari 365 GTB/4 Daytona	V12, quad-cam	4390 cc	353 bhp 7500 rpm	319 lb ft 5500 rpm	174 mph 280 km/h	5.4 sec	174.2 in 4425 mm	94.5 in 2400 mm	56.7 in 56.1 in	3530 lb 1601 kg	£6,740 (1970)
Iso Grifo	V8, overhead-valve	5359 cc	350 bhp 5800 rpm	360 lb ft 3600 rpm	161 mph 259 km/h	6.4 sec	174.0 in 4420 mm	82.5 in 2095 mm	55.5 in 55.5 in	2831 lb 1284 kg	£6,059 (1970)
Jaguar E-type V12	V12, overhead-cam	5343 cc	272 bhp 6000 rpm	304 lb ft 3600 rpm	142 mph 229 km/h	6.8 sec	184.5 in 4686 mm	105.0 in 2667 mm	53.0 in 53.0 in	3230 lb 1465 kg	£3,367 (1973)
Lamborghini Miura	V12, quad-cam	3929 cc	350 bhp 7000 rpm	271 lb ft 5100 rpm	172 mph 277 km/h	6.7 sec	171.6 in 4359 mm	98.4 in 2499 mm	55.6 in 55.6 in	2851 lb 1293 kg	£9,165 (1966)
Maserati Ghibli	V8, quad-cam	4719 cc	340 bhp 5500 rpm	326 lb ft 4000 rpm	154 mph 248 km/h	6.6 sec	180.7 in 4590 mm	100.4 in 2550 mm	56.7 in 55.4 in	3746 lb 1699 kg	£9,500 (1968)

Ferrari Daytona Data File

The 365 GTB/4 Daytona was Enzo Ferrari's way of updating and improving his top high-performance road car, the 275 GTB/4, which ran from 1966 to 1967. That was powered by a 3.3-litre quad-cam V12 engine, which itself was the update of the standard single-overhead-cam-per-bank V12 used in the original 275 GTB of 1964. The first 275 GTB was the successor to the long-lived 250 GT line and took Ferrari road cars a step forward with independent suspension all round.

By the late 1960s Ferrari could see that the 275 had reached the end of its development life, as the advent of increasingly stringent emissions-control legislation in North America, a key Ferrari market, meant that the 275's relatively small engine would lose its performance edge. The answer was a car very much in the 275 vein, again with wishbone suspension all round but with a larger, 4390-cc, quad-cam V12.

Above: Later cars, like this one, featured fully retractable headlamps rather than the Perspex covers used on the original.

Above: The overall shape was exceptionally clean and devoid of frills. Tiny bumpers were the only real concession to decoration.

Styling

Like all Ferraris since (with the exception of the Bertone-styled GT4 Dino), the Daytona was designed by Pininfarina, though actually built by Scaglietti. Although the end result is still stunning in the 1990s – the perfect realisation of the front-engined supercar theme – it was not an example of the stylist ignoring practicality. Pininfarina used the wind tunnel from a very early stage in the car's development to achieve two aims: low drag, and sufficient downforce to make the car stable at its anticipated top speed of over 170 mph. For once, clean lines did equate to aerodynamic efficiency, and not at the expense of engine cooling. The sharp-edged nose guided air over, rather than under, the car but

nevertheless the big V12 engine still had sufficient cooling air fed to it from the relatively small openings between the two vestigial quarter-bumpers. That air then exited from two vents in the body which were all that disrupted the smooth shape.

The deep crease along the side, running back from just above the bumper line, was just enough to break up what could otherwise have been too deep an expanse of curved bodywork. That was particularly important in the case of the coupé and was even seen as necessary in the convertible when the top was folded neatly down behind the front seats. It's a testament to Pininfarina's design that the Daytona looks equally good in coupé or convertible form.

Left: Vents extracted stale air and kept the cabin cool. Air conditioning was optional.

Above: Two vents set into the bonnet extracted hot air from the engine compartment.

Below: Some cars had driving lights fitted, to save raising the flaps when flashing.

Above: The distinctive nose was poorly protected by embryonic bumpers.

Below: Seats were fixed, but the pedals could be adjusted according to the driver's height. The Daytona was spacious and comfortable, and every engine function was monitored for the driver.

Above: On the Spyder the hood folded away behind the seats, flush with the body.

Below: The boot design was surprisingly practical, as the lid extended to the bumper.

Chassis and suspension

Each alloy wheel was located in accordance with accepted racing-car practice: by twin unequal-length wishbones all round and the expected concentric coil spring/damper units. Those at the front were neatly mounted between the two wishbones, allowing a low nose line, while with more space to play with at the rear, the coil springs and dampers acted on the top wishbones so that the driveshafts could reach the hubs.

From the top wishbones the coil spring/damper units went upwards, mounted on fabricated housings which were an integral part of the tubular steel chassis. Anti-roll bars were used front and rear, while the rear suspension was set up with clearly discernible negative camber, which meant that under high cornering loads the outside rear wheel would stay near the ideal upright position.

Below and right: Alloy wheels were located by racing-style twin unequal-length wishbones.

Competition record

Although the standard Daytona was not designed as an outright competition car, its combination of power, handling and strength made it a good racing car, while the special lightened and more powerful factory cars were formidable. In 1972 a competition version won its class at Watkins Glen. A similar car was a class winner at Le Mans the same year, and the NART (North American Racing Team) organisation kept the Daytona represented at Le Mans for many years. Also in France a Daytona won the Tour de France outright, just as the GTO before it had done (in 1963). The Le Mans class win was repeated in 1973 and 1974. The car ran in the Group 4 Special Grand Touring class, finishing an excellent second in the Daytona 24 Hours in 1973, while one Daytona was still going strong enough to finish second at its namesake track, Daytona, in 1979.

Above: Grip was very high and the Daytona's balance perfect – making it a good racing car.

Below: Daytonas were a common sight at Le Mans for many years, and were very successful.

Engine

The Daytona was powered by a V12 engine which could trace its evolution back to the very first post-war Ferrari V12 designed by Giachino Colombo. Granted, it was a very tenuous relationship, the first engine being only a 1.5-litre, but the heritage was there nonetheless.

The 365 engine was all-alloy with a light-alloy block and crankcase and alloy heads. As usual with alloy blocks of the era, it featured wet cylinder liners, i.e. the pistons ran in iron sleeves that were surrounded by the engine coolant, hence 'wet' rather than 'dry' liners. The combination of a bore of 81 mm and stroke of 71 mm gave a displacement of 365 cc for each cylinder (hence the 365 of the car's official name). In turn that gave an overall displacement of 4390 cc. Even with a fairly mundane specification that would have guaranteed considerable power, but the Daytona engine featured the classical type of high-performance top end in the form of twin overhead camshafts operating two valves per cylinder in hemispherical combustion chambers. Those twin-cam heads had been developed from the single-overhead-cam per-cylinder-bank heads of the 275 engine by retaining the chain drive and using it to drive idler wheels, which in turn drove the twin chamshafts by gears rather than the customary chains.

Inevitably, given the V12 twin-cam layout, fuelling was achieved by using no fewer than six twin-choke downdraught Weber 40DCN carburettors nestling in the engine 'V' and feeding the inlets, which were adjacent to the carburettors. That array of Webers was in turn fed by twin electric Bendix fuel pumps and the net result was a maximum power output of 353 bhp at a high-revving 7,500 rpm. Ferrari could easily have achieved more, but instead opted to have more torque than previous Ferrari V12 engines, with 319 lb ft at 5,500 rpm. The engine was amply strong to deal with all that power and torque too, with four-bolt main bearing caps, a crankshaft machined from a single billet of steel and forged polished con-rods, while the rigid cast-alloy dry-sump cover contributed to the stiffness of the whole assembly.

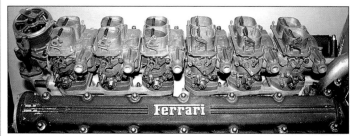

Above: Ferrari used its standard carburettor installation for the V12: six twin-choke Weber 40DCNs. Power output was 353 bhp at 7,500 rpm.

Below: Out of the car, the Daytona's 4.4-litre V12 engine appears surprisingly compact. It was of all-alloy construction with wet liners. The gear camshaft drive is to the right in the picture; it required less of a bulge in the cam covers than a standard chain drive. To the far right of the engine can be seen one of the two oil filters fitted – they can be more clearly seen in the underbonnet picture (left).

Above: Following the standard Ferrari practice of the time, the 365 in the car's name referred to the cubic capacity of a single cylinder. The camshaft drive from the earlier single-overhead-camshaft-per-bank 275 engine was retained, with the chain drive to the original single camshafts used to drive idler wheels, which in turn drove the twin camshafts for each cylinder bank via gears.

Below: Even given the substantial length of the bonnet, the 4.4-litre V12 engine was a pretty tight fit.

Below: Various different lengths of tail were studied at the initial design stage before settling on the most practical one. The Daytona remained virtually the same length as the 275.

Above: Rear springs ran from the upper wishbones, to leave space for the driveshafts to run between the wishbones.

Above left and right: Brakes were 11-in-diameter Girling ventilated discs all round, to give impressive stopping power.

Right: Daytonas may be worth a fortune, but that doesn't stop owners racing. This car has had a highly individual front spoiler fitted.

Ferrari F40

Enzo Ferrari wanted to build a special car to celebrate the 40th anniversary of the very first Ferrari, which left the factory in 1947. The resulting 200-mph F40 set new standards for supercar performance.

Above: Although the F40 is really a road car, it can give a good account of itself on the racetrack. Even when cornering hard, the F40's suspension allows very little roll and the huge tyres (245-section at the front and 335 at the rear) give the car terrific grip.

Amid all the euphoria that greeted the Ferrari F40's launch four years ago, there was a gentle undercurrent of reservation. In comparison with the technologically masterful 959, went the argument, the F40 was an unadventurous concept being sold at an ambitious price. How could Ferrari claim to be at the forefront of high-performance car design when the F40 did not even have anti-lock brakes, let alone four-wheel drive?

Ferrari had set out not to create a technological tour de force, but to build the most pure track-inspired sports car the world had ever seen. The F40 contains state-of-the-art engineering that has been directed towards the single-minded aim of packing prodigious power into a lightweight car. Thanks to the advanced use of composite materials (including carbonfibre) for its body and chassis, it weighs little more than a ton. On this super-rigid platform sits a twin-turbocharged 2.9-litre V8 engine producing 478 bhp. That made it the most powerful production engine ever developed for a road car before the Lamborghini Diablo appeared on the scene.

. . . power output of 478 bhp at 7,000 rpm

The F40 is a direct descendant of the 288 GTO, Ferrari's first attempt to build a limited-edition supercar. Launched at the Geneva Motor Show in 1984, the GTO – which took its name from the famous *Gran Turismo Omologato* model of the early 1960s – was a fascinating hybrid of road and race technology inspired by FISA's new Group B racing regulations, but, as it turned out, was never raced by the factory nor its customers.

The GTO's tubular steel chassis was nothing special, but parts of the body benefitted from knowledge gained in Formula 1 by Dr Harvey Postlethwaite, the English designer who gave Ferrari its first composite Formula 1 chassis in 1982.

The most advanced application of Postlethwaite's expertise was the bulkhead between engine and passenger compartment. Formed of an aluminium honeycomb core clad on each side with a layer of Kevlar/glassfibre composite, this bulkhead acts as a rigid structural member, an insulating barrier and a firewall. Kevlar/Nomex composite, a remarkable blend of lightness and strength, was used for the roof panel, the rear deck and the front luggage lid; this last piece, weighing only seven pounds, is so light that it cannot be slammed shut.

The GTO had its motor mounted longitudinally, Formula 1 style, in line with a five-speed transaxle extending behind the rear axle line. A pair of Japanese IHI turbos, chosen in preference to the German KKKs used in Formula 1 because of their performance across the full engine range, endowed the GTO's engine with formidable punch; an output of 400 bhp at 7,000 rpm made it the most powerful roadgoing car Ferrari had ever produced and gave figures of 0-100 km/h (62.1 mph) in 4.9 seconds, the standing quarter-mile in 12.7 seconds and a top speed of 189.5 mph. At around £90,000 a time, it proved to be so easy to sell the 200 cars required for Group B homologation that Ferrari yielded to temptation and built a few more, the final total running out at 278.

This level of interest so amazed Ferrari's senior executives that the decision to build an even more awe-inspiring successor was made a few months later.

On the face of it, the F40 was developed in a remarkably short time, just over a year elapsing between the official go-ahead and the car's press

Above: Even in the wet, the F40 can be driven safely at speeds which would see most cars spinning off into the scenery.

launch on 21 July 1987. In fact, most of the work had already been accomplished on an interim car called the GTO Evoluzione.

The F40 engine differed from the GTO's in having a wider bore of 3.23 in and shorter stroke of 2.74 in to produce even more 'over-square' dimensions. Maximum boost pressure was reduced to 1.1 bar, and with emission controls the F40's power output settled at 478 bhp at 7,000 rpm – enough to make it Ferrari's most powerful production engine ever.

That power output was not hampered by weight. The F40's body is made up from 12 pieces of Kevlar/carbonfibre/glassfibre composite.

Three times more rigid, yet weighs less

The chassis is a separate unit that essentially takes the form of a simple steel spaceframe incorporating bonded composite panels to endow greater strength. The complete structure, Ferrari reckons, is three times more rigid than a conventional steel frame would have been, yet weighs 20 per cent less. Tubular steel forms a passenger cage with outriggers to carry the engine/gearbox and suspension.

The F40 can exceed 200 mph in top gear, and cover the standing quarter-mile in 11.9 seconds. With off-the-line acceleration of 0-100 mph in 8.8 seconds and 0-150 mph in 18.5 seconds, it is no wonder that it has become the most sought-after of modern Ferraris.

Below: Ferrari developed conventional winding side windows which can be specified as an alternative to the sliding type seen above.

Right: At speed, the F40's aerodynamic shape keeps it glued to the road.

Above: The overall shape of the F40 mirrors current racing car practice. The basic wedge shape – low at the front, high at the rear – gives good aerodynamic penetration and helps to create downforce for better cornering. The rear wing smooths the airflow around the tail of the car and also generates downforce. The air inlets in the body are designed to take in the maximum amount of air while creating as little turbulence as possible.

Driving the F40: *ultimate road racer*

From the first moment you squeeze yourself into the F40's cockpit, you have no doubt that you are in the ultimate racing car for the road.

The heavy clutch bites sweetly and progressively, and the steering is pleasantly light even at a crawl. The brakes, however, require such a mighty push before the pads and discs reach operating temperature that you wonder for an instant, as the back of the lorry in front looms large, whether they work at all. Designed for three-figure cornering speeds, the suspension's kart-like stiffness gives a jarring ride over urban roads.

Flex your right foot on the throttle, and there's a blur of mind-numbing acceleration. The power is truly explosive, arriving with a ferocity that no other road car can match. The 0-60 mph sprint in 4.5 seconds sounds fine on paper, but the margin in reality is almost unimaginably massive between this figure and the 5-6 second bracket of lesser supercars.

Despite the huge 335/35 rear tyres, the wheels can spin in second, third and even fourth gears on all but the smoothest roads. Serious recalibration of your senses is needed to adjust to this Ferrari street-racer's outrageous performance.

PERFORMANCE & SPECIFICATION COMPARISON	Engine	Displacement	Power	Torque (lb ft)	Max speed	0-60 mph	Length (in/mm)	Wheelbase (in/mm)	Track front/rear	Weight total (lb/kg)	Price
Ferrari F40	V8, quad-cam, 32-valve, twin-turbo	2936 cc	478 bhp 7000 rpm	425 lb ft 4000 rpm	201 mph 323 km/h	4.5 sec	171.6 in 4358 mm	96.5 in 2450 mm	62.8 in 63.2 in	2425 lb 1100 kg	£197,502 (1991)
Aston Martin Virage	V8, quad-cam	5340 cc	330 bhp 6000 rpm	340 lb ft 3700 rpm	157 mph 253 km/h	6.8 sec	184.5 in 4686 mm	100.7 in 2558 mm	55.0 in 56.3 in	4295 lb 1948 kg	£125,000 (1990)
Honda NSX	V6, quad-cam, 24-valve	2977 cc	274 bhp 7000 rpm	210 lb ft 5300 rpm	162 mph 261 km/h	5.2 sec	173.4 in 4405 mm	99.6 in 2530 mm	59.4 in 60.2 in	3020 lb 1370 kg	£55,000 (1991)
Lamborghini Diablo	V12, quad-cam, 48-valve	5729 cc	492 bhp 7000 rpm	428 lb ft 5200 rpm	205 mph 330 km/h	4.2 sec	175.6 in 4460 mm	104.3 in 2650 mm	60.6 in 64.6 in	3474 lb 1576 kg	£158,370 (1991)
Porsche 959	Flat-six, quad-cam, 24-valve, twin-turbo	2851 cc	450 bhp 6500 rpm	370 lb ft 5500 rpm	190 mph 306 km/h	3.6 sec	167.7 in 4260 mm	89.4 in 2272 mm	59.2 in 61.0 in	3197 lb 1450 kg	£160,000 (1987)

Ferrari F40 Data File

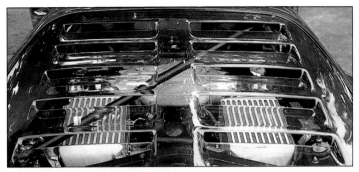

T he F40 was inspired by two things: the desire not to be outdone by Porsche in producing the world's fastest roadgoing car (it was stretching things a little to call the Porsche 959 a production car), and the requirement for something really special to celebrate 40 years of Ferrari car production (the 125 had been launched on 12 March 1947). The story has it that Enzo Ferrari wanted something in the mould of one of his favourite older Ferraris – the 250 LM, 'LM' standing for Le Mans. In other words what he wanted was a roadgoing supercar as near to a race car as possible, "a byword for technological excellence and exceptional performance". In the shape of Ferrari's short-lived Group B car, the 288 GTO, and its GTO Evoluzione development, Ferrari had just the foundation for a car to meet both requirements, but with the emphasis more on performance than technology.

Above: Bred on the track, at home on the track. Before its launch, the F40 was speed-tested at circuits in Fiorano, Nardo and Balocco.

Styling

Since much of the F40's development work had been achieved on the GTO Evoluzione, the toughest task in the 12-month timetable between the F40's official go-ahead and launch fell to Pininfarina. By any modern standards, this was a tight schedule for the design of a completely new body style, but one which a generation ago, at the time of spiritual F40 ancestors like the SWB and GTO, would have seemed generous. Years ago, Ferraris used to be created in less than a year.

Pininfarina broke with normal practice by shaping the car directly in model form. The usual procedure would be to clarify the design during sketch work, present a finished set of renderings for Ferrari's approval of the basic shape, make full-scale section drawings, and finally build a full-scale model. The F40, however, was designed in three dimensions on a polyurethane foam model, using only basic sketch work as reference. It was a risky approach, perhaps, but one which Pininfarina's designers, with 30

years' experience, and Ferrari were willing to take.

In a sense, the restrictions in the brief – this job was essentially to give an existing car a smart new suit of clothes – removed many of the choices which take up design time. The GTO Evoluzione was an ugly brute, its wings, cooling apertures and appendages the pragmatic result of three years of testing. A designer had never been near it.

Pininfarina's brief was to design new front and rear sections for the car, but to leave the central passenger cell unaltered. There was room within these constraints to adopt styling cues from Ferraris of the past, such as the three chin-level air intakes at the front (a large central opening for the radiator and smaller ducts on each side of the brakes), echoing the 'face' of countless racing Ferraris of the past. In addition, the full-width wing at the back conjures up the 312P, Ferrari's sports-prototype racer of the early 1970s.

Above: Many mid-engined cars have a vertical rear window and a horizontal engine cover, but Ferrari used a sloping window, slotted for engine cooling, which gives less turbulence.

Left: Hot air from the brakes (and spray from a wet road) flow through the slot in front of the door. Earlier cars had the mirror mounted on the quarter-light.

Below: Yet another air intake – the F40 has 13 altogether. This one is for the gearbox oil cooler.

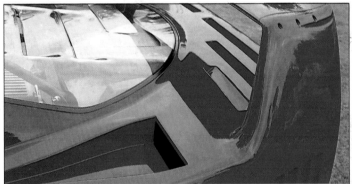

Aerodynamics

Wind-tunnel evaluation on the F40 model proceeded smoothly, most of the effort going into balancing the requirements of drag (a 200 mph top speed demanded a maximum C_d of 0.34) and downforce. One or two radical aerodynamic possibilities were tried, the most distinctive being the fitting of spats to conceal the rear wheels. These would have produced a small increase in top speed, but the practical problems – such as the inhibited flow of cool air to the rear brakes and the difficulty of changing a wheel – dictated their rejection.

The main change, in terms of aerodynamic performance, from the GTO Evoluzione was to give the rear window area a very rounded profile in plan view. Compared with the GTO Evoluzione's flat rear window, the F40's design provides a cleaner airflow over the rear of the car,

allowing the wing to work more efficiently and reducing the extent of aerodynamically undesirable turbulence in the car's wake. Beneath the tail, the tapered profile of the underbody channels on either side of the gearbox provides a small measure of ground effect.

Virtually every aspect of the F40's exterior design is dictated by function. There are 13 intakes to feed air to the intercoolers, to radiators for water, engine oil and gearbox oil, to all four brakes, and into the cabin. Slots on the rear wings, in the rear window and on the flat surface of the rear deck allow hot air to be expelled from the engine compartment, while even the tail panel is a black mesh insert to provide extra cooling. The only external feature with no functional significance is the thin black line running round the car at hip level.

Above: The GTO Evoluzione was a mobile test-bed for the F40, and was never intended for production.

Below: Powerful engines need lots of air to keep them cool, hence the vented cover.

Below: In the wind tunnel, woollen tufts show whether the air is flowing smoothly or whether there is unwanted turbulence.

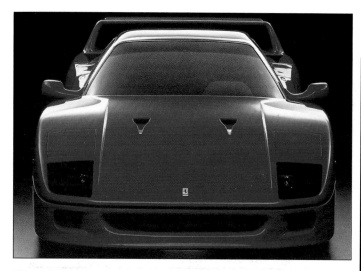

Above: Pop-up headlight pods each contain separate lights for main and dipped beams. The panels below the pods contain turn indicators, side lights, and lights for flashing when the main pods are down.

Suspension and brakes

Apart from the usual experimentation with spring, damper and anti-roll bar rates, the suspension of the F40 went ahead to production unaltered from the GTO Evoluzione's classical layout of double wishbones front and rear, with the rear spring/damper struts mounted above the upper wishbones. Koni coil-and-damper units are used, operating directly between the uprights and the chassis brackets without any intermediate levers or rockers. Each front unit runs from the base of the upright to meet the chassis between the arms of the upper wishbone, but the rears are attached at the top of the uprights and locate to the frame well above the height of the wheel rims.

Developing a braking system (in conjunction with Brembo) strong enough to handle 200-mph performance turned out to be a lengthy process. A great deal of work went into lowering pad and disc

temperatures and eliminating vibration, while an early casualty of the development process was the removal of servo-assistance. The non-servo brakes, in the end, were reckoned to give acceptable pedal effort together with the bonus of superior feel. Ferrari claims that the 92.6-lb pedal weight required to produce 1 g deceleration is comparable with the performance of some cars with servo-assistance.

The discs with which Ferrari finished up are huge, complex and expensive to manufacture. To avoid their size creating too much unsprung weight, the 12.9-in discs follow pre-carbonfibre Formula 1 practice in having an aluminium core with cast-iron friction surfaces, together with generous lateral passages and cross-drillings for cooling. Brembo four-piston aluminium calipers are fitted to the trailing edge of the front discs and the leading edge of the rears.

Below: Front suspension is by double wishbones, with coil spring/damper units and an anti-roll bar.

Below: With the engine removed, the structural details of the F40's chassis can be better seen.

Engine

The design basics of the production F40 engine follow familiar Ferrari practice. The V8's cylinder banks are angled at 90 degrees. The block, crankcase and heads are made of aluminium/silicon alloy (Silumin) cast in Maranello's foundry. Shrink-fitted aluminium cylinder liners are hardened with nickel/silicon alloy (Nikasil). Two overhead camshafts per bank, driven by toothed rubber belts, operate four valves per cylinder. With a cylinder diameter of 82 mm and a stroke of 69.5 mm, the V8 is over-square and displaces 2936 cc. The low compression ratio of 7.7:1 is explained by the presence of twin IHI turbochargers blowing at a maximum

of 16 psi, which helps give the impressive output of 478 bhp at 7,000 rpm.

The engine's detail features differ somewhat from those used in the GTO. The oil system, still dry-sump with a rear-mounted cooler and tank, was refined with enlarged lubrication passages in the crankshaft and cooling jets directed onto the piston crowns. The larger IHI turbochargers are water-cooled and supplied via larger Behr intercoolers. The wider cylinder bore allows larger valves, the exhaust ones having hollow stems. A multi-butterfly inlet system adds to the sophistication of the Weber-Marelli ignition-injection installation.

Below: Ferrari used aluminium/silicon alloy for the F40's block, crankcase and cylinder heads. Note the two overhead camshafts, each with five bearings, already installed in the cylinder head.

Below right: The large ribbed unit on top of the engine is one of the turbocharger intercoolers.

Right: Three exhaust pipes serve the F40. Wastegates dump excess turbo boost into the central pipe.

Right: Visible here between the gearbox and the right-hand rear tyre is the engine oil cooler – a vital component in a high-performance engine like this. Air enters the engine compartment through an intake in front of the rear wing and is ducted down to the oil cooler. The air then finds its way out of the grille between the rear lights. A similar radiator on the left cools the gearbox oil.

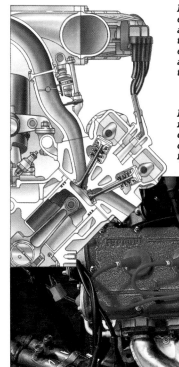

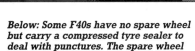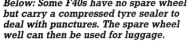

Left: Each of the four camshafts drives eight valves. Valve clearances are adjusted by changing the shim between the cam lobe and the tappet. The exhaust valves have hollow stems which are filled with sodium to help to disperse the heat.

Below: This is a completed engine, ready to be fitted into an F40. Red cylinder heads are familiar to Ferrari owners. 'Testa Rossa', the name of two famous Ferraris, is Italian for red head.

Above: Each F40 engine was built by hand by skilled Ferrari craftsmen. The completed engine was then run on the bench for four hours and thoroughly tested before it was ready to be fitted into the car.

Below: Some F40s have no spare wheel but carry a compressed tyre sealer to deal with punctures. The spare wheel well can then be used for luggage.

Above: The outer panels and floor are made of woven Kevlar and carbonfibre, which gives them great strength and lightness.

Right: The whole tail section hinges up to give access to the engine for checking routine items like engine oil level and drivebelt tension. Note the asymmetric tread of the 335/35 ZR17 rear tyres, and the two oil coolers (for engine and gearbox lubricants) on either side of the silencer.

Jaguar XJ220

When the XJ220 appeared at the 1988 Motor Show, it stopped the show. Few people believed it could be put into production, but Jaguar confounded their critics and built the 208-mph machine, the world's fastest road car.

rom a sketch on the back of a Christmas card seven years ago to becoming the world's fastest production car, the story of Jaguar's XJ220 makes extraordinary reading. Conceived by Jaguar's ex-head of product development Jim Randle as a supercar to beat the world's best, and developed initially by a team of Jaguar engineers working in their own time, the XJ220 was then redesigned from the ground up three years ago to offer a level of performance unmatched by any other car in the world.

In truth, XJ220 is not one but two cars. Randle's original vision was of a car powered by a detuned four-valves-per-cylinder version of the Le Mans-winning XJR-12 V12 engine, but with a full complement of technology to provide an immensely capable road car – it had four-wheel drive, anti-lock brakes and the potential for traction control, adaptive suspension and four-wheel steering. This was the car that made a last-minute debut at the NEC in October 1988 and quite simply stopped the show in its tracks. When Sir John Egan pulled back the dust sheet covering the immaculate silver car, a multitude of onlookers totally ignored the Ferrari F40 on the stand opposite and a beaming Egan hinted that the fastest Jaguar could possibly become a production car. The show car was already very nearly a runner, but it was still very much a one-off.

Three months later Tom Walkinshaw, head of TWR and JaguarSport, reported back to the Jaguar board that the XJ220 could be produced, and could make a decent return on the investment required, but not as it stood. A new car needed to be designed, keeping very much to the original shape but using a twin-turbo V6 and rear-wheel drive to produce a shorter, lighter vehicle owing more to Jaguar's racing experience. As Tom Walkinshaw observed about the original car: "It couldn't be V12, four-wheel-drive and have everything on it. A not inconsiderable problem was getting tyres to last under the car; we had to get the weight down even to do that. We evolved a specification and came back with a V6 car, much smaller, much shorter but retaining most of the styling cues from the original concept car."

In many ways it was very different from Jim Randle's concept; the reworked car had no place for four-wheel drive, no place for anti-lock braking and didn't even require Jaguar's famous race-winning V12 engine. Walkinshaw's explanation was that "The benefits we got from the four-wheel-drive system were so small with this type of vehicle that they didn't warrant the complexity, weight and cost. Because the car has many new features, like ground effects, then the traction it

enjoys is far superior to a conventional car and you can get as much control on your braking conventionally as you would with ABS."

As for the V12 engine, it was its size and weight that ruled it out. Jaguar's Group C race cars had just changed over to TWR's own twin-turbo V6 for similar reasons, and a 3.5-litre road-going version of that would certainly deliver the required output of over 500 bhp. According to Walkinshaw: "The styling dictated that the V6 be used; a very short engine was necessary because of the wheelbase that had been selected – a 'V' engine was about the only thing that you could actually package in the space."

Jaguar's future in the balance

Three months after chief designer Richard Owen had first sat down at a JaguarSport drawing board, the detailed engineering layout and feasibility study were on paper and a business plan completed; JaguarSport were convinced that the XJ220 was a viable proposition, but it was put on hold because not only the car's but also Jaguar's future was in the balance while Ford were negotiating to buy Jaguar. In the event, the

Above: At night, or to warn traffic of the XJ220's impending high-speed arrival, covers retract to reveal four powerful halogen lights.

Below: To help give excellent roadholding the XJ220 is very wide; at 87.4 inches it's almost 10 inches wider than the Ferrari Testarossa.

H658 KWL

XJ220 was the first project to be ratified by Ford after their takeover.

On 14 December 1989 it was announced that between 220 and 350 XJ220s would be built, with a 500-bhp twin-turbo 24-valve V6 driving the rear wheels only, at a price of £290,000, index-linked to delivery date. The response was overwhelming; only 48 hours after that announcement JaguarSport had orders for several times the maximum number of cars they were prepared to build.

The car passed its crash test first time (just as well, considering the cost. . .). It passed with flying colours too – all the glazing stayed in place and the doors still opened normally. In May the first prototype was built and the XJ220 ran for the first time on 1 June – right on schedule. The main

development thrust then switched to achieving the car's projected performance, which brought changes. Keeping engine temperatures down to acceptable levels meant adding a pair of air vents to the rear quarter-panel, for example, while the car's aerodynamics were fine-tuned in Imperial College's moving-floor wind tunnel, the 1/5 scale-model tests coming out very close to projections. According to chief designer Richard Owen, the twin underbody venturis made the XJ220 the first road car in the world to generate true ground effects. A downforce of over 600 lb presses the car onto the road at 200 mph, helping

to make the car sufficiently stable.

The XJ220's test schedule was punishing indeed; thousands of miles were covered at high-speed tracks like the Nürburgring, Nardo in Italy and Ford's Fort Stockton circuit in the USA, where the car established an average speed of 208 mph and a maximum of 212 mph in July 1991, making it the fastest road car in the world. It wasn't all high-speed work, though; weeks were spent doing cold-weather tests to make sure that whoever bought an XJ220, it would run in all climates, should he wish to take such an investment out and about in less than perfect conditions.

H658 KWL

Above: Here the XJ220 picks up speed on the test track; the light shining on the track at the rear is part of the optical speed-recording test equipment. That equipment has recorded a best top-speed run of 212 mph and a staggering 0-100 km/h (0-62 mph) time of 3.8 seconds.

Overleaf: The long and sleek XJ220 looks particularly low, but that's something of an optical illusion as it is in fact as high as the stubbier-looking Ferrari F40.

Driving the XJ220: *luxury at 200 mph*

Only a select few will get to drive the XJ220, and they will experience the fastest production car in the world. The Fort Stockton average-speed run, at 208 mph, puts other supercars into perspective and, according to chief designer Richard Owen, that was achieved with an engine down on power, so there's more to come. . .
At Milbrook with John Nielsen driving, the XJ220 has recorded a 0-100 km/h (0-62 mph) time of 3.8 seconds, a standing quarter-mile in 11.5 seconds and a standing kilometre in 20.3 seconds. The 100-mph mark came up in just 7.3 seconds, and the car could reach 100 mph and then slow to a complete stop all within 14 seconds

– an outstanding performance, and one achieved with a car that has so much handling and roadholding ability built in that it would not disgrace itself on the racetrack against genuine competition cars.

While extracting this performance from the twin-turbo V6, the XJ220 driver is cocooned in traditional Jaguar luxury rather than in a stark sports-racing car interior of bare composite panels like some of the competition; sumptuous hide covers the seats, fascia, doors and centre tunnel, while standard equipment includes air conditioning and electric mirrors, and there's space for the tallest of drivers.

PERFORMANCE & SPECIFICATION COMPARISON	Engine	Displacement	Power	Torque (lb ft)	Max speed	0-60 mph	Length (in/mm)	Wheelbase (in/mm)	Track front/rear	Weight (lb/kg)	Price
Jaguar XJ220	V6, quad-cam, 24-valve, twin-turbo	3498 cc	542 bhp 7000 rpm	475 lb ft 4500 rpm	208 mph 335 km/h	3.8 sec	194.1 in 4930 mm	103.9 in 2640 mm	67.3 in 62.5 in	3241 lb 1470 kg	£400,000 (1992)
Aston Martin Virage 6.3	V8, quad-cam, 32-valve	6347 cc	465 bhp 5750 rpm	460 lb ft 4400 rpm	174 mph 280 km/h	5.4 sec	184.5 in 4686 mm	102.7 in 2609 mm	55.0 in 56.3 in	4266 lb 1935 kg	£194,604 (1992)
Ferrari F40	V8, quad-cam, 32-valve, twin-turbo	2936 cc	478 bhp 7000 rpm	425 lb ft 4000 rpm	201 mph 323 km/h	4.5 sec	171.6 in 4358 mm	96.5 in 2450 mm	62.8 in 63.2 in	2425 lb 1100 kg	£197,502 (1991)
Lamborghini Diablo	V12, quad-cam, 48-valve	5729 cc	492 bhp 7000 rpm	428 lb ft 5200 rpm	205 mph 330 km/h	4.2 sec	175.6 in 4460 mm	104.3 in 2650 mm	60.6 in 64.6 in	3474 lb 1576 kg	£155,932 (1992)
Porsche 959	Flat-six, quad-cam, 24-valve, twin-turbo	2851 cc	450 bhp 6500 rpm	370 lb ft 5500 rpm	190 mph 306 km/h	3.6 sec	167.7 in 4260 mm	89.4 in 2272 mm	59.2 in 61.0 in	3197 lb 1450 kg	£160,000 (1987)

Jaguar XJ220 Data File

The XJ220 is a testament to personal initiative on the part of a team of Jaguar engineers led by Jaguar's erstwhile product development head Jim Randle. The original concept, hatched over seven years ago, was to apply Jaguar's endurance racing technology to the road – in other words, updating the approach that saw the Le Mans-winning D-type of the 1950s sold as a roadgoing XKSS. In some ways the road car would have been more advanced than the racer, as Randle had a supply of 48-valve V12s which in the end were never used in the Group C racing car.

The XJ220 which finally emerged was a very different machine from Randle's original concept, but without his vision and dedication it would never have appeared.

Above: Despite the XJ220's slippery looks, the car's drag coefficient is a mere 0.36, a figure beaten by many of its rivals.

Above: A straightforward yet luxurious wrap-around fascia greets the XJ220 driver.

Below: Extractor vents are placed below the rear windscreen, over the V6 engine.

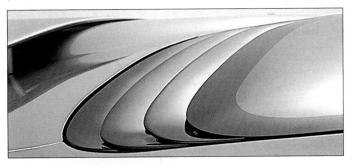

Styling

The original XJ220, the car shown at the 1988 NEC show, was designed by Keith Helfet, one of the team working under project leader Jim Randle (whose vision the car was). Drawings of the original design are shown below, but the production version was revamped by chief designer Richard Owen. Although the basic shape stayed very much the same, the massively long car was shortened, with the wheelbase being reduced by eight inches. That was possible as it

no longer had to accommodate a longitudinally-mid-mounted V12 engine. At the same time the glass area was modified and the side mirrors relocated to give acceptable angles of vision for the driver.

The body area inside the wheelbase is integrated by the bold feature of the scoop or tunnel running back to the intercooler air entry, which is a far neater design than the deliberate straked arrangement on the Ferrari Testarossa, for example.

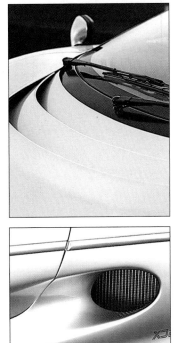

Left: The multiple rear vent treatment is echoed ahead of the windscreen.

Below: Front indicators are inset into rounded scoops next to the radiator inlet.

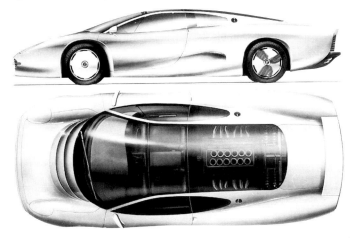

Above: The 12 intakes and exhausts indicate that this is the original V12 XJ220.

Below: The XJ220 is shown in 1989 form, after the decision had been made to go into production.

Left: Vents behind the doors feed air to the V6 engine's twin intercoolers.

Below: 17-in diameter alloy wheels are used at the front, 18-in at the rear.

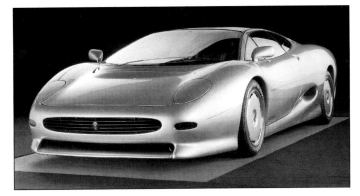

Above: The door handles are rounded to match the style of the rest of the car.

Suspension

The XJ220 runs on double wishbones all round, machined from solid alloy, with the exception of the lower pair at the rear, which are welded fabrications with an airfoil section to minimise the disruption to the airflow through the underbody venturi tunnels. At the rear, the suspension is mounted to the engine subframe rather than the transmission itself.

Rocker-arm-operated Bilstein spring/damper units control wheel travel, and anti-roll bars are used front and rear. The stub axles are beautifully-machined forgings with centre-nut wheel retention. Steering is by rack and pinion, power assistance being unnecessary since there's no drive to the front wheels. The original suspension geometry remains unchanged even after the exhaustive track and road development programme, which included extensive input from Jaguar's Le Mans-winning racing drivers John Nielsen and Andy Wallace.

Fourteen-inch-wide Speedline alloy wheels at the rear are shod with 345/35 ZR18 Bridgestone Expedia S.01 tyres. The front wheels are smaller, nine-inch-wide, alloys with 255/45 ZR17s.

Below: The massive rear brakes feature a separate caliper (on the right) for the handbrake.

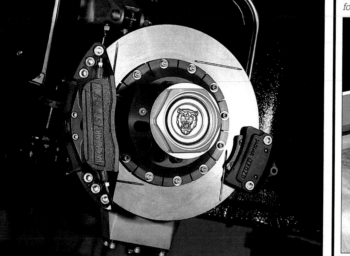

Chassis and body

The XJ220's structure is race car technology for the road. Massive two-inch-thick aluminium honeycomb panels run almost the whole length of the car, joined by both honeycomb and machined bulkheads with more honeycomb for the floor panel and centre tunnel, which houses all the wiring and pipes that run through the car. The bulkhead at the front of the driver's compartment is machined from solid alloy plate, an operation that takes 13 hours on a state-of-the-art computer-controlled machine, while more machined alloy beams run behind the cabin and under the engine. The two bulkheads behind the cabin house the 90-litre bag-type fuel tank between them, right on the car's centre of gravity.

Engine and transmission are mounted into a machined and bolted-together alloy subframe which in turn bolts to the tub behind the cabin, thus stiffening the total structure. A cross-brace connects this frame to the steel roll cage that runs up unobtrusively inside the roof pillars.

Right: The majority of the XJ220's main tub is made from an alloy honeycomb material which combines lightness with great strength. The front bulkhead is solid alloy.

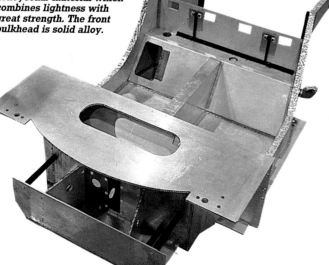

Engine

Originally the XJ220 was to have been powered by a highly developed version of Jaguar's long-lived V12; indeed the original NEC show car did have the V12. When JaguarSport productionised the car, they turned away from the 48-valve V12 to a version of the racing V6 used in Group C and IMSA. The bore and stroke of 94 mm × 84 mm are identical to that of the Gp C engine but the alloy block is a new casting to allow the normal road car ancillaries to be fitted. Its four valves per cylinder are driven by double belt-driven overhead camshafts per bank of cylinders and operate in a different combustion chamber shape, wherein the fuel injector's position is optimised for clean emissions. The valves differ from those in the race engine in being 2 mm smaller in diameter; other differences between the road and race engine include a conventional one-piece gasket for the road version compared with individual cylinder sealing.

Twin Garrett T3 turbos, water-cooled with integral wastegates, run at 1 bar pressure in an engine with an 8.3:1 compression ratio. The turbo set-up was chosen to give a good spread of torque along with economy and power. It achieved all three aims; maximum power output was 542 bhp at 7,000 rpm, maximum torque 475 lb ft at a reasonable 4,500 rpm, while the pre-production test car easily achieved 15 mpg with excellent exhaust emissions.

Above: V6 engine blocks, seen here before and after machining, make for a far lighter, more compact, unit than the V12 originally intended for the XJ220.

Above: The XJ220's engine is cooled by a front-mounted radiator, fitted at an angle within the sloping nose. Twin thermostatically-controlled electric fans are used.

Above right: The long indentations in the bottom of the doors and on the sides of the car lead to the large intercoolers; two are used, one on each side of the engine. The turbochargers can be seen behind each intercooler, towards the top.

Left: Power for the XJ220 comes from a 3.5-litre V6 which is a development of that used in Jaguar's successful racing cars; bore and stroke (94 mm × 84 mm) are the same, for example, but the block casting is new. The four overhead camshafts are belt-driven, and the engine produces 542 bhp at 7,000 rpm along with 475 lb ft of torque.

Below: On top of the engine can be seen the V6's twin intake manifolds. They are fed by twin Garrett T3 water-cooled turbos, whose location can be seen in the main cutaway diagram (bottom).

Above: The use of a dry-sump lubrication system makes the 3.5-litre V6 engine even more compact.

Below: A bulkhead separates the driver and passenger from the V6 engine, which is longitudinally mounted with the transmission (which includes a viscous-coupling limited-slip differential), towards the rear of the car.

Above: The component parts needed to assemble a 3.5-litre V6: the block and crankshaft are in the foreground, with the camshafts and heads, pistons, valves and springs on the table above them.

Below: A rounded rear wing creates rear downforce; its job is made easier by the fact that the XJ220's underbody incorporates two ground-effects venturis.

Jaguar XJR-S

The Jaguar XJ-S has been around a long time, but the attentions of Tom Walkinshaw's JaguarSport organisation have transformed its handling and, thanks to a 333-bhp six-litre V12, vastly increased its performance.

The colour brochure for the restyled, 1992, XJR-S begins with the proclamation: "The concept embodied in the Jaguar XJR-S is a simple and straightforward one. It is to combine traditional Jaguar values – craftsmanship, comfort, power and refinement – with performance that matches, or exceeds, that of the world's most illustrious sporting coupés." Few people who have driven an XJR-S would disagree with that. It is a car in the very best Jaguar traditions, and it was a logical commercial follow-up to Jaguar's re-emergence on the international motor racing scene in the 1980s.

That started in earnest in 1982, some 25 years since Jaguars had dominated sports car racing with the last of five famous victories at Le Mans, scored by an Ecurie Ecosse-entered D-type. As that first period of racing triumph had ended with a major contribution from an independent team, so the new Jaguar domination started with an outside collaboration. In this case it was the vastly experienced Tom Walkinshaw Racing organisation which teamed up with Jaguar during 1982, and by 1984 their XJ-S racing coupé had won the European Touring Car Championship, paving the way for an eventual Le Mans win with the XJR-9. That was built with a great deal of help from Walkinshaw, in this case under the banner of a new Jaguar/Walkinshaw venture called JaguarSport, which was created in May 1988. The XJR-S also emerged from JaguarSport, as a sportier version of the V12-engined coupé with

heavily revised suspension, brakes and steering, and a more-than-usually subtle body restyling to give aerodynamic stability appropriate to a quoted top speed of 150 mph.

Modified to be more exclusive and sporting

The first cars used the V12 in standard, 5.3-litre, Lucas-injected, Marelli-sparked form, with a quoted power output of 286 bhp at 5,150 rpm and peak torque of 310 lb ft at only 2,800 rpm. There were uprated springs front and rear, new and specially-developed gas dampers, modified rear trailing arms and new bushes to give the car a much tauter feel. The steering was sharpened up and given a bit more feedback, there was a sophisticated ABS braking system with yaw-control (to compensate for different wheels braking on different surfaces), bigger and rather attractively restyled alloy wheels with wide, low-profile tyres, and that aggressive new look to the body. As with all V12-engined XJ-Ss, it would be offered with three-speed automatic transmission only, but with this much power that was no great drawback, and maybe even the best solution.

It looked and felt like a very much more sporting car than the standard item, and the exclusivity was underlined by the fact that the first 100 cars would be a special limited edition, de-

signed to commemorate the Le Mans win in June. These 'Celebration Coupés' would have unique trim and colour options and individually-numbered identification plates. Number 002 went to Dutch racing driver Jan Lammers, one of the drivers of the Le Mans-winning XJR-9, which also happened to be number 2. When the celebration run had been completed, the intention was to continue with a run of broadly similar cars but without the special trim and individual numbers, for the UK market only at first and then for the USA and Europe. Tantalisingly, more power was also promised.

JaguarSport delivered that promise in quite a big way late in 1989, when they offered the first major upgrading of the V12 engine since it was introduced in 1971. By using a new crankshaft, new Cosworth pistons and new cylinder liners, they lengthened the stroke from 70.0 mm to 78.5 mm and increased the capacity from 5345 cc to 5993 cc. The bore stayed put, at 90.0 mm, which meant that the engine was still comfortably over-square and free-revving, especially with the other modifications that JaguarSport now added.

Chief among those was a completely new digital electronic ignition and sequential injection management system by Zytek, closely based on that used for the Walkinshaw Group C racing V12s. With seven-litre capacity but still with two-valve heads, the racing engines were capable of producing some 740 bhp and 550 lb ft of

Above: The rear spoiler is discreet but still plays a vital function in providing rear downforce at high speed.

18 bhp and 30 lb ft more than those for BMW's recently-announced V12 . . .

The XJR-S's performance increased to almost a 160-mph maximum speed (a figure electronically limited by the management system) with 0-60 mph times of around 6½ seconds, which allowed Jaguar to describe it as their fastest-ever road car. Happily, the XJR-S had proved from the start that with its race-developed suspension, steering and braking improvements it was more than capable of handling even that much power, and more than one magazine test now rated the XJR-S six-litre as the best overall high-performance coupé in the world.

Nothing much changed on the car for a couple of years, because nothing much needed

to, but in the middle of 1991, when Jaguar restyled the bodywork on the production XJ-S and tidied up the interior with, among other things, much-improved instruments, the XJR-S logically followed. The new version has softer, subtler bodywork add-ons (notably a much neater rear wing) and continues to look very handsome; and it is also even more powerful.

Even more effortless performance

Further revisions to the Zytek management, plus better inlet manifolds and a less restrictive catalyst-equipped exhaust system, gave another 15 bhp, to take the peak to 333 bhp at 5,250 rpm, giving even more effortless performance; and that, above all, is what makes the XJR-S great.

torque while staying reliable and fuel-efficient; using Zytek on the XJR-S was a classic example of racing technology genuinely contributing to road car development.

With its six-litre V12, the XJR-S now boasted 318 bhp at 5,250 rpm and up to 362 lb ft of torque at 3,750 rpm – improvements of 32 bhp and 52 lb ft respectively; and if the torque increase is impressive in itself, the real point was that the spread was now even flatter than on the incredibly flexible original V12, with more than 300 lb ft claimed all the way from only 2,000 rpm.

Significantly, too, the new figures were

Above: Although the basic XJ-S shape has been around for many years, the JaguarSport modifications have transformed it into a more handsome car.

Overleaf: Tom Walkinshaw's involvement in making the XJ-S go faster goes back to 1984 and the European Touring Car Championship-winning cars.

The rear wing and the side skirts indicate that this is no ordinary XJ-S.

Driving the XJR-S: *a new repertoire*

The latest, 333-bhp, XJR-S will nudge an electronically-limited top speed of 160 mph, reach 60 mph in 6.3 seconds and 100 mph in just over 15 seconds – all with a deceptive ease that comes only from so much power combined with leather-trimmed, wool-carpetted luxury. Driving hard on a twisty road, it is satisfying to use the leather-covered automatic transmission control like a manual gear change sometimes, even if only using the upper two gears, and then more for downshifts to promote engine braking than for holding the upshifts for extra performance. Left to its own devices, this automatic is superb anyway, with very quick responses but almost imperceptible full-power changes. It is fun to exploit the performance; the XJR-S soon feels smaller than it looks, the steering weight and precision are impeccable, and the brakes solid and hugely effective. Best of all is the outstanding handling, so totally different from the standard car's, with a new repertoire of ultra-sharp turn-in, massive grip, minimal roll and a balance ultimately allowing exploitable oversteer rather than frustrating understeer. It does all that with virtually no compromise to the standard ride comfort other than a noticeable increase in stiffness.

PERFORMANCE & SPECIFICATION COMPARISON	Engine	Displacement	Power	Torque (lb ft)	Max speed	0-60 mph	Length (in/mm)	Wheelbase (in/mm)	Track front/rear	Weight (lb/kg)	Price
Jaguar XJR-S	V12, overhead-cam	5993 cc	333 bhp 5250 rpm	365 lb ft 3650 rpm	155 mph 249 km/h	6.3 sec	189.7 in 4818 mm	102.0 in 2591 mm	58.6 in 59.2 in	4023 lb 1825 kg	£49,950 (1992)
BMW 850i	V12, overhead-cam	4988 cc	300 bhp 5200 rpm	332 lb ft 4100 rpm	161 mph 259 km/h	7.2 sec	188.2 in 4780 mm	105.7 in 2684 mm	61.2 in 61.4 in	4149 lb 1882 kg	£61,950 (1992)
Ferrari Mondial t	V8, quad-cam, 32-valve	3405 cc	300 bhp 7200 rpm	238 lb ft 4200 rpm	154 mph 248 km/h	5.6 sec	180.3 in 4580 mm	104.3 in 2649 mm	58.9 in 59.7 in	3560 lb 1615 kg	£69,310 (1992)
Mercedes 500 SL	V8, quad-cam, 32-valve	4973 cc	326 bhp 5500 rpm	332 lb ft 4000 rpm	157 mph 253 km/h	5.9 sec	176.0 in 4470 mm	99.0 in 2515 mm	60.4 in 60.0 in	4167 lb 1890 kg	£70,090 (1992)
Porsche 928 GT	V8, quad-cam, 32-valve	4957 cc	330 bhp 6200 rpm	317 lb ft 4100 rpm	165 mph 266 km/h	5.6 sec	177.9 in 4518 mm	98.1 in 2492 mm	61.1 in 60.9 in	3448 lb 1564 kg	£65,898 (1992)

Jaguar XJR-S Data File

The XJR-S was conceived in mid-1988, to serve a dual purpose. On the one hand it was the perfect way to celebrate Jaguar's win at Le Mans that year and, on the other, it was a relatively easy start to the new JaguarSports company's plan to produce exciting Jaguar road cars that were more performance-oriented than the then-current range. The XJ-S coupé provided the perfect base for this objective. JaguarSport boss Tom Walkinshaw knew the huge potential of Jaguar's V12 engine and felt that a faster version of the XJ-S would be a fairly straightforward proposition. The first XJR-S, however, featured the standard powerplant (although the car's suspension was uprated), but in 1989 the engine was enlarged and tuned to produce 318 bhp, a figure that rose to 333 bhp in 1991.

Above: The 1991 revamp of the XJ-S saw changes such as a reshaped rear side window, and the restyle was carried on in the XJR-S, too.

Styling

When the XJ-S was launched in 1975, its shape, especially around the oval-headlamped nose and 'flying-buttress' rear window, was controversial. And other than in the mid-1991 revamp (which mainly tidied up the rear side window line, the tail-lights and boot lid), it has changed very little; but oddly, it may be more kindly regarded now than it ever was when it was younger. For sure, an XJ-S will never be mistaken for anything else, but, as many lesser body-kits have shown, its lines are very easy to spoil. JaguarSport's uprating of the shape for the XJR-S, though, is subtle enough to give the car a much more aggressive look (and more efficient aerodynamics) without looking tacked-on or tacky. The detailing is naturally different on the original and new body shape, but the basics are very similar. There are deeper front and rear air dams with a much more integrated shape than the standard, rather heavy-looking bumpers, moulded sill panels to link the front and rear dams visually, and a low, full-width aerofoil on the rear edge of the boot – turning down at its outer ends on both new and old shapes, but rather more subtly on the latest car. The sill extensions are also a bit better integrated now, and the new car has a new-style wheel. Finally, there have been external trim options ranging from almost completely blacked-out brightwork to just enough chrome to highlight the lines, with understated 'Sport' badges for the grille, and a '6.0-litre' badge for the tail. For a 17-year-old shape, it looks great.

Above: It was criticised when new, but the XJ-S shape has stood the test of time. Redesigned rear lights (below) help maintain its appeal.

Above: Body-coloured headlight bezels on the XJR-S help disguise the XJ-S's rather clumsy standard headlamp treatment.

Right: Contrasting with the front lights, chrome was found acceptable at the rear.

Below: Larger, 8-in × 16-in, alloys are used on the XJR-S.

Below: The interior has been suitably upgraded with a thicker-rimmed, leather JaguarSport steering wheel. All XJR-Ss are automatics.

Below: Although the XJR-S is really only a 2 + 2, the rear passengers have the luxury of leather upholstery.

Chassis and suspension

Impressive as the effortless power, uncanny smoothness and tangible character of the XJR-S's uprated V12 are, the point-to-point abilities of the car are probably enhanced most of all by the brilliant changes which JaguarSport made to its suspension, steering and brakes. While retaining all the long-legged cruising refinement and most of the ride comfort of the standard model, the XJR-S adds new levels of sharpness and precision which don't quite turn it into a sports car (it's just too big for that) but do make it feel very sporty. At first glance, the changes were conventional enough, but what made them so effective was clearly TWR's vast amount of experience with preparing all manner of competition cars. The formula has remained much the same; only the details have changed. The standard XJ-S uses double-wishbone suspension at the front, and lower wishbones plus upper links and radius arms at the rear, with coil springs all round. The XJR-S retained that layout, but front and rear springs were uprated, the rear radius arms modified, the bushes changed, and special gas-filled dampers fitted. Larger-alloy wheels with wider, lower-profile, tyres were specified, and the power steering was uprated to give more feel and much sharper responses, all nicely conveyed by the smaller, thicker-rimmed leather-bound steering wheel. The brakes are discs all round, ventilated ones at the front, with ABS incorporating yaw-control. They are as excellent as the rest of the car.

Below: The XJR-S retains the twin-wishbone front suspension found on the original XJ-S.

Below: The rear suspension is held in a separate subframe, giving good noise insulation.

The 'High-Efficiency' head

When fuel consumption became a vital concern in the late 1970s Jaguar engineers redesigned the cylinder head to incorporate Swiss designer Michael May's 'Fireball' combustion chamber. That was effectively a swirl chamber, formed by deeply recessing the exhaust valve in each cylinder to give better combustion than in the Jaguar's flat, Heron head, type of chamber. It allowed the compression ratio to be increased, and fuel consumption decreased, to around 15 mpg.

Below: The HE 'Fireball' head features a swirl chamber inset below the exhaust valve.

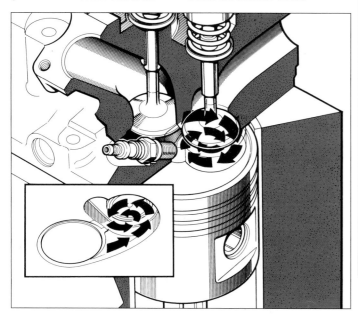

Engine

Jaguar's V12 is one of the world's great engines. It arrived in 1971, in the E-type, with a capacity of 5.3 litres and an output of some 266 bhp, using four carburettors rather than the planned injection, which had been delayed. Jaguar had used four cams on the V12 for the stillborn XJ13 racer, but the production V12 had one overhead camshaft per cylinder bank (for compactness as well as for cost) and two valves per cylinder. Being all-aluminium, it was only 65 lb heavier than Jaguar's iron-blocked six, and soon became known for its blend of smoothness and power, and in particular its astonishing flexibility. It was very thirsty, even when injection was adopted, but that was improved in 1981 with new 'High-Efficiency' heads, which gave more power for less fuel. For the first XJR-S, in 1988, the engine was left standard, with 286 bhp and 310 lb ft of torque, which wasn't quite the most it had ever offered but met current emissions requirements. Late in 1989, JaguarSport enlarged the engine to virtually six litres, stretching the stroke from 70.0 mm to 78.5 mm with a new crankshaft, while leaving the bore at 90.0 mm. There were new pistons and liners, and a new Zytek digital management system drawing closely on the lessons of TWR's racing V12s. Power went up to 318 bhp and peak torque to 362 lb ft, with a much flatter spread than before. The engine was uprated again in the new-shaped late-1991 car, and given a catalyst as standard. Most of the work was again on the management system, but there were changes to the inlet and exhaust plumbing too, to give 333 bhp at 5,250 rpm and 365 lb ft of torque, curiously enough at 3,650 rpm.

Above: The stripped alloy V12 engine shows the wet-liner construction and the duplex-chain camshaft drive for the single overhead cam per cylinder bank.

Below: The inlet and exhaust manifolding was revised in 1991 (along with the engine management) to help give the six-litre XJR-S engine as much as 333 bhp and 365 lb ft of torque.

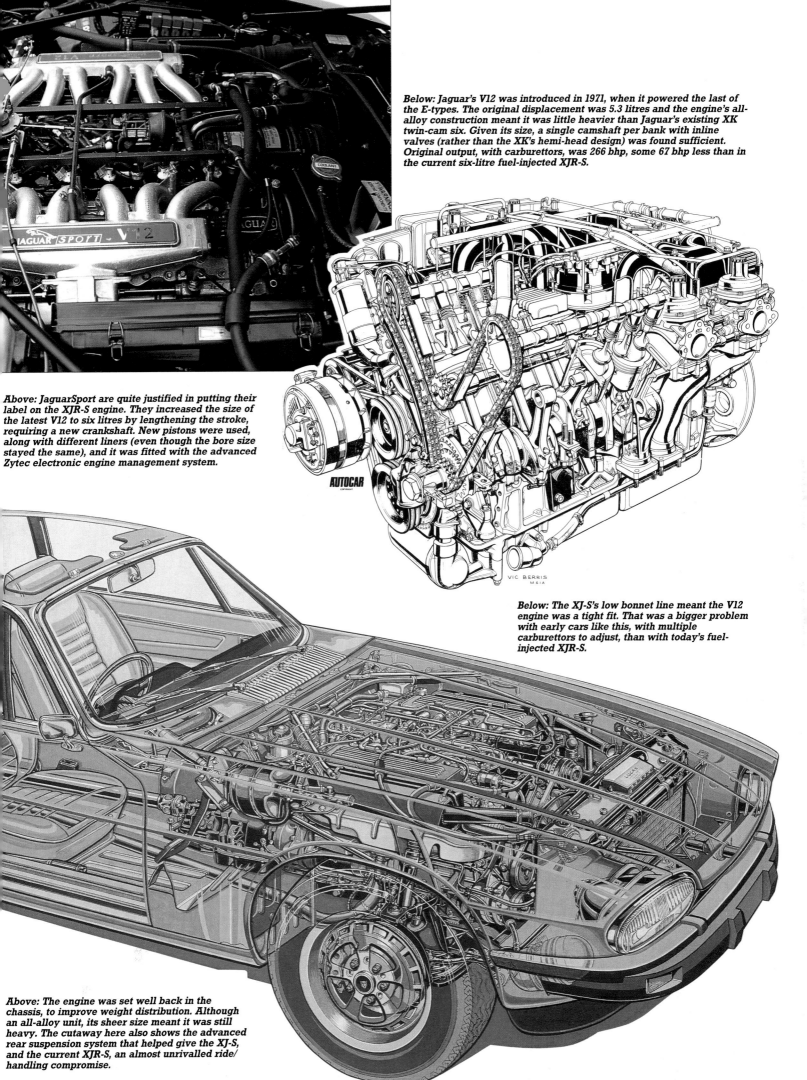

Below: Jaguar's V12 was introduced in 1971, when it powered the last of the E-types. The original displacement was 5.3 litres and the engine's all-alloy construction meant it was little heavier than Jaguar's existing XK twin-cam six. Given its size, a single camshaft per bank with inline valves (rather than the XK's hemi-head design) was found sufficient. Original output, with carburettors, was 266 bhp, some 67 bhp less than in the current six-litre fuel-injected XJR-S.

Above: JaguarSport are quite justified in putting their label on the XJR-S engine. They increased the size of the latest V12 to six litres by lengthening the stroke, requiring a new crankshaft. New pistons were used, along with different liners (even though the bore size stayed the same), and it was fitted with the advanced Zytec electronic engine management system.

AUTOCAR
COPYRIGHT

VIC BERRIS
MSIA

Below: The XJ-S's low bonnet line meant the V12 engine was a tight fit. That was a bigger problem with early cars like this, with multiple carburettors to adjust, than with today's fuel-injected XJR-S.

Above: The engine was set well back in the chassis, to improve weight distribution. Although an all-alloy unit, its sheer size meant it was still heavy. The cutaway here also shows the advanced rear suspension system that helped give the XJ-S, and the current XJR-S, an almost unrivalled ride/handling compromise.

95

Jaguar XK120

The XK120 was the model that established Jaguar as a major manufacturer of sports cars. While other carmakers were using pre-war designs, Jaguar introduced an all-new two-seater that was sleek, modern – and fast.

At the end of World War II, when Britain was faced with rebuilding a peacetime industrial economy, the government adopted the slogan 'Export or die'. It was the key to earning desperately-needed foreign currency, and the message was that those firms which didn't send a significant volume of their output abroad would not be allocated the scarce raw materials to continue operations. Nowhere was the pressure greater than on the motor industry, and no other currency was as important as the mighty dollar. That pressure put Britain's often notoriously conservative carmakers into direct competition with much more adventurous and flexible rivals, and it quickly reshaped the industry, as those who either wouldn't or couldn't adapt, soon foundered.

At the same time, in March 1945, a new name appeared in the ranks of the British motor industry, when the SS Car Company changed its name to Jaguar Cars Ltd. For one thing, SS was hardly a very desirable name by 1945, but for another, Jaguar had already become a well-respected model name on the company's most sporting cars even before the war, and it admirably suited the intended image of grace and power. The change of name would also coincide with the company's change from being an assembler of cars using other people's running gear, to a fully-fledged manufacturer in its own right. William Lyons, the company founder, obviously had more ambition and imagination than most . . .

After the war, with economies gradually recovering and people enjoying a return to peace and freedom, cars such as Lyons could offer reflected the general mood of optimism; and best of all, as GIs returned from tours of overseas duty, the American market was suddenly discovering European sports cars in a big way.

Coventry, where SS Cars was based, had suffered badly from German bombing during the war, but Lyons had even made the most of that. Like the rest of his workforce, he had taken his turn on fire-watching duty at the factory, and he made sure that he shared his weekend sessions with many of his senior design and engineering staff; in the quieter moments, they planned their new models, a new engine and the future of the company.

Near-racing performance with a stunning shape

The new engine was to be decidedly exotic for a production car – a twin-overhead-camshaft unit with plenty of power, and scope for lots of continued development; it would be the first-ever mass-production twin-cam, a layout previously associated only with racing cars and the more exotic thoroughbreds. Plans for a four-cylinder production version were soon dropped, but the six-cylinder XK engine became one of Jaguar's greatest assets, and in various forms it

stayed in production for an amazing 40 years.

The new engine and the new chassis were intended primarily for a new, 100-mph, saloon car, the Mk VII, with virtually all production destined for export, to keep the government happy. And alongside the saloon, Lyons couldn't resist the idea of building a twin-cam-engined sports car, in what he originally intended to be quite small numbers and really only for its help in publicising the Jaguar name, thereby helping to sell the 'mainstream' models.

The XK engine was first seen in public in September 1948, in two-litre/four-cylinder form, when a streamlined record-breaker driven by Goldie Gardner recorded over 176 mph on the Jabbeke road in Belgium. The following month, the 3.4-litre/six-cylinder version appeared in a stunning, two-seater sports car which stole the Earls Court Motor Show. The car used a shortened version of the saloon chassis, with deep box-section side members, substantial cross-bracing, and independent front suspension controlled by torsion bars. On the basis that it was only meant for limited production, it used an alloy body over a wooden frame. The engine produced 160 bhp and the car was dubbed the XK120, alluding to its claimed top speed. That would make it the quickest production car of its day, and lest anyone should doubt it, Jaguar took a standard example to Jabbeke in May 1949 and in front of the invited press recorded 126 mph with the car in full road trim; without the windscreen, with a cover over the passenger compartment and a smooth undertray, it managed almost 133 mph.

Above: With 160 bhp from its 3.4-litre twin-cam six, the XK120 was very fast for its day.

What's more, the near-racing performance was combined with that stunningly sleek and modern shape, excellent trim and ample comfort for two people. Most remarkable of all, a price of just £1,263 represented astonishing value for money.

Jaguar built 240 cars with the alloy bodywork on wooden frames before admitting that demand was far higher than Lyons had ever anticipated, and then a steel body was standardised. Three body styles were eventually offered: the original, sparsely-trimmed roadster (which was actually called the Open Two-Seater Super Sports); the better-equipped and more conventional convertible Drophead; and a Fixed Head Coupé. There were more potent options, too, starting with the Special Equipment model, with a 180-bhp engine, optional wire wheels, twin exhausts and the choice of aeroscreens to replace the full windscreen. Eventually, there was also a race-bred option with big-valve cylinder heads and up to 210 bhp.

The XK120 went racing; where it raced, it won

In August 1952 one of the coupés, with its superior aerodynamics, averaged over 100 mph for a full week, at the banked Montlhèry track near Paris. A heavily modified car had already achieved 172 mph at Jabbeke in 1951, and a more standard model had averaged 107 mph for 24 hours in 1950.

Naturally, the XK120 also went racing; and where it raced, it won. In 1950 it captured the Tourist Trophy and in virtually standard form came very close to winning Le Mans. In 1951 and 1953 XK120s won the RAC Rally; and in the same years the C-type, a much-modified and more aerodynamically-bodied car but still very much XK120-based, did win Le Mans, putting Jaguar firmly into the top league of sports car manufacturers and doing saloon car sales no harm at all – just as Lyons had planned.

What he *hadn't* anticipated was the sheer scale of the XK120's sales success. By the time it was replaced, in 1954, the three body styles had sold a total of over 12,000 examples – the vast majority of them for export and the majority of those for the USA, where they established Jaguar as a sporting manufacturer in the very top class. When the XK120 went out of production, the theme continued with the progressively more powerful and refined yet recognisably 120-derived XK140 and ultimately the XK150, which took Jaguar through to the launch of the next generation of sports cars with the E-type of 1961.

Left: Flowing body contours as well as superb performance made the XK120 so desirable.

Top and above: Since the huge demand had not been anticipated, early XK120 bodies were hand-formed from aluminium over a wood frame; 240 were laboriously produced before steel pressings took over in 1950. Standard cars had steel wheels, and brake fade was a problem; the introduction of optional wire wheels improved matters through better cooling of the drums. A Special Equipment package also offered even more performance, with the engine uprated to 180 bhp.

Driving the XK120: *eager and poised*

With 180 bhp and 203 lb ft of lazy torque in a car weighing just over 3,000 lb, and with that slippery shape and solid chassis, the XK120 is an entertainingly quick and well-mannered car, for all its 40 or so years. Even with its big, slim-rimmed steering wheel and relatively short cockpit, it has room enough to adopt a relatively 'modern' driving position.

Dynamically, the character of the car is set by that lovely, potent six-cylinder engine and its wide spread of torque. The car will run happily at less than 20 mph in top gear, then accelerate away with total flexibility towards that 120-mph maximum. The unassisted

steering is light enough so long as you're on the move, and the chassis is stiff enough to give a very true feel of what's happening below. Outright grip isn't great by modern standards, and tyre squeal is easy to generate, but balancing the progress of the XK120 through corners by a mixture of steering and throttle is delightfully easy – dominated in the end, not surprisingly, by predictable and very controllable oversteer.

As so often with cars of this vintage, the one thing that really betrays its age is the brakes – which will remind you to temper enthusiasm with respect . . .

PERFORMANCE & SPECIFICATION COMPARISON	Engine	Displacement	Power	Torque (lb ft)	Max speed	0-60 mph	Length (in/mm)	Wheelbase (in/mm)	Track front/rear	Weight total (lb/kg)	Price
Jaguar XK120 SE	Inline-six, twin-cam	3442 cc	180 bhp 5300 rpm	203 lb ft 4000 rpm	121 mph 195 km/h	12.0 sec	173.0 in 4394 mm	102.0 in 2591 mm	51.0 in 50.0 in	3037 lb 1378 kg	£1,953 (1953)
Aston Martin DB2/4 saloon	Inline-six, twin-cam	2580 cc	125 bhp 5000 rpm	144 lb ft 2400 rpm	111 mph 179 km/h	12.6 sec	169.5 in 4305 mm	99.0 in 2515 mm	54.0 in 54.0 in	2772 lb 1257 kg	£2,622 (1954)
Austin-Healey 100	Inline-four, overhead-valve	2660 cc	90 bhp 4000 rpm	144 lb ft 2500 rpm	111 mph 179 km/h	10.3 sec	175.5 in 4458 mm	90.0 in 2286 mm	49.0 in 50.7 in	2100 lb 953 kg	£1,064 (1953)
Ferrari 212	V12, overhead-cam	2563 cc	140 bhp 6500 rpm	159 lb ft 4000 rpm	120 mph 193 km/h	10.5 sec	146.3 in 3715 mm	88.6 in 2250 mm	50.0 in 49.2 in	2035 lb 923 kg	£3,200 (1951)
Frazer-Nash Targa Florio Turismo	Inline-six, overhead-valve	1971 cc	100 bhp 5250 rpm	118 lb ft 3750 rpm	114 mph 183 km/h	10.4 sec	152.0 in 3861 mm	96.0 in 2438 mm	48.0 in 49.5 in	1939 lb 880 kg	£3,035 (1953)

Jaguar XK120 Data File

J aguar's sporting reputation, which was well-and-truly made by the XK120, was already on the way to being established before the war, with the stylish and sporty SS100. That was the very essence of the pre-war sports car, but for the new post-war age Lyons and Jaguar wanted something different, something modern using their own engine (rather than a bought-in powerplant). This was very much the right approach in a world where most manufacturers were only concerned with putting their pre-war designs back into production. Although the new Jaguar twin-cam engine layout was established during the war, it was not until 1948 that the engine first appeared, with an output of 160 bhp, which was progressively increased.

Above: Headlight nacelles emerging from the bonnet and wing line were XK120 features. A heavier grille appeared on subsequent models.

Above: The XK120's swoopy Lyons lines were influenced by designs such as Figoni & Falaschi's 'teardrop' Talbot-Lago Goutte d'Eau.

Below: Rear spats were standard on steel-wheeled cars. Wire wheels became an option in 1950; the Fixed Head body was offered from 1951. The centre drawing is still an XK120 – the 1954 XK140 had much heavier bumpers. At the bottom is a Drophead XK150, with a wrap-around windscreen and a thicker, C-type-inspired, waistline.

Styling

One of the greatest advantages Jaguar had was the styling genius of William Lyons, which showed in all Jaguar designs right up to the 1970s. Part of his genius lay in his ability to move with the times; the contrast between the pre-war SS100 and the post-war XK120 was marked, and yet both were equally impressive designs. You could argue that Lyons gained inspiration for both cars from existing models (although the later E-type and XJ6 were unique styles), but they were still impressive for all that.

The XK120 showed the influence of two quite different cars. The beautiful Talbot-Lago Goutte d'Eau ('teardrop'), bodied by Figoni & Falaschi, inspired Lyons, who had called the design "positively indecent" but clearly

appreciated its impact and filed it away for future reference. The other influence was the streamlined BMW 328 built specifically to win the Mille Miglia, which it duly did in 1940. The BMW's modern look was recognisable in the XK120, but the Jaguar was longer and sleeker.

The first of the XK line is now regarded as the 'purest' of a range that changed with the heavier bumper treatment of the XK140 and was altered more radically with the XK150, which lost the narrow-waisted look of the original car.

Below: A Fixed Head Coupé was introduced in addition to the original roadster in 1951. The full Drophead came in 1953.

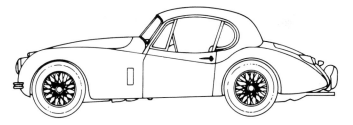

Below: Unlike later versions, the roadster (or Open Two-Seater Super Sports, to be formal) was strictly a two-seat sports car.

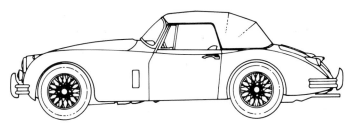

Below: On the XK120 roadster, the standard split windscreen was detachable; aeroscreens were an option.

Chassis and body

The XK120's chassis started life as a shortened version of a unit originally planned for the much heavier Jaguar saloons, so it isn't too surprising to find that it was, if anything, substantially over-engineered for the job in hand. In basic layout it was quite conventional for its day, with deep box-section side members running the full length of the car and sweeping up from behind the cockpit over the rear axle. The side rails were linked by cross-members ahead of the engine, a large box-section in the centre and another fabricated steel sheet member plus a tubular brace at the back. For the sports car, the wheelbase was shortened to 102 inches.

Essentially the same layout was used for all three models (roadster, convertible and coupé) and in each case the unstressed body was mounted at 12 points. The body itself incorporated a fabricated steel hoop ahead of the cockpit with a firewall built in, and a rear bulkhead behind the seats.

The sweeping curves of the bodywork, especially around the long front wings, made production far from straightforward, and what appear to be single panels were in fact made up from several pieces welded together and lead-loaded to achieve the final contours – including the smooth join of headlamp pods to wings. It was a labour-intensive process which Jaguar have used on many models, making their low prices seem even more remarkable. Bonnet, boot lids and the door skins were of aluminium, but the cockpit and boot floors were in wood, emphasising the 120's pre-unit-construction era.

Below: A contemporary section of the 1951 Fixed Head XK120 reveals the simplicity of the car's overall structure.

The C-type

Jaguar knew that with less weight, more power and better aerodynamics, the XK120 could offer a genuine chance of winning at Le Mans. The outcome was the XK120C (C for Competition) – or C-type. Strength and basic chassis behaviour weren't problems, but weight was, so the chassis became a tubular spaceframe and the steel body gave way to a much lighter and more slippery aluminium shell designed by Jaguar's brilliant aerodynamicist, Malcolm Sayer. The front suspension layout was retained while the rear was changed to use an 'A'-frame and radius arms for location and a single, transverse torsion bar for springing; rack-and-pinion steering replaced recirculating ball. More power was found by using bigger valves and more extreme camshafts, eventually resulting in some 210 bhp. The first three cars were ready – just – for Le Mans in 1951, where Stirling Moss took an early lead in wet weather and started to run away from the opposition. Soon, the C-types were first, second and third, but two of the cars retired with oil-pipe fractures, and it seemed the effort was doomed. The third car, however, survived for Walker and Whitehead to score Jaguar's first Le Mans win – by over 60 miles! In 1953, a C-type won again.

Below: This ghosted drawing of Rolt and Hamilton's 1953 Le Mans winner shows the C-type's strong spaceframe chassis.

Below: Malcolm Sayer designed the slippery C-type body.

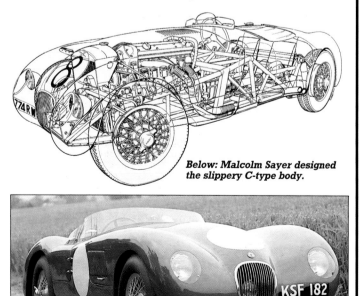

Above: A true classic in engine design, the twin-cam straight-six that made its debut in the XK120 lived on for nearly 40 years.

Above: Like many cars of the 1940s and 1950s, the XK120 had a simple, albeit well-braced, ladder-type chassis with rails arching over a live rear axle located only by leaf springs.

Engine

The 3.4-litre six of the XK120 is a classic example of what has always made Jaguars special – thoroughbred engineering on a bargain budget. XK engines formed the basis of Jaguar's success in everything from racing-sports cars to limousines right through to 1985 (when they were replaced by the modern AJ6 range of twin-cam sixes); the 120's power unit was the first of the breed. It was planned during the wartime fire-watches by William Lyons, chief engineer Bill Heynes, chief designer Claude Baily, and chief experimental engineer Walter Hassan, aided by Dick Oats and cylinder-head guru Harry Weslake. It replaced the outdated range of Standard-based engines with something that wouldn't have been out of place in a GP car not long before.

The brief was to find some 160 bhp, with flexibility and refinement but from a modest capacity – because Lyons anticipated post-war tax penalties on big engines, as well as expecting continued fuel shortages. At almost 3½ litres, the new unit was bigger than Lyons had really wanted but it met all his other criteria. The most important feature was the head design, with the chain-driven twin camshafts allowing large, inclined valves in hemispherical combustion chambers for very efficient breathing. At 83 mm x 106 mm it had a long stroke to help with torque, and with seven main bearings and a cast-iron block it was very strong. As launched, it produced 160 bhp at 5,000 rpm and 195 lb ft of torque at 2,500 rpm. Among its few faults were that, in spite of an alloy head, it was unavoidably heavy, and early engines were prone to leak oil from the front of the cam covers until Jaguar added extra studs late in 1951.

Most of the gradual XK power increases came from improving breathing and compression as better petrol became available, but for the XK120 the only big departures were the Special Equipment engine with a lighter flywheel and high-lift cams, for 180 bhp, or the C-type heads with bigger exhaust valves and bigger carburettors, for as much as 210 bhp.

Right: William Lyons entrusted development of the new Jaguar engine to a team led by Bill Heynes, including Walter Hassan and Claude Baily, and aided by Dick Oats and Harry Weslake. When it appeared soon after the war as a volume-production item, it was nothing short of revolutionary. Its dual, chain-driven overhead camshafts, light-alloy cylinder head with hemispherical chambers and large, inclined valves, and its strong, seven-bearing crankshaft would have been found only in a Grand Prix racer or expensive exotic just a few years earlier.

Below: The long-stroke (83-mm × 106-mm) 3442-cc XK120 engine had an output of 160 bhp at 5,000 rpm and 195 lb ft of torque at 2,500 rpm as standard, but was developed to achieve 210 bhp in the C-type.

Left: Slim, elegant quarter-bumpers as fitted to the XK120 were not robust enough for the US market and were supplanted by hefty girder-like bumpers on the XK140 that succeeded it in 1954.

Above left: As well as its extraordinary engine, the XK120 had a brand-new front suspension using decently wide-based unequal-length upper and lower wishbones, telescopic dampers, and longitudinal torsion-bar springs bolted under the frame rails. The XK120's Burman recirculating-ball steering box was replaced by a rack-and-pinion assembly on the XK140.

Lamborghini
Countach

Marcello Gandini's Countach is a 20-year-old design, but the Lamborghini still has the power to shock and, thanks to its 5.2-litre 455-bhp quad-cam V12, leaves most of the opposition in its 180-mph wake.

Above: The long, Testarossa-like strakes (for brake cooling) in the skirts show that this is the Anniversary model, the final variation on the Countach theme. Inset: Ferrucio Lamborghini is a Taurean, hence the bull badge, transformed by Lamborghini into a fighting bull.

When Ferrucio Lamborghini went into the car business in 1963 he adopted his birth sign, the Taurean bull, as his badge, and when he started giving his cars names, he named them mostly in connection with fighting bulls. There was one major exception. In the early 1970s, Lamborghini's second great mid-engined supercar (following in the wheeltracks of the legendary Miura) was taking shape at Lamborghini's Sant'Agata factory near Bologna, and in Nuccio Bertone's styling studios in Turin. At first, it was simply known as project number 112 and later as the LP500, for *Longitudinale Posteriore* (the Italian for its inline rear-engine layout) and the five litres of the engine in the prototype.

And then one day the first completed prototype was wheeled out of the styling shops. Bertone himself saw it in the flesh and spontaneously let out a low exclamation: "*Countach!*".

The word is from local Piedmontese dialect, with no literal translation (or no printable one!) but if you say it in the same way that Bertone said it the first time he saw the stunning new Lamborghini, you'll know what it means – and why it stuck.

...the fastest car in the world...

The Countach had a hard act to follow in the Miura, but with it Lamborghini wanted to carry his challenge to Ferrari one stage further – to take the whole concept of the Miura as state-of-the-art roadgoing supercar and to refine it even more. He wanted the new car to be more usable than the Miura, which was staggeringly fast and still unique among the most powerful supercars

in its transverse mid-engine layout, but which did have something of a reputation for being hard to drive near its limits. Now he wanted to combine this near-racing performance with the less demanding nature of a true grand touring car, to make it the sort of car that any wealthy buyer with taste but not necessarily racing driver skills could properly enjoy over long distances, at high speeds, in comfort and safety.

Most of all, he wanted it to be the fastest and best car in the world, which really meant it had to outperform any Ferrari.

Lamborghini's attitude to Ferrari was antagonistic, and it was Ferrari's attitude to Lamborghini that had turned him into a car-builder in the first place. Ferrucio had always been interested in cars and had raced, but his main business was building tractors and air-conditioning equipment. He was wealthy and he owned many fine cars, including Ferraris. Once he had cause

to complain to Ferrari about a recurring fault on one of his cars; Ferrari told him the fault was his and not the car's, that a tractor-maker could hardly understand a true thoroughbred. And so Lamborghini went off to prove him wrong.

He showed his first car in Turin in 1963, launched the Miura in 1966, and in 1971 unveiled the Countach prototype to a stunned audience at the Geneva Show. It had been styled at Bertone by the young Marcello Gandini (who had also created the Lamborghini Miura); it had an astonishingly futuristic shape with geometrically sharp lines, an openly aggressive stance, and amazing doors that opened vertically like an insect's wings.

This prototype wasn't just a pretty face, though. Under the stunning body, the Countach was already largely complete.

The prototype had a five-litre engine, but for production a four-litre was chosen – and was more than adequate. The new engine and transmission layout, with longitudinal engine and the gearbox ahead of the block for compactness and weight distribution, was a touch of genius from chassis designer and Lamborghini chief engineer Paolo Stanzani. At a stroke, that overcame several of the Miura's thornier problems; it made the Countach a better-balanced car, it separated the engine and gearbox lubrication in a way the early Miuras hadn't been able to do, and it eliminated the troublesome gear linkage that had always plagued the Miura.

It even allowed the Countach to be shorter in both length and wheelbase than its transverse-engined predecessor!

Gandini's original styling changed a little as the car was finalised, mainly in being obliged to sprout more cooling ducts (notably the scoops behind the side windows) but if anything the changes only made the car look more spectacular and aggressively unique. It obviously wouldn't have great rearward visibility, and the early prototype even had a periscope rear view mirror.

Below: If you really intended to exploit all of your Countach's 180-mph performance, Lamborghini claimed that the optional rear wing would be a sensible investment to increase its grip, albeit a rather expensive one at £1,600.

Gradually, Stanzini and chief test driver Bob Wallace, a highly talented New Zealander, made what was under the skin work, doing thousands of miles of high-speed testing, hundreds of hours of re-engineering, and finally getting the car right. By the time the car appeared at Geneva 1973 (still almost a year from production) it was very close to being finalised; in March 1974 it was launched as the LP400 Countach.

It had the 375-bhp four-litre V12, a five-speed gearbox, and an often-quoted but never proven top speed of "over 190 mph".

And from there, the Countach got better and better. First (with some assistance from Grand Prix team owner Walter Wolf) it changed onto the new lower-profile Pirelli P7 tyres, rejigged its

Power jumped to a Ferrari-beating 455 bhp

entire suspension and became even meaner looking as the LP400S, from 1978. Next, in the face of new competition from Ferrari's Boxer, it grew to 4.8 litres in the LP500S, and took the power – recently compromised by making the car more driveable – back to a quoted 375 bhp. The decline in sales which had started with the LP400S was stopped by the new '500'.

Even cars like the Countach have to stay on their toes, though, and when Ferrari launched the superb Testarossa in 1984, Lamborghini were already on their way to the next-generation Countach. That was launched at Geneva in 1985, in the guise of the heavily re-engineered *quattrovalvole*, with its capacity increased to almost 5.2 litres, and with four valves per cylinder. The power output jumped instantly to a Ferrari-beating 455 bhp, yet with cleaner emissions and better flexibility, and the Countach was once again on top.

That was the end of the major mechanical changes, even though the Countach never stood still in the area of chassis development as new tyre equipment became available. Late in 1987, the bodywork was updated with new side sills (with functional brake scoops), and late in 1988 the bodywork was more dramatically updated, with more rounded scoops and neater front and rear treatment. There were new wheels and better interior equipment, too, but the Anniversary model, as it was dubbed, was to be the end of the Countach. The Diablo was waiting in the wings.

Above: A Countach 500S in action. The 500S was powered by the five-litre 375-bhp version of the V12. The extra 825 cc over the 400S gave the Countach more torque, at over 300 lb ft.

Top: Late in 1987 the Countach
was given a neater sill
treatment, which made it the
most attractive version since the
original Countach. The
Anniversary model of 1988 can
be distinguished by its five-
spoke alloy wheels.

Above: The Lamborghini's stiff
suspension means that the
Countach can have the minimum
of ground clearance between the
Anniversary's front air dam and
the road.

Driving the Countach: an awesome heavyweight

The Countach experience begins even before you turn
the ignition key: first you have to get into the car, and
that isn't as straightforward as with some! The doors
open easily on their counterbalancing struts, and open
high, but you still have to negotiate the wide sills, and
the Countach stands only 3 ft 6 in tall. Once you're in,
though, it is a superb environment. Forward visibility is
superb, sideways is OK, rearwards is non-existent,
especially with the optional wing. The massive engine
needs care: let the pumps tick, dab the throttle a
couple of times, then turn the key, and once it bursts
into life, give it time to warm up. Then it will be

untemperamental, easy to live with. The gear change
is less friendly, with a racing-pattern 'dog-leg' first; the
clutch is enormously heavy and sensitive. Everything
about the Countach feels heavyweight and
intimidating at first, but it gets better. It needs a
positive attitude, plus respect and some mechanical
sympathy, but driven well the Countach is awesome.
It has the precise and solid feel of a racing car,
massive and flexible power, phenomenal grip and
superb brakes. It communicates everything that it is
doing, but it would take a good driver to find its true
limits – and that is the ultimate compliment.

PERFORMANCE & SPECIFICATION COMPARISON	Engine	Displacement	Power	Torque (lb ft)	Max speed	0-60 mph	Length (in/mm)	Wheelbase (in/mm)	Track front/rear	Weight total (lb/kg)	Price
Lamborghini Countach Quattrovalvole	V12, quad-cam, 48-valve	5167 cc	455 bhp 7000 rpm	369 lb ft 5200 rpm	178 mph 286 km/h	4.9 sec	162.9 in 4138 mm	96.5 in 2451 mm	58.7 in 63.2 in	3188 lb 1446 kg	£116,432 (1991)
Ferrari Testarossa	Flat-12, quad-cam, 48-valve	4942 cc	390 bhp 6300 rpm	362 lb ft 4500 rpm	174 mph 280 km/h	5.2 sec	176.6 in 4485 mm	100.4 in 2550 mm	59.8 in 65.4 in	3675 lb 1667 kg	£115,500 (1991)
Lotus Esprit Turbo SE	Inline-four, turbo, 16-valve	2174 cc	264 bhp 6500 rpm	261 lb ft 3900 rpm	161 mph 259 km/h	4.9 sec	171.0 in 4343 mm	96.0 in 2438 mm	60.0 in 61.2 in	2650 lb 1202 kg	£46,300 (1991)
Aston Martin V8 Vantage	V8, quad-cam	5340 cc	406 bhp 6200 rpm	390 lb ft 5000 rpm	170 mph 274 km/h	5.4 sec	181.3 in 4605 mm	102.8 in 2611 mm	59.3 in 59.0 in	4001 lb 1815 kg	£110,000 (1989)
Porsche 928 S4 SE	V8, quad-cam, 32-valve	4957 cc	310 bhp 5900 rpm	295 lb ft 4100 rpm	160 mph 257 km/h	5.5 sec	177.9 in 4518 mm	98.1 in 2492 mm	61.1 in 60.9 in	3488 lb 1582 kg	£64,496 (1991)

Lamborghini Countach Data File

The founder of Lamborghini was Ferrucio Lamborghini, a tractor manufacturer who decided to enter car production to outshine Enzo Ferrari after a personal argument. That's one account; another is that Ferrucio simply wanted to build the best supercar in the world, having found faults with all those he owned, including his Ferraris.

The first Lamborghini to emerge from Lamborghini's Sant'Agata plant near Bologna was the 350 GT of 1964, powered by the Bizzarini-designed 3.5-litre V12. First year's production was just 13 cars. The 350 GT was followed by the similar-looking 400 GT with an enlarged version of the quad-cam V12. That four-litre powerplant produced 320 bhp, enough to give a maximum speed approaching 160 mph. Combined production of 350 and 400 GT models was 393 between 1964 and 1968.

Next model was the Miura, which made its debut alongside the 400, in 1966. This marked Lamborghini's switch from front-engined cars to mid-engined, using the same V12 but mounted transversely behind the driver. Styled by Bertone, it was far more elegant than the earlier cars. By the time Miura development had ended in the early 1970s the SV model was producing 385 bhp from its 3929-cc V12, to give a top speed in the 170-mph bracket. Total Miura production was 765 between 1966 and 1973.

To transcend the Miura, Lamborghini needed something dramatic – the Countach, the car which provided Lamborghini with continuity from the days when Ferrucio Lamborghini himself controlled the company, through the takeovers by the Swiss Mimram family in 1980 and Chrysler in 1987.

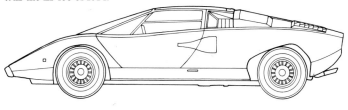

Below: First production Countach was the LP400 of 1974.

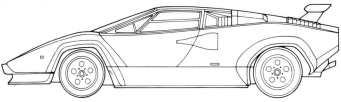

Below: Major visual change came with the LP400S of 1978.

Above: High flanks with their cooling air vents are the main reason why the rear three-quarter vision out of the Countach is so poor.

Above: The rear wing may look like the wildest of styling gimmicks but it was actually a functional option, adding rear downforce at high speed.

Top: The first Countach was shown at the 1971 Geneva Show. Designed by Marcello Gandini at Bertone, the untested prototype was finished so late that it had to be driven overnight from Sant'Agata to Geneva.

Above: By the time the Countach had reached production in 1974 it had gained those distinctive NACA ducts on the side and the top-mounted cooling scoops. The scoops meant that two small rear-side windows could be fitted.

Above: Although the engine is mid-mounted, the 'transmission tunnel', which is part of the chassis, continues under the leather-trimmed fascia.

Below: Battery and spare spacesaver tyre live under the front hatch, and there is a tiny boot in the rear behind the engine hatch.

Styling

The Lamborghini Countach was designed by one of the great Italian styling houses, Bertone. In particular it was the work of Marcello Gandini (who became well known to British TV audiences in 1990 through the ads for another car he designed years later, the Citroën BX).

The origins of the Countach's styling can be found in a Bertone show car from as early as 1968. That was the Alfa Romeo-based Carabo. The most obvious similarity was the front-hinged doors, which opened vertically from one pivot. Another Carabo element continued into the new design was the very shallow windscreen angle, the windscreen forming a continuation of the bonnet line.

The first Countach, which appeared at the Geneva Show in March 1971, was a much 'cleaner' design than the Countachs we're now

familiar with. There was none of the complicated detail which makes the car visually so interesting. There was no NACA duct cut into the side, no extra cooling scoops on the top, and just a clean line around the wheel arches rather than the add-on extensions that appeared with the LP400S in 1978. It was a pure-looking design, but it certainly lacked the dramatic appeal added by all the extra bits and pieces.

One of the more daring features, apart from those doors, was the shape of the rear wheel arch. It was a total contrast to the pure round arch at the front. One of the few drawbacks to the LP400S was how the glassfibre wheel-arch extensions masked that line. The final styling touch was the rear wing, which is actually functional as well as flamboyant. It's only an option, but the Countach would not be complete without it!

Chassis and body

The Countach chassis is a true spaceframe, a complicated lattice of straight tubes welded together in geometrically complex patterns to give immense strength for minimum weight – with much more 'space' than 'frame'. Each tube, so far as is possible, acts only in a straight line, feeding only compression or tension loads (rather than bending loads, which are harder to deal with) into its neighbours. The main elements of the Countach chassis are a large central tunnel (widening out to accept the gearbox from the centre) and two massive side sills. There are two more large side-member structures behind the cockpit to embrace the engine and to carry the rear suspension pickups, a box-like front assembly to support the front suspension, and internal panels which form the transverse bulkheads. On top of the

Above: The first Countach had a monocoque chassis but the production cars had this complicated tubular steel spaceframe, shown here from the front.

main chassis there is a lighter tubular structure which forms the basis for the bodywork, which is virtually entirely hand-formed from aluminium except for some glassfibre panels which line the floor, much of the engine bay and the front 'boot'. On late models, the additional styling panels were also in glassfibre. The hand-shaped alloy panels were then welded, rivetted or bonded on, and the car took shape. The most complex operation of all was fitting the distinctive, upward-hinging doors, no two of which were exactly identical, and that could take many hours of skilled work.

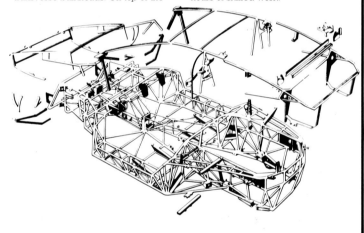

Above: The main chassis had a far lighter tubular steel superstructure, which formed the foundation for the bodywork.

Transmission

While the Miura used type numbers prefaced by TP, the Countachs are prefaced by LP – for Transversale Posteriore and Longitudinale Posteriore respectively. That is the big difference between the two cars – in English, the transverse rear-engined layout of the Miura against the longitudinal rear-engined layout of the Countach (although both are strictly mid-engined, with engine ahead of rear axle line). The Countach solution to fitting such a big engine so far forward in an acceptably compact car is brilliant. The engine and five-speed gearbox assembly are mounted apparently 'back-to-front' of the normal configuration, with the gearbox ahead of the engine and virtually between driver and

passenger, with the gear change far forward on a short extension. The drive from the engine is taken through a conventional clutch directly into the gearbox, the output from the gearbox is brought back to the engine end, taken down through a simple set of gears and to a driveshaft which passes back through a special, sealed tube in the engine's sump, below the crankshaft. At the far end of the engine, in a casing integral with the sump unit, is the final drive, from which the short driveshafts emerge to the hubs. It is marginally heavier than a conventional arrangement and the centre of gravity is very slightly higher, but overall it gives the most compact layout and best possible weight distribution.

Engine

Over the years, the Countach engine underwent enormous changes from the first two-valve-per-cylinder four-litre unit which launched the car with 375 bhp in 1974, to the 5.2-litre four-valve 455 bhp of the final 'Anniversary' models – yet fundamentally it was the same engine. It was based on the V12 that one-time Ferrari engineer Bizzarrini had designed back in 1963, and one of the finest engines in the world. Its dozen cylinders are set in a narrow, 60-degree vee, it has a light-alloy block and light-alloy cylinder heads, an immensely strong steel crankshaft with seven main bearings, and its four overhead camshafts are driven by chains. In the later quattrovalvole versions there are four

valves per cylinder and a choice of fuel systems – six twin-choke downdraught Weber carburettors for European-spec cars, or Bosch K-Jetronic injection for the more environmentally sensitive American market. The inlet tracts are in the middle of the vee and very straight, and the exhausts on the outside are like two nests of snakes. It is a very free-breathing, free-revving and efficient engine, giving an impressive 88 bhp per litre in European form. It is also immensely strong and reliable, and very refined – all characteristics, of course, that Lamborghini had insisted on in the original concept of the Countach as a supercar without vices.

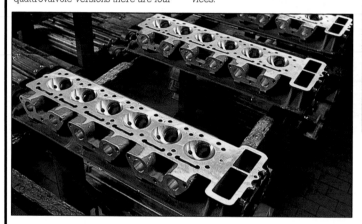

Above: Alloy cylinder heads. Note the enormous valve area, later made even bigger by fitting four valves.

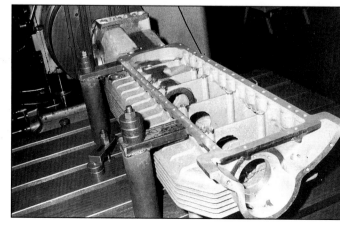

Left: To allow the gearbox to be in front of the engine and close to the driver, making for an excellent gear change, the output from the gearbox is dropped down and then fed back through a special sealed tube in the sump.

Left: The alloy block and sump of the Countach V12. Note the final-drive casing at the end of the sump, which also houses the shaft taking drive from the gearbox mounted ahead of the engine. The driveshaft flanges can be seen on the side of the final drive. The Lamborghini engine is a 60-degree V12 with twin chain-driven overhead camshafts for each bank of cylinders. At the top right of the engine are the sprockets which will drive the duplex cam chains.

Below: The Countach has always been powered by a V12 but the displacement has changed over the years, from 4.0 to 4.8 and then 5.2 litres. This is an engine from the LP500, with six sidedraught Weber carburettors. Later cars had downdraught Webers or, in North America, Bosch K-Jetronic fuel injection.

radiator cooling ducts

radiator fan

Below: Getting air to the flank-mounted radiators required NACA ducts on the side of the car and the air scoops, shown above the fans.

alloy sump and transmission shaft housing

Above: Engine and transmission are ahead of the rear axle line, making the Countach a genuine mid-engined car. Rear suspension is the expected double-wishbone system, but in keeping with other supercars from the E-type up to the Testarossa, the Countach has double coil spring and damper units on each side.

Lamborghini Miura

The Lamborghini Miura broke new ground in 1966; the first mid-engined supercar in the world, its big quad-cam V12 engine gave a claimed top speed of over 170 mph.

Above: The Miura radiates speed even when standing still. In this case, however, it's exploiting a performance potential that can see 160 mph exceeded with the greatest of ease.

When Ferruccio Lamborghini crossed swords with Enzo Ferrari in the early 1960s, the scene was set for a major shake-up in the supercar world. Lamborghini was the rich industrialist and sports car lover who had complained to Ferrari about a recurring problem with one of his cars, only to be scornfully dismissed as a tractor-maker who should leave proper engineering to proper engineers and be grateful that he could buy a Ferrari at all.

The appallingly rude reaction was by no means uncommon at the Ferrari factory, but Lamborghini's response was. He simply told Ferrari that if he wouldn't build him a car the way he wanted it, he would go away and build his own, sell it to people who wanted something better, and maybe treat them with a little respect.

He was as good as his word, and in 1963 Lamborghini the tractor-maker became Lamborghini the supercar-maker.

His approach was refreshingly different. Ferrari was the establishment, and well-known for his stubborn resistance to change; Lamborghini was the ambitious newcomer with everything to go for. He started with an ample budget, an open mind and a young, fiercely creative team. Their first car, the 350 GT, out-Ferraried Ferrari, by being significantly more modern than anything coming out of Maranello. The car was enthusiastically received, glowingly reviewed and its excellence was acknowledged pretty well everywhere save down the road at Maranello. But the 350 GT was only a start. Just two years after it had gone into full production, Lamborghini arrived at the 1966 Geneva Motor Show with their most dramatic project to date, the first mid-engined production supercar – the Miura. It took the show by storm because although it was in effect only the second distinct production model Lamborghini had built, it was a totally new philosophy: current racing technology on the road. It

really did look like a racer, with its lightweight semi-monocoque chassis, all-wishbone suspension and massive disc brakes, not to mention the familiar four-cam V12 turned through 90 degrees and mounted transversely, amidships.

The first mid-engined production supercar

That, above all, was what made people think 'racing'. In the mid-1960s, after all, that was what mid-engined cars were for. With the honourable exception of the Lotus Europa and the 'production' version of the Ford GT40, roadgoing sports cars were still staunchly front-engined. It would be almost three years after the Miura chassis had first appeared before Ferrari even introduced the classic, front-engined Daytona. Yet by the time it was shown at Geneva, the Miura really

borghini trend in names as it was borrowed from a particularly proud and aggressive breed of fighting bull; it was not just a coincidence that Ferruccio Lamborghini was born under the star-sign of Taurus.

Dallara had a great deal of help in producing the car in what was an astonishingly short time even by Lamborghini's early standards, from his assistant Paolo Stanzani (who went on to design the Countach and much later to become one of the instigators of the Bugatti revival) and from New Zealand-born test driver Bob Wallace, who put in a massive amount of time and mileage to make the theories work on the road.

Start of a new philosophy

In May 1966, Wallace drove the very first production example, immodestly finished in bright orange, from Lamborghini's factory at Sant'Agata Bolognese in northern Italy to Monte Carlo and the south of France. It was Monaco Grand Prix weekend and the most glamorous of all venues was packed with the rich, the famous and the impressionable. Wallace parked the car in Casino Square, and as he walked away, the crowds began to surround it. After giving them time to drool, Ferruccio Lamborghini himself made his way through to the car, climbed in and started the fabulous V12 engine, but even that noise was drowned out by the spontaneous roar of the crowd. Over the next few years, even in a poor economic climate, Lamborghini sold no fewer than 475 examples of the first model. Then, in 1970, in the more highly-tuned Miura S, power was increased from the original 350 bhp to 370 bhp, and, more importantly, torque was increased to 286 bhp, to improve the rather indifferent flexibility of the earlier cars. Finally, in 1971, the Miura SV appeared, with 385 bhp, a much-improved gearbox layout with its own oil

Above: The low lines of the Miura gave the driver a fine, unimpeded view forward. Although this driver looks a little cramped there is, in fact, a surprising amount of space (including head room).

system, a claimed top speed of over 175 mph and a 0-60 mph acceleration time in the order of 6½ seconds.

It was still high on the list of the fastest cars in the world, and still capable of turning heads, but in reality the Miura had always been slightly flawed. Even with Dallara's clever transverse-engined layout, space was at a premium, and so were refinement and build quality; the Miura was really quite a rough diamond. Nevertheless, nothing could stop the Miura from being one of the most significant models in supercar history, the start of a new philosophy and, with 763 cars built in total, the car that really put Lamborghini into the major league. Only one car truly overshadowed it: this was another prototype, which appeared for the first time alongside the Miura SV at the 1971 Geneva Motor Show. It was called the Countach . . .

Above: With a mid-mounted transverse engine the Miura was very well-balanced, with the main mass concentrated within the wheelbase.

Below: The view out of the back of the Miura, past the engine intakes and slatted engine cover, was poor indeed.

was a full-blown production car, with a stunning body that was the very first creation by a young designer called Marcello Gandini, then working for Bertone.

In every respect, the Miura was a major achievement. One reason why the theoretically superior mid-engined layout hadn't yet made it onto the road was simply packaging; a big V12 engine with its gearbox and final drive conventionally sprouting from its rear end could be accommodated in a racer, where there were few worries about packaging, but there was no way it would translate into an acceptably compact mid-engined road car – not until Lamborghini engineer Gianpaolo Dallara applied his stroke of genius.

Unmistakably influenced by the GT40, but actually drawing inspiration as much from the humble Mini as from anywhere else, Dallara turned the engine sideways, incorporated the geartrain into the sump, put the final drive immediately behind the block, and put the whole, compact package between cockpit and rear axle line. It sounds simple once someone has done it, but then the best ideas usually do.

It was subtitled the TP400, for *Trasversale Posteriore* four-litre, and 'Miura' started a Lam-

Above and inset: The Miura was one of the most elegant of all the 1960s supercars. The mid mounting of the V12 engine helped in that regard, allowing the bonnet line to be low. Both models shown are SV versions; the SV was the last in the Miura line, with considerably more power than the first model – 385 bhp rather than the original 350 bhp. The extra power led Lamborghini to claim a top speed in excess of 175 mph.

Driving the Miura: *prodigious power*

The Miura is a functional car, with thinly-padded seats and a surprisingly upright driving position. The thin-rimmed wheel is big enough to force splayed knees, but the controls are as well-placed as the racing feel suggests. The dash contradicts the idea somewhat, being heavily sculpted, its big, clear instruments dominated by a 200-mph speedo and 10,000-rpm tacho. There's a good view forward but not much backwards, save the top of the engine.

Even at tickover that engine has a spine-chilling noise level – big on mechanical menace, low on subtlety. There is little silencing, and little doubt in the rough and uneven idle that this is close to a full-race engine. Steering, gear change, clutch and brakes are all enormously heavy but quite progressive, and there is so much torque that a Miura is a forgiving car to drive gently, with no more than a little jerkiness from engine and transmission. Driven harder, it offers a unique experience. The power is prodigious, but the traction matches it. The engine revs like a turbine, allowing some 60 mph in first gear and 85, 120 and beyond 150 in the rest. The handling is safe and predictable, with initial understeer, scope for plenty of oversteer, but with usual mid-engined vices at the limit.

PERFORMANCE & SPECIFICATION COMPARISON	Engine	Displacement	Power	Torque (lb ft)	Max speed	0-60 mph	Length (in/mm)	Wheelbase (in/mm)	Track front/rear	Weight (lb/kg)	Price
Lamborghini Miura P400S	V12, quad-cam	3929 cc	370 bhp 7700 rpm	286 lb ft 5500 rpm	172 mph 277 km/h	6.7 sec	171.6 in 4359 mm	98.4 in 2499 mm	55.6 in 55.6 in	2851 lb 1293 kg	£10,860 (1970)
Bizzarrini GT Strada 5300	V8, overhead-valve	5354 cc	365 bhp 6000 rpm	376 lb ft 3500 rpm	145 mph 233 km/h	6.4 sec	174.0 in 4420 mm	96.5 in 2451 mm	55.0 in 55.0 in	2760 lb 1252 kg	N/A
Ferrari Daytona 365 GTB/4	V12, quad-cam	4390 cc	353 bhp 7500 rpm	319 lb ft 5000 rpm	174 mph 280 km/h	5.4 sec	174.2 in 4425 mm	94.5 in 2400 mm	56.7 in 56.1 in	2641 lb 1198 kg	£6,740 (1970)
Jaguar E-type V12	V12, overhead-cam	5343 cc	272 bhp 6000 rpm	304 lb ft 3600 rpm	142 mph 229 km/h	6.8 sec	184.5 in 4686 mm	105.0 in 2667 mm	53.0 in 53.0 in	3230 lb 1465 kg	£3,367 (1973)
Maserati Ghibli coupé	V8, quad-cam	4719 cc	340 bhp 5500 rpm	326 lb ft 4000 rpm	154 mph 248 km/h	6.6 sec	180.7 in 4590 mm	100.4 in 2550 mm	56.7 in 55.4 in	3746 lb 1699 kg	£9,500 (1968)

Lamborghini Miura Data File

One of the staggering things about the Miura was that it evolved so soon after the creation of the very first Lamborghini, the 350 GT of 1963. That was a sophisticated front-engined design with a four-cam V12 of 3464 cc producing 280 bhp at 6,500 rpm and giving a top speed of over 150 mph. The 350 GT was developed into the 400 GT in 1966; as its name implies, that had a larger version of the V12 engine, producing 320 bhp and boasting a top speed nearer 160 mph and dropping the 0-60 mph acceleration time to under six seconds. Neither model was produced in large quantities, with just 120 350 GTs being built, while production of the 400 model totalled 250. Between the two models, Lamborghini had gained sufficient experience to embark on something really impressive – the Miura.

Above: The Miura is badged as a Bertone design but the stunning shape was the work of their young designer Marcello Gandini, who later gained fame as the creator of the Lamborghini Countach.

Styling

Not least among its achievements, the Miura brought Lamborghini and Bertone together and launched the career of Marcello Gandini, the man who went on to design cars as diverse as the Countach and Diablo, the Cizeta, the Renault 5, and the Citroën BX and XM. It almost fell to Giorgetto Giugiaro to style the Miura, but the car arrived at Bertone just as Giugiaro was leaving for Ghia, and Gandini inherited it as his very first project! Ferruccio Lamborghini had used the Turin chassis as bait to lure a styling house with which he could form a long-term relationship – and he wanted Bertone. Nuccio Bertone had previously resisted offering his services to Lamborghini, because he respected Lamborghini's early relationship with rivals Touring, but by 1965 Touring were broke and Lamborghini was moving closer to Bertone. Yet Bertone didn't approach Lamborghini at the Turin Motor Show

until the two met late one night on the stand as Bertone was showing the chassis to his wife – still reluctant to 'steal' Touring's work. Lamborghini told Bertone of the real position, Bertone gave Gandini the job of styling the car, and less than four months later it was at Geneva. It is a beautifully pure shape, using the big air scoops behind the doors to tie together the upper and lower volumes, and the different-coloured sills with their dramatic scoops to balance the depths of roof and flanks. The only touches of ornamentation are in the 'eyebrows' around the pop-up headlamps and the louvres over the rear window, but in its basic simplicity the Miura will not date.

Below: This targa-top Miura was a one-off, built for the International Lead-Zinc Research Organisation in 1969, with numerous rustproof zinc-coated panels.

Above: The bonnet and engine cover could be huge lift-up panels as the front and rear wings were not required as part of the structure, thanks to the Miura's very strong chassis.

Left: These air vents were actually part of the door frame, and provided a good flow of air through to the crowded engine compartment.

Right: The sill-mounted scoop found on the Miura SV provided cooling air to the hard-worked rear disc brakes.

Right: The slatted cover was open to the engine, designed to extract the hot air in the crowded engine bay. Not surprisingly, the combination of that (and the engine intakes) made rear visibility extremely poor, one of the Miura's main faults.

Above: With a 200-mph speedo, no fewer than six minor gauges to monitor all the engine's vital functions, leather upholstery and even a grab handle for the passenger, the Miura's interior was fully equipped for its supercar performance.

Right: Early Miuras had 'eyebrows' around the lights; later examples did not.

Chassis

As well as being unique in its transverse mid-engined layout, the Miura chassis was highly unusual in its construction, which was another reason why most of those who saw it without the body at Turin in 1965 immediately thought it was a pure racer. Other Lamborghinis have used spaceframes (of amazing complexity in cars like the Countach and Diablo) but inside its all-aluminium body shell, the Miura was based on a broad, low monocoque tub, entirely fabricated in pressed sheet-steel and looking quite exceptionally strong and neat. The main elements were two very large sills with a quarter-circular section, a deep, wide centre tunnel, and substantial box-section front and rear bulkheads connecting the sides, above a sheet-steel floor. At the front and rear, there were fabricated extensions, to carry the suspension

mounting points, the engine and transmission and other components such as the front-mounted radiator. The elegantly triangulated frame at the rear completely surrounded the engine and gearbox in an immensely strong cradle, and like the rest of the chassis, virtually every sheet was liberally perforated with large holes to 'add lightness' – racing technology yet again. What made it rather strange in this context was the sheer cost and effort involved in building such a shell in such numbers, for it was neither small enough for real one-off engineering nor big enough for true series-production.

Below: The underbonnet shot shows the classic double-wishbone front suspension system, along with twin electric cooling fans.

Right: The first Miura show chassis featured far narrower, wire-spoked, wheels than the production cars.

Suspension and running gear

Oddly, the mid-engined revolution was started by the Miura some time before the most modern generation of ultra-low-profile tyres arrived, so, starting from the ground up, the Miura sat on relatively tall-profile 70-series tyres at the front and 60-series at the back – quite a far cry from, say, the Diablo's 35-series rear boots – and even the 60s, which were the lowest tyres of their day, had only appeared for the SV. They were mounted on distinctively sculpted cast-alloy wheels, retained by three-eared knock-on spinners that would send shivers through any safety legislator today, with thoughts of Boadicea's chariot! On the SV the wheels were up to nine inches wide, or a couple of inches wider than on earlier models. Big vents were there to cool the solid disc brakes all round. Steering was by rack and pinion, which didn't have

power assistance even though about 45 per cent of the Miura's weight was carried in the nose (this was in itself an admirable figure for a mid-engined car), helped by the radiator, fuel tank, battery and full-size spare wheel all sitting under the bonnet. Suspension was by double wishbones, coil springs and telescopic dampers all round, with an anti-roll bar at each end. The rear chassis members and the wishbones were uprated on later models to cope with the extra power, and the final discs were bigger too. Like so much else on this remarkable car, the fabricated wishbones look totally ready to race.

Below: The centre section of the Miura's chassis was a pressed-steel construction with a fabricated engine and suspension cradle drilled for lightness.

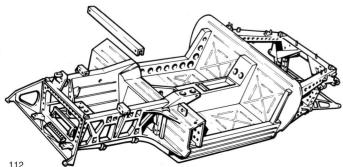

Engine

Giotto Bizzarrini left Ferrari in the mass walk-out of November 1961, worked briefly on the ATS sports car and had just finished freelance design work on a number of US V8-engined cars for Renzo Rivolta when Lamborghini recruited him as an engine designer early in 1963. Bizzarrini's credentials included designing the all-conquering Ferrari 250 GTO and he had work-in-hand on a four-cam V12 engine for the then-current 1½-litre Grand Prix formula. That was enough to tempt Lamborghini. Bizzarrini's brief was to design a similar but bigger engine for the 350 GT. His target was 350 bhp, and he would be paid by his results: more money if he beat the figure; less if he failed! He had only months to complete the project but he did it, and the first engine gave 360 bhp, or (unofficially) even a bit more. Unfortunately, Lamborghini was less impressed with the engine's refinement than with its power. Bizzarrini left as soon as he realised that Lamborghini really didn't want to go racing, and Dallara softened the engine a little for a production role, losing the racing-type dry sump and

swapping downdraught carburettors for sidedraughts. For the Miura it was back on downdraughts, with a capacity of 3929 cc from a bore of 82.0 mm and an ultra-short stroke of 62.0 mm, which allowed it to rev towards 8,000 rpm. Its four camshafts were driven by duplex chains and operated two inclined valves per cylinder, in hemispherical combustion chambers. As a pre-electronics engine, it had coil-and-distributor ignition, but in its most extreme Miura form, in the SV, it produced 385 bhp at 7,850 rpm and 286 lb ft of torque at 5,000 rpm.

Right: Despite the huge engine cover, access to the transversely-mounted all-alloy quad-cam V12 engine was not the best, particularly if you needed to reach the front bank of cylinders, which are almost masked under the rear roof line. The front air cleaner is mounted right next to the small rear window. The header tank for the front-mounted radiator is above the rearmost bank of cylinders.

Below: The Miura's mid-mounted engine was cooled by a front-mounted radiator inclined sufficiently to fit under the very low bonnet line. Air was sucked through it by two large electric fans and exhausted through two large vents on the bonnet.

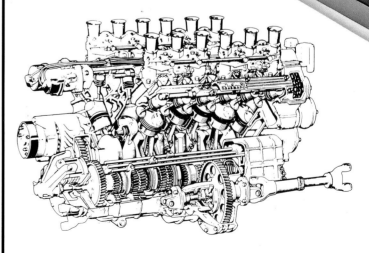

Right: Solid, rather than ventilated, disc brakes were used at the front. Those sharp wheel spinners would never be allowed today!

Above: The Miura's transmission was an extremely neat arrangement, with drop gears from engine to transmission (sharing the engine oil) and a central differential, allowing equal-length driveshafts.

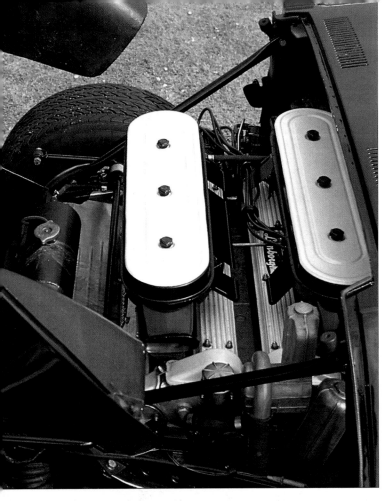

Above: A quartet of downdraught Weber carburettors sat between the chain-driven camshafts, the inlet cams driving the two distributors. The alloy casing for the transmission and differential is to the foreground. In its final SV form the Miura's V12 produced 385 bhp at 7,850 rpm.

Left: The exhaust arrangement on the Miura was necessarily complex, with the engine being a V12 and also mounted transversely. That meant the pipes for the front bank of cylinders would be near the centre of the car.

Left: The only room for the rather small silencers was parallel to the rear of the car, but silencing was not the major concern of the Miura's engineers.

Lancia
Stratos

Whether the 500 cars required for motorsport homologation were ever built is debatable, but the Stratos won three World Rally Championships and became one of the most desirable, if least practical, sports coupés of all time.

Above: Bertone's unique, stubby wedge styling gave the Stratos a tough, almost menacing, personality, and the few examples seen on the road have always looked dramatic.

Inset: Lancia-badged, the Stratos was a hybrid product of the Fiat-Ferrari-Lancia union.

s a road car, the Stratos was a short-lived but spectacularly individual creation that frankly looked more like a stylist's 'dream car' than almost anything else that ever reached production. As a competition car, it marked the beginning of a new and more sophisticated era for top-level rallying, as one of the first purely purpose-built 'homologation specials' – although there was also evidence that Lancia did, for a while at least, intend the car to be a bigger-scale production model too.

From its first win, as a prototype in Spain in 1973, through successive World Championships in 1974, 1975 and 1976, and until as late as 1979 when it scored a final, remarkable, Monte Carlo Rally victory, the Stratos became one of the most successful rally cars of all time. Yet beneath all the glamour and performance, the Stratos was a usable road car, as fine a bit of opportunist engineering as you could wish to find anywhere –

a parts-bin special of the ultimate kind.

It was conceived in the early 1970s, largely by Lancia's then competition director, Cesare Fiorio, to replace the successful but ageing Fulvia and start a head-on attack on the Special GT category of the Group 4 rallying format. That gave a fair degree of freedom in designing the car, but it did demand a minimum production figure of 500 examples, which was a fine balance to achieve on an acceptable budget – and, of course, guaranteed that the majority had to be sold as road cars.

In the end, the trigger for the Stratos came from a rather odd source; it was inspired by a Lancia-powered show car that had been built by Bertone for the Turin Motor Show of November 1970 and which was also known as the Stratos.

This futuristic, wedge-shaped creation was ultra-low; the only way to get inside it was by hinging up the whole of the front windscreen. Bertone had built the chassis, and the body, but

power came from a 1.6-litre Fulvia V4, longitudinally mid-mounted ahead of a five-speed gearbox. The car was driveable, but was obviously not a commercial proposition.

A world-beating rally car

At Turin in 1971 Bertone unveiled another show car, the Stratos HF, which looked close to the Stratos as it eventually went into production. It had Ferrari's Dino V6 engine, transversely-mounted amidships. It sat on the same stubby, 85.5-in, wheelbase as the first show car, but it was almost 10 inches taller, with real doors and windows... The promising blend of running gear was made possible by the fact that near-bankrupt Lancia had been absorbed into the Fiat empire in October 1969, alongside Ferrari, where Fiat had

actual competition debut was even earlier, back in November 1972, when a 230-bhp version retired from the Tour de Corse.

Early indications were also that the Stratos might prove quite versatile, when it finished second in the gruelling Targa Florio road race in May 1973, behind just one Porsche; and a year later Lancia went one better and won the Sicilian classic. In reality, however, although very specialised (often turbocharged) versions *were* entered in selected races over the next few years (including Le Mans in 1976 and 1977), the Stratos's main successes came, as expected, from rallying.

Status as a rare and desirable classic

The Stratos went on to win every major rally except the RAC and the Safari. Overall, it scored over 80 international wins, including 14 in World Championship events, and took three successive World Championships for Makes, in 1974, 1975 and 1976, plus numerous drivers' titles around Europe.

The Stratos's swansong came after it was supposedly outdated by newer cars. That was also, sadly, after former Grand Prix driver Mike Parkes (who had taken over the development role from Gian Paolo Dallara) had been killed in a road accident in August 1977, and after Fiat had switched all the works efforts to their own cars. One of the Stratos's greatest exponents, Bernard Darniche, took an inspired last-gasp win against

Above: As well as rallies, the Stratos won classic road races like the Targa Florio.

all the odds in the 1979 Monte Carlo Rally; he won by just six seconds, having driven like a man possessed throughout the final night.

By then, the Stratos was an old car, outdated for competition and out of fashion for the road. Like a lot of cars at the time, though, it had been something of a victim of circumstance. While it was a rally winner, it was fashionable enough to outweigh its crudeness as a road car, but it also ran head-on into the early 1970s 'fuel crisis', and that was probably the end of any plans for more conventional production. It was also, of course, the perfect foundation for the Stratos's future status as a rare and desirable classic. . .

Below: The RAC was one of the few big rallies the Stratos never won – Markku Alen and Iikka Kivimaki (here) did not finish in 1978.

taken control just a few months earlier. Lancia's president and design chief, Piero Gobbato, had previously been Fiat's man at Maranello, so all the connections had fallen into place. Finally, in the race-bred Ferrari Dino V6 engine (especially as packaged with its transmission for transverse mid-mounting in the Dino 246 GT), Fiorio had seen exactly what he needed to turn Bertone's show car into a world-beating rally car.

The need to build 500 cars in a hurry, for homologation, and to be able to sell them at an affordable price, limited Lancia's options on how to build the Stratos. They compromised, and farmed the job out to Bertone, who produced a relatively simple, fabricated sheet-steel centre section, around which Lancia could hang their running gear, and which Bertone could clothe relatively easily with glassfibre panels.

Lancia had hoped to have the Stratos homologated by March 1974, but missed that date, and the car wasn't actually accepted until October of that year. By then, it had already won its first event, running as a non-homologated prototype in the Spanish Firestone Rally in April 1973; its

Right: The Stratos was, above all, a rally 'homologation special', designed from scratch to win. This car is in the works team colours.

Above: Responsive handling and traction were Stratos design priorities. The car's Ferrari-derived V6 engine and transmission were transversely mid-mounted, and it had exceptionally wide-track, short-wheelbase proportions and compact overall dimensions (it was about the same length as a Ford Fiesta), with minimal bodywork overhang.

Inset: Although tested in 1972, the Stratos didn't gain rally homologation until October 1974.

Driving the Stratos: *raw and nervous*

Remember that the main purpose of the Stratos was competition, and you will understand much of its nature. The cabin is tight, the pedals are pushed into the centre by big front arches, three-quarter rear vision is almost zero, and the driving position is typically Italian – long-armed and short-legged.

In road trim the exotic-sounding V6 is pleasantly docile and pulls strongly from low speeds. The gear change is stiff, the brakes are solid and very effective, but the steering is light. Twitchy handling is dictated by the short-wheelbase, mid-engined layout, and becomes even more nervous if the car is not set up

absolutely precisely regarding suspension geometry and tyre pressures. A Stratos will first understeer strongly when pushed hard, but lift off suddenly and the tail will snap sharply sideways, and you must react very quickly and correctly to catch it. Nor is the grip very great by modern standards, on the relatively high-profile tyres. It is better to drive smoothly through corners and exploit the traction and power away from them. This power is impressive, and the Stratos, with its underlying rawness, feels quicker than its 0-60 mph time of around 6½ seconds and top speed of just over 140 mph might suggest.

PERFORMANCE & SPECIFICATION COMPARISON	Engine	Displacement	Power	Torque (lb ft)	Max speed	0-60 mph	Length (in/mm)	Wheelbase (in/mm)	Track front/rear	Weight (lb/kg)	Price
Lancia Stratos	V6, quad-cam	2418 cc	190 bhp 7000 rpm	166 lb ft 5500 rpm	140 mph 225 km/h	6.8 sec	146.1 in 3711 mm	85.5 in 2172 mm	56.4 in 57.5 in	2160 lb 980 kg	£7,000 (1975)
Alfa Romeo Montreal	V8, quad-cam	2593 cc	200 bhp 6500 rpm	173 lb ft 4750 rpm	137 mph 220 km/h	8.1 sec	166.0 in 4216 mm	92.5 in 2350 mm	54.3 in 52.5 in	2811 lb 1275 kg	£4,999 (1973)
Ferrari 308 GTB	V8, quad-cam	2927 cc	255 bhp 7700 rpm	210 lb ft 5000 rpm	154 mph 248 km/h	6.5 sec	166.5 in 4229 mm	94.1 in 2390 mm	57.9 in 57.5 in	2870 lb 1302 kg	£11,997 (1976)
Lamborghini Urraco S	V8, quad-cam	2463 cc	220 bhp 7500 rpm	166 lb ft 5750 rpm	143 mph 230 km/h	8.5 sec	167.3 in 4249 mm	96.5 in 2451 mm	57.5 in 57.5 in	2884 lb 1308 kg	£9,385 (1974)
Maserati Merak	V6, quad-cam	2965 cc	208 bhp 5800 rpm	188 lb ft 4500 rpm	143 mph 230 km/h	7.7 sec	170.4 in 4328 mm	102.2 in 2596 mm	57.8 in 57.0 in	3062 lb 1389 kg	£18,987 (1981)

Lancia Stratos Data File

 efore the Stratos, Lancia's reputation was firmly established as a maker of very finely engineered sporting (rather than sports) cars. Cars like the Fulvia were good enough to be turned into competitive rally cars, but when rallying became more advanced with the advent of Group 4 in the early 1970s, Lancia needed something dramatically different to compete. The Stratos marked a departure for Lancia in that it did not use a Lancia engine – the V6 was a Ferrari engine (Ferrari and Lancia having become part of the Fiat empire) – and it was also the first Lancia to use glassfibre bodywork. In fact it was unlike any previous Lancia and was inspired by a Bertone styling exercise first seen at the 1970 Turin Motor Show. From that base evolved a World Championship-winning rally car – one that would set the scene for Lancia's later domination of the world rally scene with the four-wheel-drive Deltas and Integrales of the 1980s and 1990s.

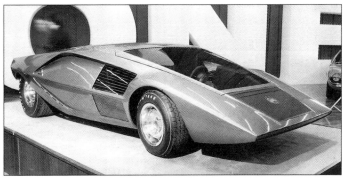

Above: Bertone's 1970 Turin Motor Show styling exercise provided at least a hint of inspiration for the real Stratos rally car.

Above: Side-on, the Stratos's chunky wedge shape is accentuated; it still looks striking now, but in 1972 it was sensational.

Styling

In 1970, Bertone showed their Stratos 'ideas car' in Turin. Wedges were in fashion and so was the mid-engined layout, both thanks to racing. In 1966, Lamborghini had put mid-engines on the road, with the Bertone-styled Miura; alongside the first Stratos, Bertone showed a Lamborghini prototype called the Countach. Wild as it was, the Countach was the one that went into production – the show Stratos was even more outrageous. It was angular, with a flat needle-nose and an amazingly low profile. There were no side doors; access was via the windscreen, which hinged up from its top edge. The mock-up interior was typically futuristic; an electronic dash and minor switches were in the huge pillar to the driver's left, and the pedals sat high up by the bottom edge of the lifting windscreen. Pulling back on the steering wheel closed the front hatch. The driving position was exaggeratedly forward, with one's feet positioned ahead of the front wheels. The compact, longitudinal V4 was situated far enough back to allow space for the fuel tank and near-horizontal spare wheel between it and the steeply-

reclined seats. The flanks had deep recesses for airflow (and styling), but the only glass was located ahead of the driver, above and below the waistline.

This first car was driveable, but it obviously wasn't practical. A year later, the second Stratos looked almost exactly like the car as it went into production. The wheelbase was the same as on the first show car, but this version was taller and the driver sat further back. The wedge was just as severe, but now it was topped by a narrow cabin, with a steeply-raked windscreen sweeping up into dramatically-curved side windows, to give it an even more stubby look. In production, very little changed; proper windscreen pillars appeared, the front louvres became smaller but more numerous, there was one wiper instead of two, the arches were integral rather than bolted on, and the rear end was properly detailed, but the car still looked much as it had at Turin in 1971.

Below: One of the Stratos's most distinctive external features was its radically-curved windscreen.

Above: Even in a roadgoing Stratos, the interior was strictly functional.

Left: A spoiler fitted close to the rear of the roof proved an important aerodynamic aid.

Right: Bertone probably selected the round rear lights for the Stratos from the Ferrari parts bin.

Below: Rear bodywork, including the louvred engine cover and the roof aerofoil, was a one-piece assembly.

Chassis and body

Lancia and Bertone's solution to the awkward production numbers required for the Stratos was one of the most distinctive chassis ever made. The centre section was a steel monocoque, fabricated from relatively simple pressings. Essentially, it comprised the floor, roof and door/screen pillars, and front and rear bulkheads – with extensions at the front to support the suspension and steering and the front bodywork. A massive frame at the rear accommodated the engine/transmission and suspension mounts.

The rear structure made the Stratos chassis unmistakable. It looked like the edges of a large crate, fabricated in steel box-sections and completely surrounding the transverse engine and gearbox, to above the level of the tops of the carburettors. It also formed the pick-up points for the rear suspension, and mounting points for most ancillaries. This construction was not only tremendously strong, but with

the rear bodywork removed it also provided excellent access to most of the main assemblies. The shape was still a distinct wedge, and the narrow, steeply-raked wrap-around top demanded some very interesting glass curvatures!

The bodywork effectively comprised just four main parts: two doors, a one-piece nose and a one-piece tail; the last two hinged from the ends of the car, emphasising the short wheelbase. All the panels were in glassfibre, and very light. Early cars came virtually unadorned; later ones grew additional spoilers (notably the hoop aerofoil on the trailing edge of the roof) as they were homologated for competition. With or without these, there's little danger of mistaking a Stratos for anything else.

Above and left: Front and rear bodywork (all glassfibre) hinged up for easy access.

Suspension

The first Stratos prototype used wishbone suspension front and rear, but that was changed for the production cars, to become yet another of the Stratos's distinctive features. At the front, it retained conventional, unequal-length double wishbones and coil spring/damper units, plus an anti-roll bar. At the rear, the double wishbones were replaced by a layout using a single lower reversed wishbone plus radius arm, and a huge coil spring/damper strut unit, mounted almost vertically between the top of the hub-carrier and the box-frame above the engine. The struts provided both springing and damping media, plus the top suspension links, while leaving ample room for the driveshafts. There was also an anti-roll bar at the rear, and, as befits a competition car, the suspension was fully equipped with adjustable joints, allowing careful geometry tuning.

Although the wheelbase was only 85.5 inches, the front and rear tracks were 56.4 and 57.5 inches, giving the Stratos a very square and purposeful stance. The brakes were all ventilated discs, mounted outboard all round, but without servo-assistance. The transmission was also pure Dino, with the five-speed Ferrari transaxle mounted in unit below the engine, the final drive being just behind the bottom of the block, for a remarkably compact package and, yet again, acceptable access. Steering was by an unassisted rack-and-pinion layout, and the road cars used bolt-on 14-in diameter Campagnolo alloy wheels.

Above: Stratos prototypes had wishbone suspension all round; this was retained at the front, but the rear design (left) was changed to struts for the sake of strength.

Engine

The final appearance of the Dino V6 wasn't in the baby Ferrari, nor even in its front-engined Fiat cousin, but in the Stratos – launched after the others were discontinued. The Dino engine had originated in 1966 and was built in large enough numbers to qualify for the production-based Formula 2 of the time, while still being close to a pure racing engine. The Stratos used the second version: not the original all-alloy two-litre unit but the later, iron-blocked, alloy-headed 2.4-litre engine. Fiat had prompted that change, for lower production costs and quieter running; the extra capacity helped offset about 45 lb more in weight.

This engine had the same slightly odd 65-degree 'V', a six-throw, four-main-bearing crank, and four chain-driven overhead camshafts operating two valves per cylinder. Bore and stroke increases took the unit's capacity to 2418 cc. In Fiat form, the 2.4-litre V6 gave a claimed 180 bhp

and in Ferrari form, with detail changes, 195 bhp. In both cases, torque was much better than in the smaller engine, at 159 and 165 lb ft respectively – albeit at quite high revs. The Stratos version seemed identical to Ferrari's, with similar carburation by three twin-choke downdraught Webers, but it boasted 190 bhp and 166 lb ft of torque.

That, of course, was just for starters, because the Stratos was mainly a competition car. Conventional tuning gave it up to 240 or 250 bhp, and in 1974 the works team could call on a 290-bhp version with fuel injection and four-valve heads, or even (where regulations allowed) a one-off 350-bhp turbo; an even more extreme model was built for racing, with as much as 580 bhp in high-boost form for short events! Both four-valve and turbo engines were outlawed for rallies by 1977 – the beginning of the end of the Stratos's competition career (road-car production had already stopped).

Above: The 'Dino' logo tells the story of the Stratos's power unit: the four-cam V6 was the 2.4-litre version of the Ferrari/Fiat engine.

Above right: The transversely-mounted Dino engine was imported to the Stratos along with the five-speed Ferrari transaxle, giving an unusually compact driveline package, arranged just as in Ferrari's 246 GT. A substantially-proportioned square subframe carried the drive assembly and provided suspension mountings.

Right: Large, ventilated 11-in Girling discs provided ample braking capacity, though for better feel there was no power assistance.

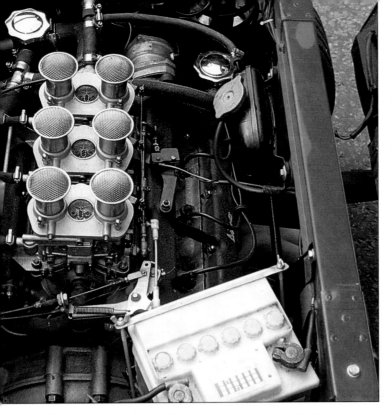

Above: With a trio of twin-choke Weber carburettors as used in its Ferrari and Fiat Dino applications, the 'standard' Stratos engine produced 190 bhp at 7,000 rpm, with a broad torque spread peaking at 166 lb ft at 5,500 rpm. Fuel-injected 24-valve rally versions were far more powerful, with outputs of up to 290 bhp.

Below: The engine chosen for the Stratos was the 2418-cc iron-blocked Fiat-built development of the two-litre aluminium Ferrari quad-cam V6 originally designed for Formula 2 racing and then used in the Dino 206. In standard form it had two valves per cylinder and breathed through three downdraught 40-mm twin-choke Weber carburettors. It was used both in Ferrari's 246 series and in Fiat's own Dinos, but by the time the Stratos was homologated in 1974, neither was in production.

Above: Bertone built the Stratos around a central cabin monocoque. Strong roll-over protection was incorporated.

Right: The Stratos was created to be a winner of international rallies, and that's what it became: in the hands of drivers like Sandro Munari and Bernard Darniche, it scored over 80 international wins, and took three successive Makers' World Championships, in 1974-76.

McLaren F1

When McLaren, seven-times World Championship winners, built the ultimate road car, the 550-bhp, 200-mph-plus three-seater was named after the sport which inspired it.

Gordon Murray has always been one of motor racing's original thinkers. Between 1973 and 1989, with Brabham and McLaren, the laid-back, South African-born designer stood Formula 1 on its ear – with concepts like fan-assisted ground effects, carbon-composite chassis structures and pull-rod suspension. But Murray is a lot more than just another innovative race-car engineer, he is a visionary; and one of his visions has been to build what he describes as "the pinnacle of 20th century high-performance sports car design". He had been thinking about it, in one way or another, since the 1960s – even before he moved from Durban to Britain, to start his career as a racing car designer with Brabham. And he was thinking about it towards the end of the 1980s,

when he became technical director at McLaren International, overseeing the GP design programme which won four world titles in the next five years.

By then, for all McLaren's success, Murray was increasingly frustrated by the way the rule-makers stifled original thinking in Grand Prix racing. But he had his escape route, because McLaren were finally ready to build his ultimate road car.

In March 1989 McLaren Cars Ltd was launched, as an offshoot of GP manufacturer McLaren International, with the intention of leading the supercar elite with the best supercar of the lot. It would be created using Formula 1 technology and steered by Murray's key philosophies. Those were to build a car virtually without

compromise, with minimum weight, with maximum driveability and practicality, and above all with driver appeal.

Gordon Murray laid down the main parameters for the car in one long session around May 1990, when the concept was already firmly fixed, but before the team even knew whose engine they would use. Whosoever it was, it would be large in capacity but compact and light, naturally-aspirated, and very powerful – with a target of well over 500 bhp. The car would be equally light and compact, with a target weight of just about a ton, including full creature comforts. It would be sophisticated but simple, without complexities like four-wheel drive, traction control, or even ABS for the brakes.

An all-new four-cam, 48-valve, six-litre V12

Packaging was the keyword, and Murray took the radical approach. Normally, to keep the wheelbase (and the car) short with a mid-engined layout, the cockpit needs to be pushed well forward between the front wheels, but that compromises footwell space, usually demanding offset pedals and a less than perfect driving position. Murray's solution was to put the driver on the centre-line of the car, well forward and with space for *two* passengers, one on either side and set slightly back. Thus the driver had an ideal control layout with fine visibility, and the pas-

Left: The F1 driver's central and forward position means that visibility is excellent. Plasma sprayed on the inside of the outer screen laminates provides tint, and there is a heating element for speedy defrosting and demisting.

Left: Form follows function in the F1, but its sleek shape, ultimately styled by the wind tunnel and Peter Stevens, has a lot of personality. The light, all-composite body and chassis comprise over 90 components made with advanced moulding techniques.

Right: The F1 is low, wide and compact, with a clean, uncluttered body design. The scoop on the roof supplies air to the engine, and the small panel behind the louvred engine cover is the 'brake-and-balance' foil which rises automatically under heavy braking.

sengers would have ample space. Fuel could be housed centrally behind the cabin, luggage could fit into compartments flanking the engine (all near the centre of gravity) and all the major components could be laid out virtually within the wheelbase, for the desirable effect of low polar moment of inertia, and optimum handling.

In February 1991 McLaren Cars announced that they would be using an all-new four-cam, 48-valve, six-litre V12, designed and built to McLaren's brief by BMW Motorsport in Munich – the company that had built the engines for Murray's championship-winning Brabhams in 1983. The power unit was to produce no less than 550 bhp.

While BMW were finalising the engine, McLaren could get on with the rest of the car, both on the bench and using first one and finally two mobile test-beds to put mileage on transmission and brake components and latterly on the BMW engine.

The first of the test-beds, built in mid-1991 immediately after the basic layout of the F1 had been approved, was nicknamed 'Albert', after the company's address in Albert Drive, Woking.

Greeted by stunned approval

It was based on a spaceframed Ultima kit car and used a 7.5-litre Chevrolet V8 truck engine – which was the only way of finding enough torque seriously to test the new transmission. That test-bed was crucial to the F1's success, in its contribution to the car's compact size and 'low-polar-moment' balance. Developed by McLaren and the American company Traction Products, it answered the old problem of mid-engined packaging by mounting the six-speed gear cluster transversely in a magnesium casing attached directly to the V12, and, uniquely, by placing the final drive assembly alongside the clutch. This avoided all the pitfalls of an inline layout (which could be too long) or a gears-under-engine configuration (which could be too tall), and it would also provide pick-ups for the cleverly-engineered rear suspension.

Both at front and rear, Murray would use conventional double-wishbone layouts, with ultra-lightweight spring/damper units, but by two clever (and patented) mounting systems he would achieve racing levels of rigid control with road standards of comfort and refinement. The all-composite chassis/body unit (made up from over 90 components compared with the seven or so of a typical single-seater monocoque) came together brilliantly and was built in the large 'autoclave' curing ovens at Guildford.

By February 1992 BMW had their first engines running and McLaren built a second Ultima-based car for them (nicknamed 'Edward') to test the engines and transmission.

Meanwhile, the car was shaped in a moving-floor wind tunnel, with the emphasis on balance rather than just low drag, and with several other Murray innovations. The fan-assisted ground-effects layout was finalised, the balancing features were completed, and Peter Stevens gave the compact, low-overhang shape its styling touches – including doors which opened forward and upwards for maximum compactness.

The F1 was unveiled on 28 May 1992 in a glitzy ceremony at the Monte Carlo Sporting Club, on the Thursday evening before the Grand Prix weekend. It was greeted by stunned approval. None of those who had placed deposits wanted their money back.

On the Sunday, Senna took the other McLaren F1 to its first win of the year, and by Monday, Murray and his team were back at work finalising the first running prototypes of the new supercar. It first ran on the road, right on schedule, as 1992 slipped into 1993, with Gordon Murray taking it for its first outing.

Above: This is the view which most drivers will get, probably shrinking rapidly, of the McLaren F1. The Inconel rear silencer box also doubles as a crash structure. Most of the monocoque's main structure composite panels (left) are double-skinned and stiffened with aluminium honeycomb.

Above: The sculpted, wing-like doors rise automatically when released and are then pulled down by hand once one has entered the car. The doors' shape means only the lower section of the side windows are retractable, and the onboard computer ensures that they are unopenable at speeds of over 130 mph. The front composite moulding doubles as a crash structure and the passenger compartment is an enormously strong 'survival cell', thanks to the cockpit bulkheads, roof pillars and roll-over protection.

Driving the F1: *the ultimate supercar*

Gordon Murray wanted the car to be light, compact and super-quick, but also practical. That meant proper luggage space, good all-round visibility, and a driving position with none of the usual supercar compromises of limited space or awkward pedal offset. The F1 is also sophisticated simplicity at its best – aimed, as Murray put it, "at minimum weight, maximum driveability and practicality, combined with our company heritage of exceptional performance, painstaking build quality and uncompromising safety standards". For those very few lucky enough to drive one, the F1 offers a unique driving environment; its

central driving position will allow perfect pedal, wheel and control layout, and excellent visibility over the small, neat dashboard as each car will be tailored for its owner. More than 550 bhp in almost exactly a ton of car gives the best power-to-weight ratio a road car has ever achieved, and five closely-spaced gear ratios will make the most of that up to around 160 mph (the high sixth ratio will be for cruising – potentially at more than 200 mph). The handling and braking should approach race-car standards, with comfort, and the F1's aerodynamics also promise fine manners, whatever the speed or conditions.

PERFORMANCE & SPECIFICATION COMPARISON	Engine	Displacement	Power	Torque (lb ft)	Max speed	0-60 mph	Length (in/mm)	Wheelbase (in/mm)	Track front/rear	Weight (lb/kg)	Price
McLaren F1	V12, quad-cam, 48-valve	6064 cc	550 bhp 7000 rpm	442 lb ft 5500 rpm	200+mph 322+km/h	3.9 sec	168.8 in 4288 mm	107.0 in 2718 mm	61.7 in 58.0 in	2244 lb 1018 kg	£530,000 (1993)
Bugatti EB110	V12, quad-cam, quad-turbo	3500 cc	560 bhp 8000 rpm	451 lb ft 3750 rpm	213 mph 343 km/h	3.4 sec	173.2 in 4400 mm	100.4 in 2550 mm	61.0 in 63.7 in	3571 lb 1620 kg	£292,000 (1993)
Ferrari F40	V8, quad-cam, twin-turbo	2936 cc	478 bhp 7000 rpm	425 lb ft 4000 rpm	201 mph 323 km/h	4.5 sec	171.6 in 4358 mm	96.5 in 2450 mm	62.8 in 63.2 in	2425 lb 1100 kg	£197,502 (1991)
Jaguar XJ220	V6, quad-cam, twin-turbo	3498 cc	542 bhp 7000 rpm	475 lb ft 4500 rpm	208 mph 335 km/h	3.8 sec	194.1 in 4930 mm	103.9 in 2640 mm	67.3 in 62.5 in	3241 lb 1470 kg	£400,000 (1992)
Lamborghini Diablo VT	V12, quad-cam	5729 cc	492 bhp 7000 rpm	428 lb ft 5200 rpm	205 mph 330 km/h	3.9 sec	175.6 in 4460 mm	104.3 in 2650 mm	60.6 in 64.6 in	3578 lb 1623 kg	N/A

McLaren F1 Data File

The McLaren F1 stemmed from Gordon Murray's vision to build the best supercar in the world. That meant it had to be not only better than such established production models as the Ferrari F40 and the Lamborghini Diablo, but also superior to the new breed of supercar – like the Jaguar XJ220 and the quad-cam, quad-turbo EB110 from the revived Bugatti marque. Apart from anything else, this aim guaranteed that McLaren's car would be expensive, but even with a price tag of around £530,000 there was good demand for the planned annual production, scheduled to be no more than 50 cars a year.

Right: The powerful headlamps are faired into the wings to maximise the aerodynamics.

Right: Louvres behind the front wheels allow egress of hot air from the brakes and radiators.

Left: Combined tail/brake lights and indicators are duplicated for clarity.

Left: Air is fed to the engine through this shallow duct, which also forms the F1's roof.

Above: McLaren drew heavily on their immense Formula 1 experience in developing the F1 – a mid-engined, six-litre, three-seat supercar.

Styling

The F1 was partly shaped by its minimalist packaging and partly by the dictates of the wind tunnel, but it was given its style by Peter Stevens. You might not spot that the body (integrated with the chassis) is moulded in carbon composites and finished with new-generation, environment-friendly coatings, or that it has moulded carbon crash beams and carbon doors and sills to resist side impact, that the thin, tinted-and-laminated glass has an in-built electrical demisting system, that the catalyst assembly doubles as a rear crush structure, or that the F1 has racing-style skid plates underneath; but you will certainly notice how compact and neatly detailed the car is. It is form following function. Low drag is only part of aerodynamic excellence; positive control of the car's balance is equally vital. The F1 has true ground effects, using the shape of the underside of the car and its airflow to create downforce without using aerofoils above the body. Two powerful electric fans suck 'boundary-layer' air from the diffuser tunnels below the car, and a small 'brake-and-balance' foil on the rear deck is raised automatically under braking – to expose additional brake cooling vents, to increase rear downforce and thus resist wheel locking, and also to help minimise forward movement of the centre of pressure in dive, thereby optimising stability. The driver can also partly deploy the brake-and-balance foil at high speed, in a 'high-downforce' mode, which improves traction.

Above: The F1 designers were concerned with CoP, or centre of pressure; this foil rises automatically under heavy braking, putting pressure on the rear and cancelling any tendency to nose-dive.

Right: The gear lever, carved in African blackwood, with a red starter and controls for the air conditioning, windows and fan.

Below: The 1+2 cockpit has racing-type harnesses, a Nardi F1 steering wheel and a minimal fascia (bottom).

Below: The beetle-wing doors lift automatically when opened, and well clear of the openings. The passenger compartment is very strong.

Chassis and running gear

The F1's integral chassis/body is built from carbon composites around aluminium and Nomex honeycomb sections – in some cases foam-filled for ultimate rigidity. The floor is a carbon-skinned honeycomb, and skinned honeycomb beams run from the rear bulkhead to the nose. A magnesium front bulkhead includes the casing for the unassisted rack-and-pinion steering, and the engine and six-speed gearbox are load-carrying. Uniquely, the final drive is offset alongside the clutch, which keeps the wheelbase short, the centre of gravity low and the transverse gearbox casing both compact and stiff. The F1 uses double wishbones all round, with horizontal coil spring/lightweight co-axial damper units operated by rocker arms. The brilliance of the set-up is in its mountings, which give isolation from road noise and harshness, plus a

degree of compliance, while retaining solid location. The front wishbones pick up via rigid bushes on an aluminium-alloy subframe, and four flexible subframe mountings give compliance and insulation, but with exceptional control of the tyre contact area. McLaren call the system 'Ground-Plane Shear Centre'. Another innovation, dubbed 'Inclined Shear Axis', is used at the rear, whereby the suspension mounts directly to the gearbox and engine casings, the V12's mass acts as a vibration damper, and the engine/gearbox mounts (to the rear bulkhead and the longitudinal beams) control drive, braking and torsional loads. Iron-disc Brembo brakes with four-pot alloy calipers are used all round (without ABS or assistance), and the car sits on ultra-light five-spoke magnesium wheels shod with 235 and 315/45 ZR17 tyres, developed by Goodyear for the F1.

Engine

True to the F1's philosophy, its powerhouse is a strictly no-compromise unit, specially commissioned by McLaren and designed and built by BMW Motorsport in Munich. Designated type S70/2, the all-new engine is a 60-degree V12 with four chain-driven overhead camshafts operating four valves per cylinder, with continuously variable inlet valve timing. The bore and stroke of 86 mm × 87 mm give a capacity of 6064 cc, but in a package that is little bigger than many current 3.5-litre GP engines. The block and heads are in aluminium alloy, with Nikasil-coated bores; the cam-carriers, oil-pump and variable-valve-timing housings, and the casing for the dry sump are all in magnesium, while the flywheel is aluminium and the intake air-box is in carbon composite – all contributing to very light weight

for such a large capacity. The V12 uses a management system developed by TAG Electronics Systems; it has transistorised ignition by 12 individual coils, fuel injection with 12 single-throttle valves, and in addition to the usual management features it incorporates a 'get-you-home' function plus electronic data-logging with onboard data acquisition and direct data-download facilities – the latter linked to the factory (via modem), for diagnostic purposes. The engine is clean (running on unleaded petrol, with four catalytic converters, lambda sensors and secondary air injection); it is also efficient, as well as very powerful. With a 10.5:1 compression ratio, it produces more than 550 bhp at 7,000 rpm and more than 440 lb ft of torque on a flat curve from 4,000 to 7,000 rpm – and it weighs just 573 lb.

Below: The V12's alloy block is well-cooled, but the heat has to escape; this is the V12 at full rpm at BMW Motorsport's test centre.

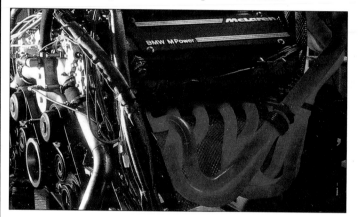

Below: McLaren has applied for a patent for the GPSC front suspension system, which features compliant wishbone mounts for reduced noise.

Above: The composite monocoque's strength is based on two floor beams, with a sturdy pier behind the driver's seat, integrated into the roof pillars.

Right: A brake assembly is tested to red heat on the dynamometer.

Below: A side view of the mid-engined F1, in which virtually all the weight is between the wheels. Note how low the V12 is sited, and how the three-into-one exhausts rise over the rear axle and then down into the silencer.

Below: The wide vents in front of the wheels feed air through the the oil and water radiators on each side, and then through to the brakes. Under the front bonnet are the fluid reservoirs and a small storage space.

Left: The S70/2 6064-cc V12 is a unique design, immensely powerful and yet not much larger than contemporary 3.5-litre F1 racing engines. This view reveals how compactly the ancillaries and exhausts are mounted. There are individual water pumps for each cylinder bank, and dry-sump lubrication to ensure good flow under high cornering loads. Weight is remarkably low, and each engine, which is hand-assembled, has an alloy block and magnesium-alloy sump, variable-valve-timing housings, cam-carriers and cam covers.

Right: The BMW Motorsport V12 with ancillaries, carbon-composite air-box and cam covers removed, revealing the 12 single throttles, with the TAG fuel injector systems on each side. Also visible are the lobes of the four chain-driven cams which operate the 48 valves. The engine is very clean in terms of emissions and has particularly efficient heads, continuous variable-inlet-valve timing and an emissions-control system with a secondary air supply and four catalytic converters, plus an exhaust-gas analysis control.

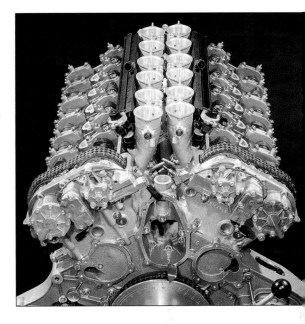

Below: The F1's interior is finished in hand-stitched Connolly leather, and the driving seat, steering wheel position and pedals are tailored to the driver for the finest ergonomic match.

Below: On the roof is a discreet high-efficiency air intake for the engine behind. The 'dihedral doors' form the outer sections of the roof, part of the composite monocoque's 'survival cell'.

Below: The 'brake-and-balance' foil, here retracted, is activated automatically by electronic sensors during heavy braking.

Above: The F1's specially-designed Goodyear tyres have asymmetric and directional treads, and are all different; no spare is carried, and thus a puncture-sealant aerosol is supplied.

Above: At speed, the F1 is remarkably stable, because air beneath the car is compressed against the road and released via an expanding-section channel at the rear. There a three-part diffuser generates downforce, while two powerful electric fans suck air from the outer reflex diffuser sections.

Marcos Mantula

The story started in the early 1960s, with the nimble Marcos GT, superbly styled and aerodynamically efficient. Two decades later its good looks were reborn in the Mantula, a 133-mph British supercar with Rover V8 power.

Car critics suffer from attacks of unrealistic nostalgia perhaps more than most. From time to time they are prone to claim that if only so and so were to put a certain model back into production it would still sell. The reality is that cars usually outstay their welcome and by the time they go out of production it's for a very good reason. When the MGB, for example, finally died it was totally obsolete, and had to be somewhat modified when Rover revived it in 1992 for a small niche market.

There was a precedent for Rover's actions, and it was one supplied by a relatively obscure manufacturer based in Westbury, Wiltshire. In the 1960s Marcos had produced a sports car with lines as striking (if perhaps not as beautiful) as the E-type Jaguar – the rather prosaically-named Marcos 1800. That had its ups and downs before

production ended in 1971. And yet, in 1981 the company's founder Jem Marsh decided the time was once again right for the Marcos and it was duly reborn; its derivative, the Mantara, is still around today.

No-one would pretend that early Marcoses were attractive; they may have been aerodynamically efficient thanks to the work of the ex-de Havilland aerodynamicist Frank Costin, but they looked bizarre. By the early 1960s Jem Marsh had realised that what was needed was a combination of aerodynamics and aesthetic appeal; in other words, the cars also had to look sleek. The result appeared in October 1963 in the form of the Marcos 1800, styled by Dennis Adams. The connection with Costin had not been totally lost, however, despite his lack of enthusiasm for Adams' flamboyant creation, as the chassis was

wooden. Costin had always stressed the advantages of wooden construction, pointing to the success of the de Havilland Mosquito in World War II. The use of wood for the chassis was not the only novelty in the Marcos's refreshing design. It was decided to have the seat assemblies as a fixed integral part of the rear bulkhead to give the structure greater stiffness, and that posed obvious problems for short drivers – tall ones were automatically catered for, as Marsh himself was over six feet. Those not so blessed had recourse to a hand wheel under the steering wheel; turning it moved the whole pedal assembly towards the driver.

Stressed the advantages of wooden construction

The combination of a wooden chassis and a glassfibre body meant that, almost whatever the engine chosen, the power-to-weight ratio would be very good indeed. Marsh had looked at the inline four-cylinder BMW overhead-cam engine (the block of which was later used for BMW's Formula 1 engines) but that would have been too expensive, and the choice fell on Volvo's rather more ordinary four-cylinder, along with its overdrive-equipped transmission.

At this stage Marcos were still discovering what the real market for the car was, and that pushed them to simplify the car somewhat, with the original de Dion-type rear suspension being dropped after the first 30 or so cars in favour of a cheaper live axle, while the Ford Cortina engine seemed a logical powerplant to offer.

Apart from its dramatic good looks, the GT shared another feature with the E-type (and, to be fair, less exotic models like the Triumph Spitfire, GT6 and Vitesse): the whole front section of

Left: Low, light and easily tuned, the Marcos GT was a success in sports car racing; here, 1966 and 1967 models corner at Silverstone.

Above: The ultra-low Mantula Spyder was a very successful model; the substantial increase in rear width and track over the years is obvious from this rear view.

Above: The classic lines of a 133-mph 1991 Marcos Mantula, with prodigious Rover V8 power and styling based on the 1963 Marcos.

the bodywork hinged forward to reveal a large, easily accessible, engine bay. The room within it meant that Marcos's plan of fitting whatever engine seemed appropriate was a viable one. In could go the tunable Ford cross-flow overhead-cam unit, a straight-six Volvo engine or, briefly, even Ford's unloved V4.

Not only could engines be switched with seeming ease but the chassis itself was replaced in 1969 when a more conventional tubular steel design supplanted the wooden original. It might be thought that such an adaptable design would live on and on, but over-expansion with the move to a bigger factory, poor cashflow and declining sales saw the company itself go under in 1970. Within five years, however, Jem Marsh felt confident and financially secure enough to relaunch the firm; when another five years had passed he was ready to bring back the evergreen Marcos, this time re-engineered yet again to accept V6 Capri running gear. The three-litre Capri V6 engines were tough, very reliable and reason-ably powerful but they were undeniably heavy, so the logical step was taken to fit the engine that just about every other small-scale sports car manufacturer in the country used – the alloy pushrod Rover V8.

By this stage Adams' original design needed a revamp, which Adams himself undertook, to produce the Mantula. The most obvious differences were the deeper front bodywork, required to accommodate a larger radiator, and rear wheel-arch extensions to cover far larger wheels and tyres. The remodelling proved very successful, and adaptable too, and in 1986 a convertible version was introduced. That was a relatively easy exercise structurally, as the glassfibre body contributed little to the car's overall stiffness compared with the tubular steel chassis.

An extremely low centre of gravity

It was an inspired move; the Mantula convertible seemed to have everything required: looks, performance and handling. Performance was guaranteed by the 3.5-litre Rover V8 in Vitesse trim with 190 bhp at 5,280 rpm and 220 lb ft of torque at 4,000 rpm. That was enough to give a top speed of 133 mph with 0-60 mph acceleration in under six seconds and 0-100 mph being possible in less than 15 seconds, which was outstandingly quick. The handling matched the car, helped no doubt by an extremely low centre of gravity, well-balanced weight distribution and the front wishbone suspension which, even if it was derived from the ancient Triumph Spitfire/GT6 line, worked well. Admittedly, the rear suspension was still an uncomplicated live-axle arrangement, but it was located well enough by four trailing arms and a transverse Panhard rod. There was still scope for improvement, however, and independent rear suspension appeared in 1989.

The current model, the Mantara, made its debut at the 1992 Motor Show, and was revealed as the formula as before with some changes. The body had grown wheel-arch flares to accommodate wider wheels and tyres, the ride height had been increased over the bare minimum of the Mantula, and with the loss of the distinctive transparent headlamp cover, the Mantara had a slightly bug-eyed look. Under the spreading glassfibre, Marcos had finally discarded the old front wishbone arrangement in favour of struts. The modifications made an interesting design a better, more driveable, car, which was just as well as the optional 450 engine delivered over 300 bhp. So good did the new car appear that there was confident talk of entering one at Le Mans where L'Auto Club de l'Ouest, organisers of the 24 Hours, had gone back to their roots in throwing the race open to the most powerful of roadgoing GTs. A good performance there in 1994 would serve to bring the Marcos name to more people's attention and preserve the lines of a model first seen 30 years earlier.

Top: A classic sports car race at Thruxton in 1984. The Lotus Elans were good, but the Marcos GT driven by Roger Ealand was better, and was first across the line. This Marcos was fitted with the Volvo 1800-cc four-cylinder.

Above: The Mantara of 1992 had lost some of the clean styling but was tremendously fast, with either a 3.9- or 4.5-litre Rover V8.

Overleaf: The Mantula Spyder was launched in 1986, with the 3.5-litre, fuel-injected Rover V8 engine.

Driving the Mantula: *low-line ride*

In the 1960s racing drivers drove Marcos almost lying down with arms outstretched; they would have been at home in the Mantula, but that's no surprise, as the design concept dates from 1963. The Mantula does suit taller drivers, and the driving position accentuates the awkwardness of some very heavy steering at slow speeds (the current Mantara has much-needed optional power assistance). That problem disappears at speed though, where the Marcos demonstrates an excellent blend of ride (at least on smooth surfaces) and handling, helped by the precise quick-ratio steering.

It's basically neutral until very high cornering speeds

are reached and then it's the back which moves out of line, but only at the sort of speeds reached on a track rather than on the road, and then not viciously. The large V8 is mated to the usual Rover five-speed gearbox and allows over 130 mph, while as a testament to the original aerodynamics the Mantula can be driven with the top down at 100 mph without the slipstream threatening to tear your hair out and stop you breathing. And if you want to get to those speeds as quickly as possible, 0-100 mph can be achieved in 14.4 seconds with three gear changes and some brutality, by which time the car would have covered the standing quarter-mile.

PERFORMANCE & SPECIFICATION COMPARISON	Engine	Displacement	Power	Torque (lb ft)	Max speed	0-60 mph	Length (in/mm)	Wheelbase (in/mm)	Track front/rear	Weight (lb/kg)	Price
Marcos Mantula Spyder	V8, overhead-valve	3946 cc	190 bhp 4750 rpm	235 lb ft 3600 rpm	133 mph 214 km/h	5.4 sec	163.5 in 4153 mm	89.5 in 2273 mm	50.5 in 54.3 in	1960 lb 889 kg	£28,159 (1992)
Caterham Super Seven HPC	Inline-four, twin-cam, 16-valve	1998 cc	175 bhp 6000 rpm	155 lb ft 4800 rpm	126 mph 203 km/h	5.2 sec	133.5 in 3391 mm	87.8 in 2230 mm	48.8 in 52.2 in	1384 lb 628 kg	£18,255 (1992)
Lotus Elan SE	Inline-four, twin-cam, 16-valve	1588 cc	165 bhp 6600 rpm	148 lb ft 4200 rpm	136 mph 219 km/h	6.5 sec	149.7 in 3802 mm	88.6 in 2250 mm	58.5 in 58.5 in	2253 lb 1022 kg	£22,490 (1992)
Morgan Plus 8	V8, overhead-valve	3946 cc	190 bhp 4750 rpm	235 lb ft 2600 rpm	121 mph 195 km/h	6.1 sec	156.0 in 3962 mm	98.0 in 2489 mm	54.0 in 54.0 in	2059 lb 934 kg	£24,821 (1992)
TVR V8S	V8, overhead-valve	3950 cc	240 bhp 5750 rpm	275 lb ft 4200 rpm	146 mph 235 km/h	5.2 sec	155.8 in 3957 mm	90.0 in 2286 mm	56.6 in 56.6 in	2249 lb 1020 kg	£23,595 (1992)

Marcos Mantula Data File

The first Marcos in the range that has led to the current Mantara was the 1800, launched in October 1963 with a wooden chassis, glassfibre body and Volvo engine. The 1.5-litre Cortina GT engine was offered in 1966. That unit was enlarged to 1650 cc and revised to produce 120 bhp in 1967, the same year that the Ford 1600 cross-flow powerplant became available. By 1969 Ford's V4 engine (versions of which saw action in Saab 96s, as well as Ford Corsairs and Transits) was offered, along with the three-litre Ford V6, and the wooden chassis was discarded in favour of a tubular steel type. The next year the Volvo three-litre straight-six became available and was fitted to 200 cars in all. In 1971 Marcos production ceased after around 1,000 models had been built, 11 with Triumph's 2.5-litre straight-six. The car was re-introduced in kit form in 1981 with a range of engines, including the 1.6-litre cross-flow Ford, and the three-litre Volvo and Ford units. The Mantula appeared in 1984 with a Rover V8; the convertible Spyder followed in 1987, and was further improved by being given independent rear suspension in 1989, and finally a comprehensive change saw the 3.9-litre Mantara appear at the Birmingham Motor Show in October 1992.

Above: The front and rear of a 1966 GT; from the front there were hints of the E-type Jaguar.

Below: The 1992 Mantara Spyder was faster than ever, but the shape had been compromised.

Above: A 1991 Mantula Spyder. It was an efficient, aerodynamic shape and proved extremely stable even beyond 130 mph.

Styling

It's most unlikely that the Marcos would have looked the way it did if the E-type Jaguar had not already appeared. That's not to say that Marcos's stylist Dennis Adams copied the E-type, but the influence of the Jaguar's long, slim bonnet and enclosed headlights is clear. Adams opted for twin headlights under the clear covers, but the whole front of the car hinged forward just as it did on the E-type. Again like the Jaguar, the body seemed to be stretched tightly over the running gear beneath and so shared a similar bulge in its haunches for the rear wheels. But despite all the parallels that can be drawn, no-one could mistake one car for the other and the Marcos was one of the most unique styles to emerge in the 1960s.

It was clearly a very sleek design but, like Alfa Romeo's Disco Volante from the previous decade, it looked as though it should generate far too much lift at speed. In fact, even without any

front spoiler the car stayed very stable even at the very high speeds its shape permitted. Over the years as the original design transmuted into the Mantula, and today's Mantara, the basic contours stayed recognisably the same, although the Mantula could be recognised by its far deeper nose section. The Mantara did depart from the original style in a more obvious way; its wider track meant the front wheel arches had to be considerably more flared than before, and the rear arches had more exaggerated lips. The clear headlight covers had been discarded and the twin headlights were made more prominent. The Mantara was undoubtedly striking but lacked the clean lines of the earlier, prettier, models.

Below: In 1963 the smooth Marcos profile attracted much interest; few could have guessed it would sell for decades to come (bottom).

Below: The V8 Mantula's 133-mph performance dictated a boot-lid rear wing to keep the back down.

Above: Ventilation slots on the bonnet assisted egress of hot air from the engine bay.

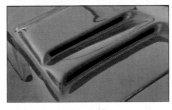

Right: Marcos fitted many types of wheels over the years; this Mantula has split-rim alloys.

Left: Aerodynamic Perspex light covers were standard on earlier cars, but not the Mantara.

Left and below: The Mantula's cockpit was tastefully finished in figured veneer and leather.

Chassis and running gear

The Marcos 1800 of 1963 was one of the very few cars to feature a wooden chassis, following the principles proven in the first Marcos of all – the bizarre-looking gull-wing GT of 1961. This model had shown that, using a sandwich of marine ply, it was possible to build a monocoque structure as strong as a steel one. The key to its strength was threefold, in having the grain of the middle layer of ply run at 90 degrees to the outer layers, in using it in layers up to 3 mm thick, and in making it into a very boxy structure. The plywood was formed into large box-sections running longitudinally, for the sills and the transmission tunnel. That did little for space-efficiency inside the Marcos, but for a two-seater sports car that hardly mattered. Bulkheads front and rear resulted in a stiff yet light monocoque, one which stood the test of time and survived the ravages of the English damp extremely well.

The front suspension was held in a tubular steel frame rather than being mounted directly to the central monocoque and was originally lifted out of Triumph's parts bin, along with the GT6/Vitesse-type twin wishbones and concentric coil spring/dampers. They had been used in countless models and worked extremely well. Originally the rear suspension

featured a clever de Dion-axle design with a telescopic transverse link, and two radius arms for longitudinal location, together with coil springs and dampers. Eventually, after over 30 cars had been so equipped, this system was discarded on grounds of cost and complication in favour of a conventional live axle, which was secured as precisely as possible by four leading links, while lateral location was provided by a Panhard rod. The penalty of such an arrangement in a lightweight car is excessive unsprung weight, and that did require a fairly stiff spring/damper set-up. Eventually, however, the car's performance dictated the switch to an independent double-wishbone, coil-sprung rear end in 1989.

The arrival of the Mantara in 1992 marked the end of the Triumph-derived front-suspension components in favour of Ford Sierra-sourced parts, and that in turn meant the ditching of wishbone front suspension for a modified MacPherson-strut arrangement with twin wishbones, coil springs and dampers at the rear.

Other aspects of the running gear have been regularly updated. The original 9.25-in diameter front discs and 9-in rear drums grew as the power increased until the Mantula was given larger, ventilated front discs.

Below: Early on, Marcos adopted a live axle with leading arms and a Panhard rod for lateral location.

Right: From 1989 the Mantula's handling was improved with the adoption of independent rear suspension, with twin wishbones and the coil spring/damper unit mounted behind the driveshafts to allow more spring travel.

Above: The Mantula was built on an extremely solid and adaptable square-section steel chassis.

Engine

No other car has been fitted with the vast range of engines that have appeared under the Marcos's distinctive bonnet. The number of different configurations, let alone actual engines, is impressive; there have been Ford inline-fours, a Ford V4 and V6, inline-fours and sixes from Volvo and finally the perfect solution, the Rover V8. Their difference in size, shape and power shows the enormous adaptability of the Marcos design, and the contrast in power outputs is marked. In 1965 the Marcos 1800 was powered by a tuned Volvo 1780-cc inline unit which was a conventional pushrod overhead-valve design used in the Volvo P1800. Given twin Stromberg carburettors and revised inlet and exhaust porting, Marcos extracted some 114 bhp at 5,800 rpm, along with 110 lb ft of torque at 4,200 rpm. That was enough to give a top speed of 116 mph and a 0-60 mph time of 8.2 seconds.

By the early 1970s the straight-six Volvo engine had found favour, originally for the US market, but it proved popular in the UK too. That was a 2978-cc unit with bore and stroke of 88.9 mm × 80 mm, and with more power and torque than the smaller four, at 130 bhp at 5,000 rpm and 152 lb ft at 2,500 rpm. This again improved performance, dropping the

0-60 mph time to 7.5 seconds. Yet more power came from Ford's V6 and more again from the Rover V8 which was first fitted in 1984. When the tuned Vitesse-spec engine became available, that was incorporated into the ageless design, producing 190 bhp at 5,280 rpm and 220 lb ft at 4,000 rpm. Up went the performance again, with maximum speed climbing to 133 mph and the 0-60 mph time dropping to 5.4 seconds, while 0-100 mph took only 14.4 seconds.

The Mantara uses a yet bigger engine, the current 3.9-litre version of the V8, but although displacement is larger (thanks to a bigger bore), power output is little different from the Vitesse spec, although the maximum power comes in at a far lower 4,750 rpm and there's 7 lb ft more torque, at 3,600 rpm rather than 4,000 rpm. If that's considered insufficient, there is also the 4.5-litre version of the V8, as modified by JE Engineering and offering 302 bhp at 6,000 rpm and 320 lb ft at 4,000 rpm – enough to give a top speed of over 150 mph and 0-60 mph acceleration in well under five seconds.

Below: The Mantula's all-alloy 3946-cc Rover V8 had a 9.7:1 compression ratio, Lucas fuel injection and mapped ignition.

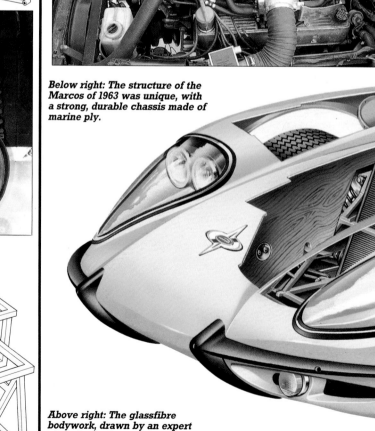

Below right: The structure of the Marcos of 1963 was unique, with a strong, durable chassis made of marine ply.

Above right: The glassfibre bodywork, drawn by an expert aircraft aerodynamicist, was distinctive and efficient. The engine was set well back, thus leaving much scope for future development.

Above right: The well-proven twin-wishbone front suspension, steering rack and anti-roll bar were Triumph GT6/Vitesse parts.

Above: This is the Volvo engine of one of the 99 Marcos 1800s built. It was a well-proven cast-iron pushrod unit, orthodox in design and exceptionally reliable. With slightly revised manifolds and Stromberg carburettors, power rose slightly to 114 bhp and 110 lb ft of torque, and the very light Marcos 1800 offered stunning performance for the mid-1960s, with a top speed of 116 mph.

Below: As the decades passed, expectations of performance rose, and the Marcos proved capable of handling considerably more power. Rover's Buick-derived 3.5-litre alloy unit was at one time the smallest-capacity production V8, though there have been smaller ones since. As fitted to the latest Mantara, it has been expanded to 3.9- and even 4.5-litre form.

Below: Many early models used the four-cylinder Volvo P1800S engine which, in the light wood and glassfibre Marcos, gave impressive results.

Below: The Webasto roof was wide enough to give an open-top sensation. Note that the seats were structurally important and thus not adjustable.

Below: The live rear axle was held with leading rather than trailing arms because of a lack of space in front of the wheel arches.

Right: A highly-tuned, Volvo-engined 1800GT with Minilite wheels leads the pack in a classic sports car race.

Maserati Ghibli

Although eclipsed by cars like the Lamborghini Miura and Ferrari Daytona, Maserati's lovely Ghibli was one of the most beautifully-proportioned supercars of all, as well as one of the most satisfying to drive.

Above: Ferrari's similar but even quicker Daytona and Lamborghini's revolutionary Miura restricted the Ghibli's success, but it was a lovely, fast and well-balanced car.

Inset: Maserati's trident was taken from a statue of Neptune on a fountain in Bologna.

L ate in 1957, Maserati went to Venezuela with their team of sports-racing cars, still with a chance of winning the world title. Having already won the Formula 1 World Championship with Fangio driving, they needed to win the Sports Car Grand Prix of Caracas to clinch the sports car title too. They took four cars, but only a matter of minutes into the race, all four were eliminated; two of the awesomely fast but hard-to-handle Tipo 54 450Ss had individual accidents, and the third 450S crashed into the fourth works car, a 300S.

It couldn't have happened at a worse time for Maserati; it marked a sudden and sad end to the marque's patchy but often brilliant racing history. It also, indirectly, opened a new chapter in the Maserati production car story.

For many years, Maserati's staple power units, for road and track, had been various versions of their classic twin-cam six-cylinder; the ill-fated 450S had been the first Maserati to use a V8 since the mid-1930s. Around 1955, American racing team patron Tony Paravano (whose drivers included Carroll Shelby) had approached Maserati to see if they would build two alcohol-burning 4.2-litre V8s for Indianapolis, and his money gave Maserati the chance to build an engine they had long planned. In the end, Paravano had his 4.2-litre engines just in time to run into financial problems in 1957; he had

already taken delivery of a 4.5-litre version in one of the first 450Ss in 1956, the year before the works used it. With a displacement of 4½ litres, twin plugs and four gear-driven overhead camshafts it could offer some 400 bhp at 6,700 rpm in race tune. After Maserati's withdrawal from racing, the V8 found a new career as a road car engine, launched again in 1959 in the 5000GT at the Turin Motor Show, and used in the first Quattroporte of 1963.

Its elegant lines were extravagantly praised

That initially had a four-litre engine, with chain-driven cams and a softer state of tune. It was enlarged first to 4.1 litres and then to 4.7, and in that capacity Maserati obviously saw it as an ideal basis for a more compact two-seater GT. At the Turin Show in 1965 they launched a two-door, four-seater coupé based on a shortened version of the Quattroporte chassis, known as the Mexico, and this made the perfect foundation for the forthcoming Ghibli.

The Mexico reverted to a simple live axle on semi-elliptic springs, plus a well-proven double-wishbone and coil-spring layout at the front, and disc brakes all round. The chassis, while retain-

ing its basic tubular layout, was comprehensively strengthened by the addition of welded-in sheet and box-sections, to make it one of the stiffest production chassis Maserati had ever built.

To create the Ghibli, the Mexico chassis was shortened by another 3½ inches, the engine was given another 40 bhp, to take it to 340 bhp, and a dry sump was added to allow it to be mounted as low down and as far back as possible, to help both weight distribution and aesthetics.

The latter factor was entrusted, in 1965, to Ghia, and to the man recently appointed as their chief designer – Giorgetto Giugiaro, then only in his 20s. His stunningly beautiful coupé was shown for the first time at the Turin Motor Show late in 1966 and went on sale in 1967. Like many Maseratis, it was named after a famous wind, in this case the Ghibli. Its elegant lines were extravagantly praised, and even Giugiaro himself was rather proud of it; in 1984 he commented: "Of all the cars I designed for Ghia, the only two I'm sorry I don't own are the Ghibli and the Mangusta."

The Ghibli was much the most expensive of Maserati's generally pricey range, but it was so well-received that before long, orders were coming in faster than Ghia could build bodies – which only amounted to three or four cars a day on a small line within their main factory. Nevertheless, Maserati sold 87 cars in the rest of 1967, 276 in 1968 and 270 in 1969.

Also in 1969, Giugiaro added another fine version of the Ghibli to the line, in the form of a supremely elegant drop-head Spyder, with the options of a neat detachable hard top, automatic transmission and power steering. The Spyder was even more expensive than the coupé, but was a car that had been almost universally well-received by testers and owners alike, making it even more desirable.

Just ahead of Ferrari's mighty Daytona

The Ghibli's problem was nothing to do with the car itself, but primarily with the opposition. It had appeared at almost exactly the same time as Lamborghini's Miura and just ahead of Ferrari's mighty Daytona – the former making mid-engined sophistication the way ahead for exotic car builders, the latter marking the absolute pinnacle of the big, front-engined GT car. In spite of their totally different layouts, the Ghibli's modern Giugiaro styling ironically forced comparisons with the futuristic Miura, which the conservatively-engineered Ghibli had no chance of beating; and the Daytona simply had the measure of both in terms of outright performance. And although you might argue that the Ghibli was aimed at a subtly different customer who placed more importance on style and comfort than on speed and racing technology, the competition was still winning.

Maserati's necessarily limited response was to introduce the larger, more powerful and even torquier-engined Ghibli SS in 1970; although this was primarily in reaction to increasingly stringent American pollution-control requirements, it also brought a small gain in performance. By lengthening the stroke of the 4.7-litre V8 by 4 mm, displacement was increased (growing to 4930 cc) and the engine gained some 15 bhp, to take its claimed peak in European tune from 340 to 355 bhp at 5,500 rpm, but the sales peak had already been passed by 1969.

Production finally came to an end in 1973, when the last five coupés were built. In total, Maserati had sold 1,274 Ghiblis – 1,149 of them coupés and just 125 Spyders.

Left: Under its exceptional skin, the Ghibli was essentially a variation on the formula of the mundane-looking 1965 Mexico four-seater, itself developed on a shortened version of the chassis and powertrain devised for the Quattroporte (four-door) of 1963.

Below: The Ghibli Spyder was considerably more expensive than the coupé, and only 125 were built. Its convertible top stowed out of sight beneath a hinged panel to the rear of the cockpit, and a hard top was available as an optional extra.

Overleaf: The Ghibli was designed by Giorgetto Giugiaro, at that stage of his career still relatively unknown and working for the well-established styling house, Ghia of Turin (where he also created the De Tomaso Mangusta at around the same time). The Ghibli's long, gently-dipping nose and equally subtly-curved fastback tail made it one of the most elegant and refined front-engined GT designs of all time, and to begin with, orders came in faster than Ghia could build bodies for it.

Driving the Ghibli: *thoroughbred luxury*

The Ghibli might not have been quite so fast as some V12-engined contemporaries, but what it lacked in outright speed (and that wasn't much) it made up for with a unique character. This was a *genuine* luxury car which drove like a thoroughbred. The superbly-fitted cockpit, with its deep centre tunnel, wood-rim wheel and full complement of instruments, was classically sporting. With deeply padded seats and an adjustable steering column, it was a car which held no threat of discomfort even over great distances; you could even see out of it.

The Ghibli's V8 had every bit as much character as rival 12s – there was no mistaking the engine's racing origins, even though it relied more on thunderous torque at relatively low revs than a more high-revving V12. The power was smooth and progressive but there was enough of it to reach 60 mph in a little over six seconds, and to go on to 160 mph with ease, yet the car remained unflustered in traffic. Clutch and gear change alike were light and precise, the ride was exceptional for such a car, and the handling way beyond what the simple chassis might suggest. The steering was superb, there was very little roll, and lots of grip; even the brakes inspired confidence.

PERFORMANCE & SPECIFICATION COMPARISON	Engine	Displacement	Power	Torque (lb ft)	Max speed	0-60 mph	Length (in/mm)	Wheelbase (in/mm)	Track front/rear	Weight (lb/kg)	Price
Maserati Ghibli coupé	V8, quad-cam	4719 cc	340 bhp 5500 rpm	326 lb ft 4000 rpm	154 mph 248 km/h	6.6 sec	180.7 in 4590 mm	100.4 in 2550 mm	56.7 in 55.4 in	3746 lb 1699 kg	£9,500 (1968)
Bizzarrini GT Strada 5300	V8, overhead-valve	5354 cc	365 bhp 6000 rpm	376 lb ft 3500 rpm	145 mph 233 km/h	6.4 sec	174.0 in 4420 mm	96.5 in 2451 mm	55.0 in 55.0 in	2760 lb 1252 kg	N/A
Ferrari Daytona 365 GTB/4	V12, quad-cam	4390 cc	353 bhp 7500 rpm	319 lb ft 5000 rpm	174 mph 280 km/h	5.4 sec	174.2 in 4425 mm	94.5 in 2400 mm	56.7 in 56.1 in	2641 lb 1198 kg	£6,740 (1970)
Jaguar E-type V12	V12, overhead-cam	5343 cc	272 bhp 6000 rpm	304 lb ft 3600 rpm	142 mph 229 km/h	6.8 sec	184.5 in 4686 mm	105.0 in 2667 mm	53.0 in 53.0 in	3230 lb 1465 kg	£3,367 (1973)
Lamborghini Miura	V12, quad-cam	3929 cc	350 bhp 7000 rpm	271 lb ft 5100 rpm	172 mph 277 km/h	6.7 sec	171.6 in 4359 mm	98.4 in 2499 mm	55.6 in 55.6 in	2851 lb 1293 kg	£9,165 (1966)

Maserati Ghibli Data File

I n the 1990s, Maseratis are being mass-produced, but this is in complete contrast to the bulk of the company's history. Maserati made their name producing Grand Prix and sports-racing cars; much like Ferrari, manufacturing road cars was not the firm's primary interest. Nevertheless the company did produce some powerful and desirable coupés and spiders in limited numbers – cars such as the A6/1500 of the late 1940s, and the 3500GT and Sebring of the 1950s and 1960s. By the mid-1960s Maserati were building the Mexico, a four-seater coupé with rather mundane Vignale styling. The Mexico had certain assets, however – a production version of Maserati's racing V8 quad-cam engine, and a good chassis. Both were used as the basis for the marque's new top-of-the-line two-seater, the Ghibli. The Ghibli was almost the end of a traditional line of powerful front-engined cars and, with its Giugiaro styling, was easily the most beautiful.

Above: Some V12 rivals could outrun it, but the Ghibli was no mean performer, with a top speed approaching 160 mph.

Styling

There are many who argue that the Ghibli was the most beautiful Maserati ever; some would even say that it was the most beautiful sports car of all time. Certainly it had the touch of a master – designed by Giorgetto Giugiaro while he was chief stylist at Ghia. The Ghibli killed any notion that Maserati styling was inevitably a bit dull alongside the opposition. Although the wheelbase was shorter than that of the 2+2 Mexico it was markedly longer than that of its two-seater sibling, the Mistral, so the look was dominated by an extraordinary sleekness. The car's proportions were classically long-nosed and bob-tailed, and the Ghibli was the longest, lowest, widest two-seater Maserati ever made.

While Ferrari and Lamborghini tended towards soft-edged designs, the Ghibli was, though curvy, elegantly angular and shark-nosed, with minimal ornamentation and an unmistakable hint of aggression – it really did look fast even when it was standing still! Details like the long,

shallow air vents in the front wings and the gentle full-length crease below the waistline were exactly enough to break up the slab sides and emphasise the length and lowness even more; the full-width black grille, big flip-up headlamps and low bonnet bulge were as subtle as could be, but again the message was of power and speed. The coupé was superbly impressive and almost perfectly proportioned from every angle, and, at least with its soft top down, the Spyder very nearly maintained the same level of gracefulness. Even the optional hard top didn't upset the car's visual balance.

Below: Closed coupé and open Spyder models of the Ghibli looked equally handsome. The Ghibli was the first Maserati styled by Giugiaro and was such an aesthetic success that elements of its shape were carried over to the later, mid-engined, Bora.

Above: Lockable fuel filler flaps were built into the Ghibli's rear quarters.

Right: Maserati had traditionally used a trident in their badge. On the Ghibli, as on the earlier Sebring and Mistral models, the motif was made bigger and bolder, and set centrally in the grille without a surround.

Below: Inside the cabin, the Ghibli was a typical 1960s luxury Grand Tourer.

Ghibli Spyder

Looking at Giugiaro's original fastback coupé design, it's hard to imagine that anyone would think of changing it, but demand dictated that an open Spyder version be produced. Usually in such conversions extra chassis strengthening has to be added along the sills and across the rear ahead of the boot opening. The Ghibli Spyder needed none of these additions. Apart from the absence of a roof, the lines of the two cars were the same. The Spyder had a folding canvas top and a smart removable hard top. The production total for the Spyder, at 125, was virtually the same as for its rival, the convertible version of the Ferrari Daytona.

Below: The Ghibli Spyder was unveiled at the 1968 Turin Motor Show and went on sale in 1969.

Below: Very little modification was necessary to turn the coupé into the Spyder. The petrol filler flaps were relocated on the flat deck between the soft-top stowage panel and the boot lid.

Maserati Ghibli Spyder

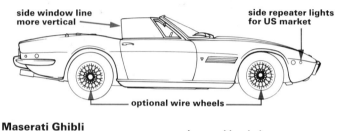

side window line more vertical

side repeater lights for US market

optional wire wheels

Maserati Ghibli

fuel filler cap

chrome side window surround

Above: Wire-spoked wheels were offered as an option on the Ghibli Spyder in place of the usual cast-aluminium ones.

Below: For a powerful car with leaf-spring rear suspension and a live axle, the Ghibli handled extraordinarily well.

Engine

The Ghibli engine was a classic example of the race-bred Maserati V8, and the most powerful yet put into production. It had an alloy block with a 90-degree 'V', and a five-bearing crankshaft. The alloy cylinder heads carried two inclined valves per cylinder, operated through inverted-bucket tappets by four overhead camshafts, driven by a long, complicated run of duplex chain. The valves were set in hemispherical combustion chambers around central plugs – easily accessible between widely-spaced cam covers. Early Ghiblis had a bore and stroke of 93.9 mm × 85.0 mm for a capacity of 4719 cc, but for the SS the stroke was lengthened by 4 mm, to 89.0 mm, to take capacity to 4930 cc. Mainly to reduce the overall height of the engine, but also obviously drawing on its racing origins, the V8 used dry-sump lubrication. In the centre of the 'V', under a single huge air-cleaner-cum-air-intake box, were four twin-choke downdraught Weber carburettors. The exhaust system used intricately-bent tubular manifolds – which on engines with the emission systems demanded by America had a close-fitting second skin to improve the efficiency of the emissions control. Quoted power for the 4.7-litre engine was 340 bhp at 5,500 rpm. For the 4.9-litre engine, output rose yet again, up to 355 bhp at the same rpm. Torque output increased to over 350 lb ft.

Left: The quad-cam V8 that Maserati used in road cars from the Quattroporte onwards was derived from the racing engine designed by Giulio Alfieri in the 1950s

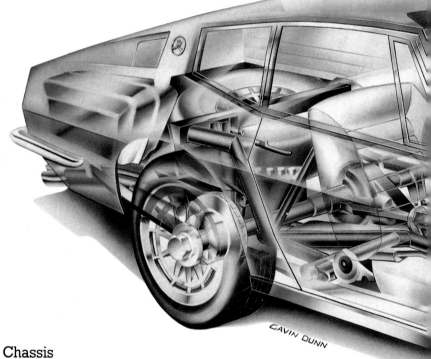

GAVIN DUNN

Chassis

Underneath the heavy steel shell (built at the Ghia factory, not at Maserati) was an essentially simple, front-engined, rear-drive chassis that placed more emphasis on strength than on lightness. That meant a tubular frame, the main elements of which were centre and side rails, transverse triangulated hoops front and rear, plus a substantial extension at the front to carry both engine and front suspension. The tubes were mainly oval, and generous in size (not like Maserati's famous 'Birdcage' racer with its complex lattice of tiny tubes). The basic layout dated back a long way, but by the mid-1960s it had been further strengthened by welded-on sheet metal fabrications, forming stiff box-sections and angles – and the deep, structural centre tunnel allowed the car to have low and non-intrusive sills, while still having sufficient torsional rigidity.

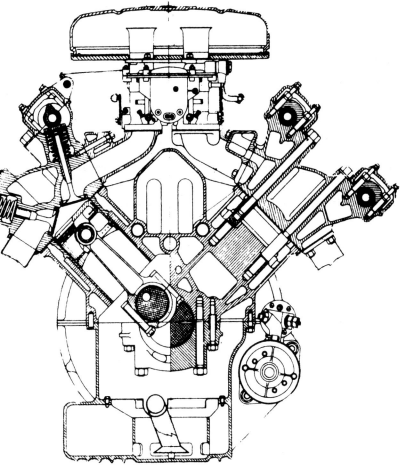

Below: The 90-degree Maserati V8 was a strong and untemperamental power unit. Made of aluminium alloy throughout, as adapted by Alfieri for roadgoing use it had duplex chain drive to the pair of overhead camshafts on each cylinder bank, rather than the gear drive of its competition forebears. In 4719-cc form, its bore and stroke dimensions were 93.9 mm × 85.0 mm.

Above: As initially installed in the Ghibli, the V8 had a displacement of 4719 cc, producing, in European-market form, 340 bhp at 5,500 rpm and 326 lb ft of torque at 4,000 rpm. It also had a terrific spread of torque, giving loads of low-down urge and making it less hard work to drive than some of the higher-revving V12s in rival supercars. Later, in 1970, capacity was increased to 4930 cc, mainly to compensate for American emission-control requirements, and power rose to 355 bhp.

Below: By 1960s standards the Ghibli's windscreen was expansive and steeply raked, and its roof line was low.

Below: The Ghibli application of the V8 breathed through four downdraught twin-choke Weber carburettors.

Below: Electric fans pushed air through the radiator, which was inclined to fit the sleek nose.

Above: A strong spaceframe and central tunnel meant the Ghibli didn't need massive sills.

Mercedes-Benz

540K

The 540K was fast and the epitome of the Teutonic sports car, solidly built around a superb supercharged 5.4-litre straight-eight, with all-independent suspension, a luxury interior and some of the finest-ever pre-war styling.

I ron fists were seldom concealed within such impeccably-tailored gloves as with the 500K/540K Mercedes of the 1930s, for the bodywork designed by Hermann Ahrens for the Mercedes body works at Sindelfingen had a balanced elegance of line that few could match. And though the chassis design of the Mercedes with all-round independent suspension was ahead of most of its contemporaries, the supercharged engine was a power unit that exuded might and arrogance. "All brute force and pigskin" was *The Autocar*'s disdainful verdict on the 540K.

But the car merited kinder judgment, for it was the ultimate development of the supercharged Mercedes line that had its origin in the company's World War I aero engines. It was the need to make Germany's warplanes fly faster and higher than the fighting aircraft of the Allies that led Paul Daimler, son of the company's founder, to experiment with superchargers.

What set the supercharged Mercedes of the 1930s apart from the big blown Mercedes of the previous decade was the nature of their chassis, which, oddly enough, resulted from Mercedes' first venture into the economy car class with the Type 170 of 1931. This popular 1.7-litre six-cylinder model was the Stuttgart company's first car with all-round independent suspension,

employing parallel transverse springs at the front and swing-axles at the rear.

The 540K was a development of the blown 380K of 1932, but supercharging could not conceal the fact that the 380K was overweight – and fewer than 160 had been built by the time Mercedes decided to cure the problem of the poor power-to-weight ratio by upping the engine size to five litres, thus creating the 500K. This was rather more like it: H. S. Linfield, road-test editor of *The Autocar*, summarised it as "a master car for the very few; the sheer insolence of its great power affords an experience on its own."

Elevated to a place among the immortals

Not everyone could handle such insolence on the open road, so British Mercedes retained the racing driver Goffredo 'Freddy' Zehender as technical adviser and demonstration driver. The designer of the 500K was Hans Nibel, but he died in November 1934 and the development of the subsequent supercharged Mercedes was carried out under the direction of former racing driver Max Sailer.

Though it was one of the very few cars of the

1930s capable of 100 mph on the open road, it was still overweight, scaling nearly 2.5 tons empty. Again, Mercedes-Benz countered by developing a larger-engined version, the 5.4-litre 540K, which duly appeared in late 1936. Its engine gave 115 bhp unblown or 180 bhp blown, and the need for the added urge of the supercharger was clearly shown when a Cabriolet B was road-tested by *The Autocar*. Tests in those polite days only obliquely hinted at shortcomings, but here the opinion was quite obvious: "Without the supercharger this is a quiet, docile carriage, the acceleration from low speeds being then quite mild. It will amble around town and along by-ways with scarcely a hint of its latent performance. Bring in the supercharger and it becomes another machine, with fierce acceleration." Most of the time, latent performance was all you got . . .

Advanced though the Mercedes chassis was, it was the bodywork which elevated it to a place among the immortals of motoring history – and that was the work of the young head of the *Sonderwagen* (Special Cars) body shops at Sindelfingen, Hermann Ahrens. Just 28 years old, Ahrens had already worked in the body design departments at Deutsche Industriewerke and Horch before taking over the new custom body division at Sindelfingen in September 1932. With an initial staff of only five draughtsmen, the divi-

Above: This 540K two-seat Cabriolet A, capable of 105 mph, has a one-piece windscreen rather than the 'V' screen of the Special Roadster.

sion had a capacity of five bodies a month (rising to six at the peak).

A custom body could be completed in as little as 10 weeks, but that was the exception rather than the rule, and of the 1,000-odd supercharged Mercedes built between 1933 and 1940, some 100 to 150 were fitted with Sindelfingen-built custom coachwork. Customers included racing drivers Rudy Caracciola and Manfred von Brauchitsch, who had handsome hard-top coupés built on the 500K chassis. Hard-top K-Series Mercedes of all kinds were a rare minority, representing less than 14 per cent of production but they included the stunning and influential 500K *Autobahnkurier*, built in 10 weeks for the 1933 Berlin Show. With its spatted wheels and streamlined fastback body, it stands as one of the most beautiful closed cars of all time.

Then there were the series-produced bodies, made in small numbers to Ahrens' designs by the Mercedes-Benz 'serial-production division'. These were predominantly cabriolets, and the handsomest of all were the 'V'-windscreen Special or Sport Roadsters. Of these, the company boasted: "The Sport Roadster has been distinguished in numerous international coachwork awards . . . its graceful lines, elegantly-designed bonnet, drawn-out mudguards and its divided 'V'-shaped screen all impart to this car a distinctive sporting character." Such exclusivity – the cars were finished to meet the customer's every whim – cost a hefty £2,250 on the British market (28,000 Reichsmarks in Germany). In contrast, the flat-screen standard 540K Roadster was priced at a slightly more affordable 22,000 Reichsmarks on its home market.

A thirsty car for rich owners

In the long-dead days of petrol costing less than two shillings (10p) a gallon, the mighty thirst of the blown Mercedes counted for little with the fortunate (and wealthy) private owners who were able to afford the asking price, which was close to that of a new custom-built Rolls-Royce Phantom III. An echo of those days was heard in 1986 when a 540K Cabriolet which had been standing in a Denham, Buckinghamshire, barn since its fuel consumption of 8-10 mpg put it off the road during the post-Suez fuel crisis of 1957 was unearthed and auctioned in London. Its 77-year-old owner, John Fraser, said: "I can remember going to pick it up from the Mercedes depot opposite Battersea Power Station in exchange for two crisp, white £1,000 notes." Mr Fraser, the only man apart from Mercedes service staff ever to drive the almost forgotten car, added: "One of the best trips I remember was to Monte Carlo in 1946, just after the war. The Cabriolet was the ideal car for such a journey."

The big blown Mercedes enjoyed much success as the preferred transport of the upper echelons of the Nazi party; Hermann Goering, for instance, drove a 500K, and when Mercedes showed a prototype '580K' at the 1939 Berlin Show the humourless Korpsführer Huhnlein, head of the NSKK (or *Nationalsozialistische Kraftfahr-Korps*, the National Motor Corps, a para-military Nazi unit), annexed it for his personal use.

Nor was the 580K the ultimate expression of the supercharged Mercedes; that honour was reserved for the 600K, first seen in 1938, which had a 6.0-litre V12 and was intended to replace the mighty 770K Grosser Mercedes as exclusive transport for the leaders of the Third Reich; blown V12s have always been a scarce commodity and the 600K (of which none is now known to survive) was no exception. Just 23 are believed to have been built between 1939 and 1942, of which 10 were, it seems, armour-plated six-seat Type F Cabriolets destined for top Nazis and heads of state of countries sympathetic to the Axis cause. One was found in Berlin at the end of the war, said to have been used by Admiral Doenitz during his week-long reign as Hitler's successor in May 1945; others were delivered to the likes of Hitler, Goebbels, Himmler, Generalissimo Franco of Spain, Marshal Mannerheim of Finland and 'Iron Guard' Antonescu of Romania. Tested briefly on the Berlin autobahn, the 5.5-ton car reached 110 mph.

Left: Mercedes offered two 540K Cabriolet versions as well as the Roadster; this car, with a more upright screen, is the more spacious Cabriolet B type, with room for four.

Above: The epitome of elegance, Ahrens' Special Roadster gained numerous coachwork awards for Mercedes-Benz.

Above: The Autobahnkurier, or Motorway Express, was a streamlined coupé ideal for rapid progress along Germany's new roads of the 1930s. Note the split windscreen.

Overleaf: A sleek chrome-lined 540K Special Roadster. Although Germany was not a country renowned for car styling, the young Hermann Ahrens created a series of cars whose appeal has never waned.

Driving the 540K: *for the experienced*

The road manners of the Mercedes-Benz 540K have always aroused controversy, and it was the car's weight that was chiefly to blame, leading some critics to claim it "had neither the performance nor the tautness of the old SSK". Nevertheless, vintage car expert Cecil Clutton was probably being too harsh when he described it in 1942 as "a miserably bad car with few, if any, commendable qualities".

Contemporary road-testers spoke with awe of the ride of the all-independent Mercedes, one observing that "even a severe deflection is not felt, and on normal road surfaces the ride is mostly level and

steady so that the car can be cornered very fast indeed". However, the handling seems to have been somewhat unpredictable at the limit, as *The Autocar* remarked that the 540K was "not a machine that helps the driver by indicating, as it were, the sort of speed at which it likes to be taken into a fast corner. The explanation probably lies almost wholly in the fact that the margin of safety lies extremely high up in the speed range, but a driver who does not know the car well needs to be convinced of this . . ." The magazine also observed that the big Mercedes "inspired confidence at speed, even flat-out at Brooklands".

PERFORMANCE & SPECIFICATION COMPARISON	Engine	Displacement	Power	Torque (lb ft)	Max speed	0-60 mph	Length (in/mm)	Wheelbase (in/mm)	Track front/rear	Weight (lb/kg)	Price
Mercedes-Benz 540K	Inline-eight, over-head-valve, s/c	5401 cc	180 bhp 3500 rpm	N/A	105 mph 169 km/h	16.4 sec	207.0 in 5258 mm	129.5 in 3289 mm	59.5 in 58.8 in	5796 lb 2629 kg	£1,890 (1938)
Bentley 3½-litre	Inline-six, overhead-valve	3669 cc	120 bhp 3500 rpm	N/A	92 mph 148 km/h	15.8 sec	192.0 in 4877 mm	120.0 in 3048 mm	56.0 in 56.0 in	3500 lb 1588 kg	£1,380 (1937)
Bugatti Type 57SC	Inline-eight, twin-cam, s/c	3257 cc	200 bhp 5200 rpm	N/A	110 mph 177 km/h	10.0 sec	159.0 in 4039 mm	117.5 in 2985 mm	53.0 in 53.0 in	2127 lb 965 kg	£860 (1938)
Delage D8-120	Inline-eight, overhead-valve	4750 cc	142 bhp 3750 rpm	N/A	98 mph 158 km/h	16.6 sec	200.0 in 5080 mm	130.0 in 3302 mm	56.0 in 56.0 in	3585 lb 1626 kg	£1,495 (1938)
Delahaye 135M	Inline-six, overhead-valve	3557 cc	110 bhp 3850 rpm	N/A	105 mph 169 km/h	12.5 sec	155.9 in 3960 mm	115.0 in 2920 mm	54.0 in 54.0 in	2072 lb 940 kg	£868 (1937)

Mercedes-Benz 540K Data File

Produced in limited numbers as the flagship models of the Stuttgart company's complex range, the supercharged Mercedes-Benz cars of the 1930s represented a dramatic combination of arrogant brute force cloaked in some of the most gorgeous coachwork ever created. Like the contemporary Mercedes 'Silver Arrows' racing cars, they were intended to promote the image of German technical superiority. The Mercedes *mit Kompressor* were designed as the ultimate fast touring cars of their day, though their performance was somewhat compromised by the massiveness of their construction. Of the series, the peak was represented by the 540K, launched in 1936 at the beginning of the autobahn era. But the concept of a supercharger that was only engaged at full throttle proved a technological dead-end and the line died out early into World War II.

Above: A 1936 500K Roadster, with the five-litre straight-eight; the styling was virtually identical to that offered on the 540K models.

Styling

Mercedes-Benz were remarkable in offering 'in-house' bodywork which was fully a match for the products of outside coachbuilders. The secret was the unerring skill of Hermann Ahrens who headed the Mercedes Sonderwagen (Special Cars) body shops at Sindelfingen. Originally built as a World War I aeroplane and aero-engine works, Sindelfingen had converted to coachbuilding to maintain employment when Germany was banned from building aircraft by the 1919 Versailles Treaty.

Concentrating on coachbuilt bodies for limited-production Mercedes-Benz chassis, Ahrens had an impeccable eye for shape and form. With total responsibility for both design and production in this exclusive 'works within a works', he pioneered the continuous wing line, with front and rear wings and running board forming a sweeping, sinuous curve. This was used to stunning effect on the supercharged Mercedes of the 1930s, particularly on the Special Roadsters. They were lower than the standard Cabriolets and the wing line deliberately more flamboyant, noticeably so on the rear wings, which swept down to a sharp point aft of the bumper line. One of the most successful styling features was the combination of having the imposing radiator set well back, actually behind the front axle line. That allowed the front wings to sweep in towards the centre in unbroken curves, the huge headlights being accommodated on a bar ahead of the radiator.

Below: The 'V'-shaped radiator, between broad wings, gave the impression of a ship's hull cutting through bow waves.

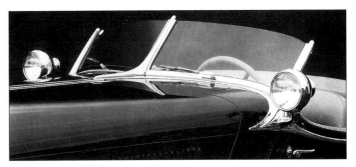

Above: In an era before curved glass, the split windscreen aided streamlining and, with the three raked pillars, looked very stylish.

Below: The interior was trimmed simply in fine veneers and hide, with clear instrumentation.

Above: Spare wheels were usually mounted in front wing recesses, or at the rear.

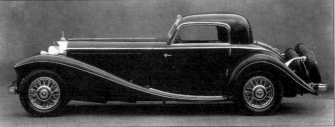

Above: A long bonnet and short hard top distinguished the Sport-Special two-door coupé model.

Below: A Berlin coachbuilder's Saoutchik-inspired roadster did not surpass Ahrens' own designs.

Above: The Autobahnkurier was a streamlined, supercharged coupé offering limousine comfort.

Below: A works-built blown Streamlined Special coupé, with an unusual sloping grille.

Chassis and running gear

When the 540K's direct ancestor, the 380K, was unveiled in 1938 it was its chassis that caused the most comment, being a considerable step forward from previous models. Like the small 170 family car, it had independent rear suspension with swing-axles and coil springs; that complemented a new front suspension system of double wishbones and coil springs. The 170 was renowned for its handling and roadholding, and the design of the 380K was even better; unfortunately that advantage was lost simply because the car was so heavy. That led to the adoption of first a five-litre, then a 5.4-litre engine to create the 500K and 540K respectively, and the great weight also meant that the steering was of necessity low-geared and that servo-assistance was needed for the drum brakes. The original 540K was intended to have de Dion rear suspension rather than swing-axles, but a lack of development time compelled Mercedes to retain the swing-axles although a de Dion system was later adopted by designers Sailer, Wagner and Hess for the new W125 Grand Prix car of 1937. The 540K chassis started as a ladder frame with box-section side members, but late in 1938 Mercedes introduced a revised model with oval-section chassis tubes similar to those used on the Grand Prix car.

The 540K had a four-speed transmission, with fourth gear being direct rather than overdriven as on the 380K and 500K. The gearbox was a semi-automatic in that it allowed clutchless gear changes between the top two gears. The gate was laid out as a normal three-speed; fourth was engaged somewhat clumsily by moving the lever right and then forward from third gear and releasing the throttle pedal. At the beginning of 1939, the final batch of 540Ks were fitted with five-speed 'autobahn' transmissions.

Below: The long straight-eight sat within massive chassis rails, flanked by the upright scuttle supports.

Below: The 540K chassis was very sturdy, with deep main members, but it and the bodies built on it were very heavy, which is why Mercedes continued to increase engine size and power.

Engine

Under the striking bodywork of even the most imposing 540K Special Roadster was a very conventional engine. It was a cast-iron monobloc straight-eight with just two valves per cylinder, operated in the traditional way by pushrods and rockers via a single block-mounted camshaft. That was in stark contrast to some previous Mercedes engines, which had been overhead-cams, and certainly to the likes of the early four-valves-per-cylinder Bentley engines. The substantial crankshaft was supported by nine main bearings and was strong enough to stand supercharging of up to 180 bhp (for limited periods).

The engine's most distinctive feature was its supercharger installation, derived from Mercedes World War I aero-engine design. The blower was only intended for occasional use, to boost output for rapid acceleration, and was engaged by a multiple clutch actuated by pressing the throttle hard down beyond its normal limit, much like kickdown on a modern automatic. Prolonged use of the supercharger increased top speed by around 15 mph but invited mechanical failure, even after Mercedes switched to racing-type sodium-filled exhaust valves with better heat dissipation.

Above: A side view of the 5.4-litre block: note the supercharger, carburettor, and inlet and exhaust manifolds on the same side of the engine.

Below: The independent rear suspension featured twin coil springs on each side, and half-axles secured by trailing arms.

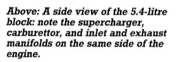

Below: The engine was mounted well behind the front wheels, helping the front/rear balance.

Above: The 540K straight-eight was an orthodox and massively engineered water-cooled design with two valves per cylinder, a block-mounted camshaft and pushrods. Logically, the twin ignition system of coil and magneto was mounted on the same side of the engine as the spark plugs.

Below left: Through the passenger seat can be seen the twin rear coil springs, used in conjunction with semi-trailing arms.

Below: The bulkhead helped reduce engine noise and heat reaching the passenger compartment; the straight-eight was, however, very smooth.

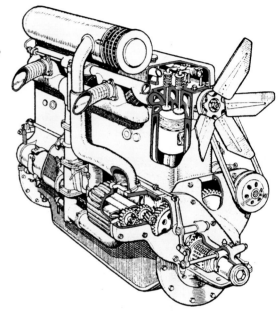

Below: The Mercedes-Benz supercharger revealed: note the inlet port, twin rotors, gear drive, control rod and, to the left, the updraught carburettor.

Right: This cutaway of the 540K monobloc straight-eight engine shows the gear drive to the supercharger from the front of the nine-bearing crankshaft. Note too the rod assembly which operated the supercharger clutch at the front of the shaft. Above, behind the fan, can be seen the vertical valve arrangement, the pushrod-operated rockers and the large air-filter box.

Below: The 540K was designed as a true prestige car, hence the broad wings, large headlamps and imposing upright radiator.

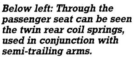

Above: The twin external exhausts were very characteristic of the model; under the bodywork they joined into one pipe.

Right: Note the sturdy twin wishbones and coil spring; on the other wheel can be seen one of the large finned brake drums, which were servo-assisted.

Above: At the front the girder-like chassis rails tapered into supports for the heavy wings and the sprung mountings for the chromed bumpers.

Morgan Plus 8

A 1930s design, built 60 years after its time, yet with enough V8 power to out-accelerate the most sophisticated supercars, the Morgan Plus 8 is a unique mix of old-fashioned romantic roadster and bone-shaking muscle car.

Above: This 1985 Plus 8 has the classic lines of a 1930s two-seat roadster. With its Rover V8 giving 0-60 mph in under seven seconds, the Morgan can initially out-accelerate far more exotic rivals, but at higher speeds the car is slowed by its lack of aerodynamics.

Where else but in a Plus 8 will you find supercar performance in a contemporary car that was launched in the mid-1930s and has been in continuous production ever since? If Darwin's theories were right, the Morgan roadster should have vanished long ago, along with the old wire-wheel MGs and Sunbeams; but whereas they adapted and became extinct, the Morgan refused to change and survived. The factory at Malvern Link, under the hills, founded in 1910 by H. F. S. Morgan, has hardly changed either, nor have the construction methods. Only the engines have been replaced as other cars came and went, and they have all

been bought-in proprietory units easily adapted to the basic chassis.

The family business has always maintained the view that if the product is good, and people want to buy it, why change it? In the early 1990s the company has a six-year waiting list of eager buyers, drivers who feel that the countless improvements in car design have also smoothed much of the pleasure out of motoring, and that if you have a car with real performance, you need to be able to feel it to be able to experience it. Which is where the Morgan Plus 8 gives all of its value, with breathtaking acceleration, an intimate sensation of the road surface, and more

wind in the hair than most heads can tolerate.

Morgan had been building three-wheelers for 25 years before venturing to add the extra wheel, and the first four-wheelers were rather sedate machines. The original 4/4, shown at the 1935 Motor Show, was an up-to-the-minute design, with an 1122-cc Coventry Climax four-cylinder engine under the classic two-seat roadster bodywork, with a narrow bonnet, cycle-type wings and a flat, sloping rear with recessed spare wheel. Development was slow, to say the least, and by 1950 the same car was powered by a 2.1-litre Standard engine, with a slightly lengthened wheelbase, hydraulic brakes and telescopic dampers. In those days the Morgan was already rather old-fashioned, but the customers were as eager as ever. Four years later, and amid much protest from Morgan enthusiasts, the old flat grille was revised and curved, and the headlamps faired into wings which joined the bonnet sides. In 1957 came the 100-bhp Triumph TR3 engine and in 1960 Morgan adopted a four-speed gearbox for the first time. Then, in 1967, when the founder's son, Peter Morgan, was in charge, Rover approached them with a view to taking over and thereby gaining itself a sporting image. Fortunately, Peter Morgan rejected the

Left: The Plus 8 can bring all the pleasures of top-down motoring on the open road, but its ride over less than smooth surfaces is brutally hard.

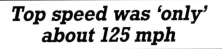

idea and instead asked Rover to supply the company with its alloy 3.5-litre V8, to replace the Triumph four-cylinder unit. Surprisingly, although Rover's overtures had been spurned, they agreed, and a legend was born.

It did not take Morgan's engineers long to widen and lengthen the ladder-frame chassis so that it could carry the 3528-cc engine, mated to the Moss four-speed gearbox. With all that extra power, it made sense to have disc brakes fitted at the front, along with servo-assistance (the latter was later dropped). As soon as it was launched the Plus 8 showed itself to be astonishingly quick, and ever more buyers came to inscribe their names on Morgan's waiting list.

Top speed was 'only' about 125 mph

Here was a truly unique car, pre-war in construction, design and styling, yet able to out-accelerate the E-type Jaguar, if not match its ultimate top speed. Aerodynamics, or the virtual lack of them, meant the top speed was 'only' about 125 mph. In those days its sibling, the Morgan Plus 4, had the 1600-cc Ford engine, and compared with that the Plus 8 offered 55 per cent more bhp, 60 per cent more torque, and yet weighed only three per cent more. And all for just £1,477 18s 6d, some £640 less than the cost of an E-type.

Since the late 1960s the world has changed much, but the Plus 8 is still with us. In 1972 the Rover four-speed gearbox replaced the cruder Moss type, and that was followed by Rover's excellent five-speed in 1976. In 1983 came Rover's

Vitesse engine, with the advantage of fuel injection and 200 bhp, and by the early 1990s the V8's displacement had been increased to 3947 cc, with catalytic converter and the capability to run on lead-free fuel. As a result, power went down marginally to 190 bhp, but torque rose to a massive 235 lb ft at 2,600 rpm, as you would expect from the larger engine.

A jolting, bumpy ride over uneven surfaces

The Morgan Plus 8 is still hand-built just like the pre-war roadsters, although there have been many detailed changes under the skin. The basic layout, however, remains, and the Plus 8 sits on a sturdy ladder-frame chassis with girder-like 'Z'-section longitudinal members with box-section cross-members. The rear axle is still a live unit and will doubtless always remain so, even when no other manufacturer is building one. Nevertheless there has been progress; the Plus 8 now comes with a limited-slip differential and telescopic dampers; the first Plus 8s still had lever-arm dampers at the rear. At the front the car has the system Morgan used on its first three-wheelers from 1909 – vertical sliding pillars with coil springs, but now accompanied by telescopic dampers. Its survival has proved very worthwhile, for it ensures that the front wheels are always vertical to the road – an excellent characteristic for modern tyres, which do not function so well when their camber is altered. One of the few advantages of the live rear axle is that it has that same characteristic.

Whereas the wheelbase of the original 4/4 was 92 inches, and then 96 inches for the Plus 4 of 1950, the Rover engine required only a further

two inches of wheelbase, while the track has been widened slightly over the years, to accommodate wider, low-profile tyres.

The bodywork has always been built in the time-honoured tradition derived from carriage construction, the steel panels laid over a carved ash frame and the dimensions of each car thus slightly different. It takes Morgan's craftsmen about two months to build each car, and the production maximum is only some 10 cars a week, even in the early 1990s. In standard form the panels are steel, although an aluminium bonnet and front wings are optional extras, as is a mohair hood.

On the road the Plus 8 offers the same back-to-basics feel that all Morgans have had, with a jolting bumpy ride over uneven surfaces, a tendency for the suspension to bottom occasionally (front-wheel travel is only 4.5 inches), along with wind noise, scuttle shake, rattles and other discomforts which most car manufacturers overcame decades ago. For many, however, the performance makes that irrelevant; its acceleration leaves Porsche turbos behind at anything up to 80 mph, the handling is exhilarating even in the dry, the sensation of speed tremendous, and the feel of the road transmitted through the steering wheel unrivalled, as is that wonderful view over the tapered, louvred bonnet, with the flowing wings topped with their side lights.

No matter that there is no luggage space to speak of, especially if the hood is stowed behind the seats. That only leaves the glovebox and your pockets, but Morgan owners learn to travel light; the main thing is to drive rather than to arrive. The wind-noise levels also mean that there is no point in such modern contrivances as radio-cassette players – instead you have the singing of that burbling V8, and the rushing sights and sounds of the world around.

Above: A Plus 8 of 1983, the first year that the car was offered with the fuel-injected 190-bhp Rover Vitesse engine.

Overleaf: One of the first Morgan Plus 8s, from 1968; note that the rear lamps, fuel caps and bumpers were later restyled.

The brute power of the V8 in a small car created a fast racer. Note the inflated hood; the top speed was higher by around 7 mph with the hood up.

Driving the Plus 8: ancient and modern

The Morgan Plus 8 offers an authentic taste of pre-war roadster motoring, but with performance which in the old days was confined to a few supercharged works racers.

Start the engine and there's a slightly uneven burble from the exhaust; slip into first, release the rather heavy clutch and the car simply leaps forward. The torque is astonishing, and progress through the gears very rapid indeed. At higher speeds the engine begins to sound a little harsh, but by then the world is rushing by at such speeds and the road transmitting so many sensations that you hardly notice; everything becomes a blur of noise and wind.

Front/rear balance is good and the Morgan can be thrown into corners with real zest, assuming the road is smooth; the Plus 8 has a bone-shaking ride and is easily thrown off line by bumps. The understeer is very manageable and any tendencies for the rear to slip out of line can be adroitly controlled with the throttle. In the wet, the car has to be driven more carefully, and the crude pre-war suspension also makes long, high-speed journeys advisable only for the hardened. In the dry, though, on curving country roads and lanes, the Plus 8 offers immense driving pleasure.

PERFORMANCE & SPECIFICATION COMPARISON	Engine	Displacement	Power	Torque (lb ft)	Max speed	0-60 mph	Length (in/mm)	Wheelbase (in/mm)	Track front/rear	Weight (lb/kg)	Price
Morgan Plus 8	V8, overhead-valve	3946 cc	190 bhp 4750 rpm	235 lb ft 2600 rpm	121 mph 195 km/h	6.1 sec	156.0 in 3962 mm	98.0 in 2489 mm	54.0 in 54.0 in	2059 lb 934 kg	£24,821 (1992)
Caterham Super Seven HPC	Inline-four, 16-valve, twin-cam	1998 cc	175 bhp 6000 rpm	155 lb ft 4800 rpm	126 mph 203 km/h	5.2 sec	133.5 in 3391 mm	87.8 in 2230 mm	48.8 in 52.2 in	1384 lb 628 kg	£18,255 (1992)
Ginetta G33	V8, overhead-valve	3946 cc	198 bhp 5280 rpm	220 lb ft 3500 rpm	137 mph 220 km/h	5.3 sec	150.9 in 3833 mm	87.6 in 2225 mm	54.4 in 54.6 in	1927 lb 874 kg	£20,470 (1992)
TVR V8S	V8, overhead-valve	3950 cc	240 bhp 5750 rpm	275 lb ft 4200 rpm	146 mph 235 km/h	5.2 sec	155.8 in 3957 mm	90.0 in 2286 mm	56.6 in 56.6 in	2249 lb 1020 kg	£23,595 (1992)
Westfield SEiGHT	V8, overhead-valve	3946 cc	273 bhp 6100 rpm	285 lb ft 4500 rpm	140 mph 225 km/h	4.3 sec	139.4 in 3541 mm	93.3 in 2370 mm	52.4 in 54.3 in	1521 lb 690 kg	£20,888 (1992)

Morgan Plus 8 Data File

The Morgan Plus 8 was introduced in 1968 and was basically the Morgan four-wheeler 4/4 of pre-war days (launched in 1936) fitted with Rover's 3.5-litre V8 engine. The car is a high-performance two-seat roadster, hand-made over a simple ladder-frame chassis and with the suspension little changed in 50-odd years. The first Plus 8s were fitted with the Moss four-speed gearbox, which was replaced by the Rover four-speed in 1972, and the five-speed in 1976. In 1983 the Plus 8 was offered with the Rover V8 in Vitesse tune, with electronic fuel injection and ignition. Disc brakes were fitted at the front, and rack-and-pinion steering appeared for the first time on a Morgan. By the early 1990s the Plus 8 had the 3.9-litre version of the V8, with fuel injection and a catalytic converter.

Above: A return to pre-war motoring. No modern car offers anything to compare with the view over the long bonnet, traditionally louvred.

Above: This 1990 Plus 8 was built in exactly the same way as the pre-war Morgans, with a separate chassis and an ash wooden frame under the bodywork.

Styling

The appearance of the current Morgan Plus 8 is little different from that of the 1930s Morgans, except for the lower bonnet line, integrated wings and sloping, curved grille introduced from 1954. It has survived so long because it looks exactly right.

At the front, the simple grille with vertical slats is surrounded by a plain cowling, with flowing wings on each side within which are faired-in headlamps and indicators; each wing is topped by a streamlined side light. The bonnet comprises two curved tapered panels with a central hinge, just 36 inches above the road, giving very little indication of the large V8 engine beneath.

The doors are front-hinged in the pre-war fashion, cut away to allow elbows to rest on them. Below these are equally traditional narrow running boards flowing from the front wings to

the rear. The rear wings, like those, are separate from the main bodywork and linked at the rear by the flat, sloping panel that hides the fuel tank and surrounds the recessed spare wheel. The rear lamps are set in horizontally-mounted chrome tubes, and the rear bumper, a simple horizontal bar without overriders, is very similar to that at the front.

The Morgan's styling dictates that the windscreen is a flat pane; the fascia below it is also flat to match, surmounted by a padded lip.

Despite being a styling exercise 60 years behind the times, the Morgan Plus 8 looks perfectly homogenous, well designed and unfussy, and in the early 1990s it was clear that, having resisted change for so long, it never would evolve in styling terms, and would be produced in exactly the same way into the 21st century.

Right: A modern alloy wheel, but mounted in the traditional way, on the roadster's petrol tank.

Below: The simple fascia has a large speedo and rev-counter with gauges in between.

Below: No modern assembly line in the paint shop at the Malvern works, where cars like the Plus 8 have been hand-built since 1910.

Below: Similar in style if not in power: an early 1930s Morgan three-wheeler with a Ford 933-cc engine (background), and a 1980s Plus 8 with a 3.5-litre Rover V8.

Chassis and running gear

The Morgan Plus 8 remains one of the very few cars built with a separate chassis and body; the chassis is a simple ladder frame with two longitudinal 'Z'-section girders, with the upper flanges pointing outwards and the lower ones inwards. That's mated to tubular and box-section cross-members, and while it is an extremely tough chassis, it is not particularly rigid; this is deliberate, to complement the suspension set-up in a way that was common pre-war.

A considerable amount of wood is used in the construction of the bodywork, with wooden floorboards below and behind the seats and a traditional ash frame to support the steel body panels. The frame comprises carved and jointed pieces of ash around and inside the doors and supporting the rear bodywork. The front wings and bonnet can be supplied in aluminium as optional

extras; otherwise they are steel. Virtually all of the assembly and finishing of a Morgan is still done by hand, each car taking between six and eight weeks to complete.

The layout is traditional, with the engine mounted between the front chassis members, the gearbox in unit, and a propeller shaft leading to the live rear axle located and sprung by underslung semi-elliptic leaf springs allied to telescopic dampers. At the front, the car retains a version of the sliding-pillar suspension that was used on the first-ever Morgan in 1909, with a coil spring around the tube and a telescopic damper mounted in front. The system ensures that the front wheels always remain vertical to the road, as do the rear wheels; this of course works favourably with modern tyres. Front brakes are 11-in discs, and on later Plus 8s there is no servo-assistance.

Below: The ladder-frame chassis is very basic, offering strength and durability but only a limited degree of torsional rigidity.

Right: Hard-sprung sliding-pillar front suspension does not give much wheel travel, hence the Morgan's notoriously harsh ride, but it does keep wheels vertical at all times, useful with modern tyres. Note how the front chassis rail is very deep, for strength.

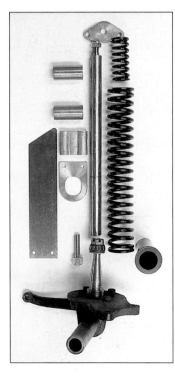

Left: Sliding-pillar components, with the stub-axle (bottom) and king-pin at centre, which fits inside it, through bronze bushes. There are two springs, the smaller rebound unit and the larger top spring, with a dust cover below it.

Right: The 72-piece, hand-crafted ash frame has always been made in the traditional coachbuilder's fashion, screwed and jointed together, providing a light, sturdy structure for the body panels. Labour-intensive methods like these were phased out by other manufacturers when mass-production of cars began.

Engine

The Rover V8 engine, like the roadster it powered, has a long history, being a discarded General Motors design for a compact model. It was abandoned because GM concluded that there was no justification for the extra expense of its all-alloy construction when the thin-wall cast-iron units they had pioneered were nearly as light, and far cheaper. The displacement of 3.5 litres was also rather small for the mainstream of US cars. After the design was acquired and modified by Rover, however, they used it in several models and it was first installed in the Morgan in 1968.

It was a classic 90-degree unit with a bore and stroke of 88.9 mm × 71.12 mm. Valve gear was via pushrods and rockers, with hydraulic tappets and a centrally-mounted camshaft. The compression ratio was a relatively high 10.5:1 and the 100-octane fuel was fed through twin SU HS6 carburettors. The result was an easy 160 bhp at 5,200 rpm with maximum torque of 210 lb ft at just

3,000 rpm. Fuel consumption in the Morgan was about 21 mpg.

From 1983, Rover's high-performance Vitesse engine was fitted, along with its Lucas fuel injection and electronic ignition. That produced 190 bhp at 5,280 rpm and 220 lb ft of torque at 4,000 rpm.

With the arrival of lead-free fuel and new emissions legislation, the engine received a catalytic converter, but by then its capacity had grown to 3946 cc, the bore having been increased to 94 mm. The compression ratio was reduced to 9.35:1 and although maximum power remained unchanged at 190 bhp, torque rose to 235 lb ft at 2,600 rpm.

The first Plus 8s were fitted with the Moss four-speed gearbox, with no synchromesh on first gear; that was replaced by Rover's four-speed all-synchromesh gearbox in 1972, and the five-speed in 1983. Top gear offers 27.6 mph per 1,000 rpm, and the torque is such that the car can be driven in top from very low speeds and cruise at very low revs.

Right: The cutaway reveals how the ash frame sits on the chassis and supports the body panels. Behind the rear axle can be seen the 12-gallon fuel tank; luggage space is behind the two seats.

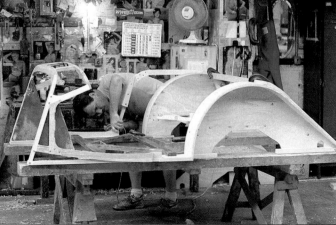

Left: Modern Morgan Plus 8s are fitted with the enlarged form of the original Rover 3.5-litre V8, displacing 3.9 litres. It's now fitted with Lucas electronic fuel injection (the plenum chamber of which can be seen above the cylinder heads) with mapped electronic ignition rather than the twin SUs and mechanical ignition of the original installation. Although its outright maximum power of 190 bhp is not enormous, the torque output of 235 lb ft is what guarantees the Morgan's fierce acceleration.

Below: Erecting the hood is quite simple, and when up it makes the car more aerodynamic; the side screens attach to the door tops.

Below: Triple two-speed wipers are required because of the width of the low, flat windscreen. The hood attaches to the screen top with studs.

Above: The Rover V8 engine can trace its origins back to a General Motors design of the early 1960s fitted to the compact Buick Skylark. It appeared in the Plus 8 in 1968. Block and heads are alloy, and valve actuation is by a central camshaft via pushrods, rockers and hydraulic tappets.

Above: The long V8 and five-speed Rover gearbox are a tight fit, low between the chassis rails. This demanded that the lever went directly into the gearbox. Note the engine air filter assembly tucked behind the cylinder heads.

Above right: Morgan's sliding-pillar suspension is a compact design; the gas-filled damper is mounted in front of the long coil spring. The steering track-rods are to the front of the wheel hubs.

Above: Owing to the narrow bonnet, the radiator is fairly deep. The curved grille dates from 1954.

Plymouth Superbird

Take a huge seven-litre V8 engine producing as much as 550 bhp, surround it with aerodynamic bodywork and give it wings to keep it on the track, and you have one of the most outrageous performance cars of all time.

Above: A Plymouth Superbird in its natural element, on a banked oval. The car was designed to run at speeds of up to 200 mph around the banked oval tracks used in American NASCAR stock car racing in 1970. That distinctive rear wing was a more effective aerodynamic device than the pointed nose.

I n the late 1960s race-goers the world over suddenly saw wings sprouting from hitherto smooth racing cars. Colin Chapman started it in Europe with the Lotus 49, but in this instance America had not really lagged behind. In 1969 the Dodge Charger Daytona had an aerodynamic device just as startling as the high-mounted and flimsy-looking wings on the Lotus. Inside the Chrysler empire the Charger then gave birth to the Plymouth Superbird, which reigned supreme in American stock car racing in 1970.

An outrageous-looking machine, the Plymouth Superbird could trace its evolution back to 1963. That was when Chrysler made the formal decision to engage Ford in NASCAR (National Association for Stock Car Auto Racing). Chrysler hadn't officially raced since early 1957 with the Chrysler 300C, a potent car which probably would have gone on to dominate the Grand National season had not the American carmakers adopted their famous 'ban' on factory-supported racing.

By 1963, things had changed and with Chrysler's new 426-cu in (seven-litre) hemi-head V8 engine, Plymouth and Dodge in theory had sufficient power to guarantee NASCAR supremacy. The 'Hemi' engine powered the first three cars at the 1964 Daytona 500, but that did not lead to the expected NASCAR dominance. Sheer power

was not enough. At the speeds reached round the stock car ovals (the fastest Ford qualified for the 1968 Daytona 500 at 189 mph, against the Dodge Charger's 185 mph) aerodynamics were vital. The Charger needed to be cleaned up . . . The air intake was minimised, the headlights were faired-in and a front spoiler was added, along with a sloping backlight from the Charger 500. The car was faster, but it was a struggle to keep the slippery shape on the ground at high speed. That was where the high rear wing came in, to keep the rear wheels on the track. The package worked, to the extent that the winged Charger was a significant 5 mph faster than before around the Daytona oval.

A struggle to keep it on the ground at high speed

To satisfy NASCAR regulations, 500 roadgoing Charger Daytonas had to be sold – that was no problem at all, and Chrysler almost immediately had orders for 1,200. The magazines soon had their hands on such a dramatic car, *Road Test* managing a standing quarter-mile in 14.5 seconds at a terminal speed of 96.15 mph. That was with the 440-cu in V8 allied to Tor-queFlite transmission. The racing cars used the

426 Hemi instead, with a close-ratio four-speed gearbox and Hurst shifter, and were immensely fast. At Talledega one set a new closed-lap speed record of 199.996 mph but, owing to tyre problems, did not end Ford's racing stranglehold; as one of its designers put it: "Firestone could not, and Goodyear would not, build a tyre that could stand up at 200 mph."

Nevertheless Chrysler did build a car to take over where the Charger Daytona left off, and that was the Plymouth Superbird. At first glance, to the uninitiated, the Plymouth looked identical to the Charger. Both being Chrysler products, naturally they were near enough the same under the skin, but there were differences – differences which in normal conditions were purely cosmetic but in the context of aerodynamic efficiency at 200 mph proved significant. The Plymouth's front bumpers were deeper and avoided the lift introduced by the shallower front of the Charger. The Superbird's air intake was different too, with a broad scoop under the nose. There were streamlined mouldings on the 'A' pillars and the side windows were flush-mounted.

All the aerodynamic addenda tacked onto the Plymouth made the Superbird over 17 inches longer than the standard Plymouth Road Runner and it was sold with three engine options, not that any of them were low-powered. The choice was

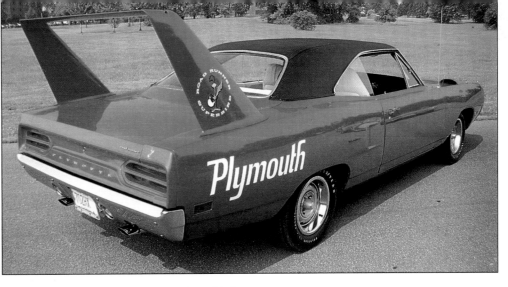

Above: It's hard to imagine that the Superbird's rear fins were not designed that way for dramatic effect, but Chrysler engineers would argue otherwise. The road runner symbol may look silly, but there was nothing frivolous about the Superbird's performance, with a 140 mph top speed and 0-60 mph acceleration in 6.0 seconds.

average speed of 149.601 mph, ahead of three Charger Daytonas and a lone Ford. Every other finisher was at the very least a lap behind. Plymouth did have the huge advantage of having Richard Petty involved in the Superbird project. If you look at the side of the racing Superbirds, you'll find the slogan 'Plymouth by Petty', and at that time Petty was the undoubted 'King' of NASCAR. His technical input helped to make the design ultra-competitive and had he not been injured for some of the season following a bad

accident at Darlington, he would have been NASCAR champion yet again.

Despite its success, it wasn't long before the high-winged Superbird disappeared from the racetracks. That was a reflection on NASCAR's determination to keep racing as equal as possible, to maintain the interest of the fans. The Association ruled that if Chrysler wanted to run the cars in 1971 they would have to reduce engine size by 25 per cent to compensate for the aerodynamic shape. "They were out to get us," said one project official, "and that just put everybody flat on their backs. Nevertheless one of the race people built a 305-cu in engine for the 1971 Daytona that gave away 100 cubic inches. During the race it led for seven laps and scared NASCAR no end!" That car crashed, however, and with it went the Superbird programme and the most exciting car ever to wear the Plymouth badge.

between the 440-cu in wedge-head V8 with either a four-barrel carburettor or three two-barrel carbs, and the engine the racers had – the 426-cu in Hemi. Standard equipment included heavy-duty suspension, front disc brakes and power steering. You had to pay extra, of course, for the added power and performance, but not a great deal by current standards. The list price was $4,298, some $1,300 more than for the standard Road Runner.

The road car was almost irrelevant to Chrysler (almost, but not quite; they did, after all, sell 1,971 of them). The Superbird was designed to win, and win it did, taking 21 Grand National wins in the 1970 season. That total included the most important victory of all, in the Daytona 500 where Pete Hamilton's Superbird cruised home at an

Above: Cornering one of the roadgoing Superbirds at speed produced a dramatic amount of roll, even though the suspension was far stiffer than on other American cars of the era.

Overleaf: This example lacks the small spoiler usually mounted under the nose (as on the car above), which was very effective in decreasing front-end lift.

This NASCAR action from the Charlotte track in 1970 shows a Superbird coming up on a Dodge Charger Daytona.

Driving the Superbird: *handle with care*

Although a good number of roadgoing Superbirds were built, the car was first and foremost a racing car, and it was only on the high-speed ovals that its aerodynamics were designed to work. The rear wing generates no downforce below around 80 mph and really only begins to work effectively past 125 mph or so. Effectively, that makes the Superbird a standard American muscle car of the old school, with all that that implies. Acceleration is dramatic; if you load the transmission in drive with your foot on the brake until wheelspin just starts, and then release the brake, the Superbird rockets away to return a standing quarter-mile figure of 13.9 seconds (with the 426 Hemi engine), having passed 100 mph in a mere 13.8 seconds.

Although contemporary road tests spoke of sensitive steering and very controllable handling, modern drivers would find the steering devoid of feel, and the roadholding limited indeed, although the far stiffer than normal suspension set-up helps considerably. Great care has to be taken in applying all the enormous torque so readily on tap in order to prevent the Superbird's rear from slewing violently sideways and to keep all the car's considerable length pointing straight ahead.

PERFORMANCE & SPECIFICATION COMPARISON	Engine	Displacement	Power	Torque (lb ft)	Max speed	0-60 mph	Length (in/mm)	Wheelbase (in/mm)	Track front/rear	Weight (lb/kg)	Price
Plymouth Superbird	V8, overhead-valve	6974 cc	425 bhp 5000 rpm	490 lb ft 4000 rpm	140 mph 225 km/h	6.0 sec	218.0 in 5537 mm	116.0 in 2946 mm	59.7 in 58.7 in	3841 lb 1742 kg	$5,342 (1969)
American Motors AMX	V8, overhead-valve	6391 cc	340 bhp 5100 rpm	430 lb ft 3600 rpm	130 mph 209 km/h	6.7 sec	180.0 in 4572 mm	97.0 in 2464 mm	58.5 in 58.5 in	3395 lb 1540 kg	$3,395 (1969)
Chevrolet Camaro Z28	V8, overhead-valve	5735 cc	245 bhp 5200 rpm	285 lb ft 4000 rpm	123 mph 198 km/h	6.7 sec	188.5 in 4788 mm	108.0 in 2743 mm	61.3 in 60.0 in	3689 lb 1673 kg	$4,855 (1972)
Chevrolet Corvette Stingray	V8, overhead-valve	5735 cc	350 bhp 5600 rpm	380 lb ft 3600 rpm	135 mph 217 km/h	5.5 sec	182.5 in 4636 mm	98.0 in 2489 mm	58.7 in 59.4 in	3390 lb 1538 kg	$5,269 (1969)
Shelby Mustang GT500	V8, overhead-valve	7016 cc	355 bhp 5400 rpm	420 lb ft 3200 rpm	128 mph 206 km/h	6.5 sec	186.6 in 4740 mm	108.0 in 2743 mm	58.0 in 58.0 in	3370 lb 1529 kg	$5,043 (1967)

Plymouth Superbird Data File

The Plymouth Superbird was created in an attempt by Chrysler (the company controlling Plymouth) to dominate NASCAR stock car racing in the late 1960s. NASCAR had (and to a large extent still has) the highest profile of all racing formulas in the USA and success on the oval tracks brought great rewards in terms of extra sales of the company's ordinary cars. With the American manufacturers' 'ban' on factory involvement in motorsport which ended Chrysler involvement in 1957, sales had declined and by the 1960s the decision was taken to get back on the oval circuits. The Superbird was preceded by the very similar-looking Dodge (another Chrysler division) Charger Daytona in 1969 but both were evolved from standard Chrysler products; the outrageous bodywork which greatly increased aerodynamic efficiency was grafted on to avoid expensive retooling for what were very limited-production runs. Although the object of the Superbird was to win in NASCAR, a street-legal roadgoing version was also built.

Above: The new nose section was made of glassfibre and required pop-up lights to be fitted.

Below: One reason for the high rear wing was to allow room for the boot lid to be opened.

Above: Despite its great length of over 18 feet, the Superbird was not even built on one of Chrysler's full-size chassis.

Styling and aerodynamics

The Plymouth Road Runner Superbird (to give it its full title) was a drastic adaptation of Chrysler's existing corporate 'B'-type body that was also the basis for the Dodge Charger. Although the Charger had appeared before the Plymouth, in similar winged style, the Plymouth was significantly different. The most obvious changes from the standard body was the addition of that long, pointed nose and the two rear fins supporting a high-mounted wing. There was also a small spoiler fitted under the nose to overcome front-end lift and to decrease the amount of air flowing under the car. Chrysler had other aerodynamic tricks up its sleeve even that far back; the front windscreen 'A' pillars, for example, had aerodynamic mouldings and the side windows were flush-mounted. Chrysler used the wind tunnel at Wichita State University to test the modifications and that told them they

could have made the package even more efficient, for example by having the rear wing operating directly over the back axle (but that would have meant a non-opening boot).

The vertical rear fins were not there just to hold the rear wing; they also served to decrease yaw, enhancing side stability.

The glassfibre front section added another 17 inches to the car's overall length, making it an enormous 218 inches long – at well over 18 feet it was two feet longer than a Jaguar XJ12, and remember that the car was an 'intermediate' rather than a 'full-size' car. American cars of that era featured a long overhang front and rear, and the extended nose accentuated that look, making the car look slightly ridiculous to modern eyes. But with its aerodynamic changes helping it achieve a top racetrack speed of nearly 200 mph, that view is misplaced.

Below: The Superbird's basic interior was typical of American design, although there was a full array of instruments.

Below: Two Chrysler divisions, Dodge and Plymouth, built aerodynamic NASCAR racers. The Dodge Charger Daytona came first, and although at first glance it looks identical to the Plymouth Superbird, there were significant differences – in the rake of the rear fins, for example. The Superbird was more aerodynamically efficient.

Above: The Plymouth Road Runner, from which the Superbird was developed, was introduced in 1968 with the 383-cu in V8 engine, as an intermediate two-door coupé.

Plymouth Road Runner

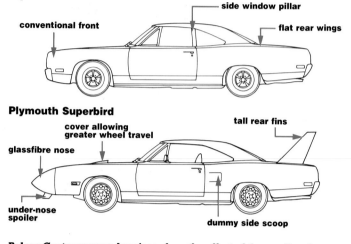

side window pillar

conventional front

flat rear wings

Plymouth Superbird

cover allowing greater wheel travel

tall rear fins

glassfibre nose

under-nose spoiler

dummy side scoop

Below: Contemporary drawings show the effect of the small under-nose spoiler and the high-mounted rear wing, both of which increased downforce at very high speeds.

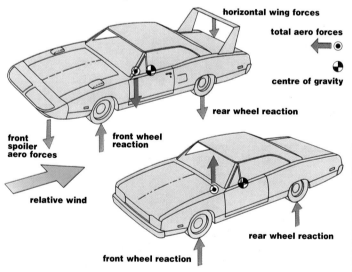

horizontal wing forces

total aero forces

centre of gravity

rear wheel reaction

front spoiler aero forces

front wheel reaction

relative wind

rear wheel reaction

front wheel reaction

Below: With side fins, the aerodynamic centre of pressure was moved closer to the centre of gravity, yaw was decreased (along with oversteer), and directional stability was greatly enhanced.

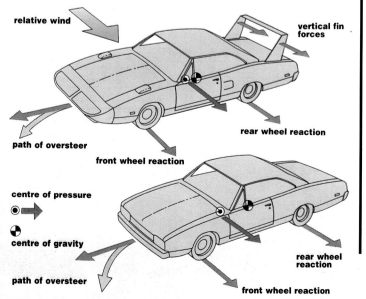

relative wind

vertical fin forces

rear wheel reaction

path of oversteer

front wheel reaction

centre of pressure

centre of gravity

rear wheel reaction

path of oversteer

front wheel reaction

Engine

The racing Superbird had the great advantage of being powered by Chrysler's superb 'Hemi'. Hemi was shorthand for its hemispherical combustion chambers, Chrysler following a pattern more commonly found on high-performance European engines. The advantage of the hemi-head was that it allowed the largest possible valve area; the disadvantage was that it was far more complex to build, in that the valves had to be angled rather than inline. The normal way to operate such valves was by twin overhead camshafts, but Chrysler preserved the usual American V8 practice of using just one camshaft, mounted in the depths of the 'V' and operating the valves by pushrods. This did require the exhaust-valve pushrods and rockers to work at strange angles, but the result was very successful.

Another way in which the Hemi differed from European performance engines was that it was made of cast-iron rather than light alloy.

The engine could trace its roots back to the FireDome unit of the early 1950s, which made its performance even more remarkable. In its NASCAR form it displaced seven litres (6974 cc) with virtually 'square' dimensions of a bore and stroke of 95 mm × 95.25 mm and could rev to 7,200 rpm, by which time it was producing an excellent 550 bhp. The roadgoing street version of the Hemi was claimed to produce as much as 425 bhp and even though that was measured according to the generous SAE gross reckoning then used by the American industry, it would still be a lot of power under the more stringent modern net DIN rating.

The Hemi was only an option on the roadgoing Superbird, which came with a 440-cu in V8 with wedge-shaped combustion chambers as standard; a six-barrel 440 was another choice.

Above: A huge air cleaner cover masked the multiple carburettors needed to fuel the 426-cu in (seven-litre) Hemi engine which, although large, was almost lost in the Superbird's vast engine bay.

Right: The cutaway shows how Chrysler achieved a hemi-head design, with pushrods operating inclined valves on either side of the combustion chambers from one central camshaft.

Below: The height of the rear wing meant it operated in 'cleaner', less disturbed, airflow.

Above: The Chrysler Hemi was in some ways typical of American V8 design in having a cast-iron block and heads and pushrod overhead valve gear. Its large displacement guaranteed enormous torque along with great power – as much as 550 bhp in racing trim. Access was more than adequate despite the engine's size, although reliability was so good that there was little need for constant attention to the engine.

Below: With the Superbird, Chrysler made some attempt at producing individual sports seats but there was very little to hold the driver and front passenger securely in place.

Left: The Superbird's rear suspension was very simple, with a live axle on underslung semi-elliptic leaf springs. The rear brakes were drums, rather than discs as at the front.

Right: This Chrysler publicity shot shows an array of Superbirds filling a banked oval as far as the eye can see. Almost 2,000 examples of the winged wonder were produced, the vast majority for road use rather than racing.

Porsche 911 Turbo

Porsche's 911 Turbo was an unruly interloper among the supercar elite – stunningly quick, superbly engineered, but bad-mannered due to its anachronistic rear-engined layout. For 1991 it grew faster still, but more sophisticated too.

Above: Like the latest model, the earlier Porsche 911 Turbo looks purposeful in profile, due in no small part to the large tail-mounted wing breaking up what would otherwise be a clean shape, differing only in detail from that of the original 911 of 1964.

D r Ernst Fuhrmann's original prediction in the early 1970s that it would be difficult to sell 500 911 Turbos (type 930) showed he was a better engineer than corporate strategist and was soon refuted in the marketplace.

Porsche needed to manufacture 500 of the Turbos during 1975 in order to race the type 934 and 935 derivatives the following year, but so rapturous was the public response that 1,300 were sold in the first 24 months! Demand has continued unabated, and some 15,000 of them will have been made in Zuffenhausen by the end of 1991.

Porsche's engineers wanted to offer the Turbo as a spartan, lightweight road-racer, a successor to the Carrera RSR 3.0, but Dr Fuhrmann reasoned that the customers, wealthy as they must be, would demand a luxury model. The Turbo was offered with leather upholstery, electric windows and air conditioning at an initial price of DM67,850 – nearly double the price of a 2.7-litre 911.

Porsche's goal was to dominate the World Championship for Manufacturers, the so-called 'silhouette formula' which came into being in 1976. The Group 5 racing car development, the 935, won the first title in 1976 after a tough battle with BMW, then dominated the series over the next three years.

The 935's crowning glory was to win the Le Mans 24 Hours in 1979, the Kremer K3-prepared car being the first production-derived car to win the classic for many a year, and the last. With equal ease the Group 4 derivative, the 934, so dominated the Grand Touring class that the European series was abandoned by the FIA at the end of 1978, and has never been revived.

Porsche's Turbo model has a platinum-plated pedigree, but what sort of car is it? Curiously old-fashioned in some ways, it's almost the antithesis of such modern rivals as the Ferrari Testarossa, the Lamborghini Diablo and even the Chevrolet Corvette ZR-1.

The German contender can never shake off the fact that the basic design was created over 25 years ago, even though a modernisation was carried out in 1988 and the latest, fastest, version appeared in 1991. Even the current model is unfashionably narrow inside the cabin, the windscreen is more upright than is usual nowadays, and the once-handsome dashboard is now a mess of switches and knobs that need to be learned, as a newly-blind person learns to read braille.

That's the first reaction, and it's a turn-off to some people with more than £70,000 to spend. But patience is rewarded. Just hear the solid 'thump' as the doors are closed. Just smell the leather upholstery . . . just flick the gear lever around, to appreciate what is now one of the most precise shifts in the sports car industry.

The new chassis, a modification of the greatly developed chassis used on the 911 Carrera 2, offers some benefits that aren't noticed straightaway. Extra space was afforded to move the 13-litre dry-sump oil tank forward, alongside the gearbox, and that released space for a fully-efficient exhaust system with three-way catalytic emission controls.

Significantly faster than before

The Turbo's weight rose, inevitably, by 10 per cent to 3,216 lb but this was offset by a gain of 20 horsepower, to 320 bhp. In the emission-controlled markets, however – most of the world, nowadays – the gain is greater, up to 315 from a previous 285 bhp, and the Turbo is significantly faster than before.

Polyurethane front and rear body sections improve the Turbo's aerodynamics and promote the 'family' look, in common with the 928 S4 and the four-cylinder 968, and the wheel diameter

Left: At the front, the latest 911 Turbo's elegantly remodelled looks give it a 'family' resemblance to other recent Porsches, including the mighty 959. The deep, body-colour bumper with neatly integrated wrap-around side/turn lights produces much purer lines than those of the old-style Turbo.

has now crept up to 17 inches, with the fitting of classic-looking forged-alloy rims shod with uni-directional, ultra-low-profile tyres.

Initially, the engine is a disappointment. The noise level is extremely low, the famous flat-six being partially encapsulated, then finally muffled by heavy silencing and an efficient, all-metal catalyser. Nor does the engine feel very flexible below 3,000 rpm, despite the promise of the written specification.

The brakes are simply astonishing . . .

Where conditions allow a full-throttle exercise, it's fascinating to see how quickly the white needle flicks around the face of the tachometer, transforming this luxurious cruiser into a lusty thoroughbred that wouldn't be disgraced if let loose on a racetrack.

When a four-speed gearbox was all that customers could have, it was offered as a virtue – so much torque, you see, you don't need to change gear very often . . . The introduction of the five-speed transmission can now be judged as an unmitigated blessing, closing up the spread of ratios and enhancing the sporting nature of the Turbo.

Power steering and power brakes would have been greeted as an abomination two decades ago, but so refined are the systems that

they suit the nature of the Turbo perfectly. The steering is extremely responsive and well-weighted, by no means featherweight, while the ABS-assisted, Brembo-calipered brakes are simply astonishing for their sheer power. The wide wheels and tyres offer levels of adhesion far beyond the normal limits on public highways, but the high bump-thump factor gives unwelcome harshness at low speeds.

That's easier to come to terms with now, as the 911 Turbo's other traditional faults have been smoothed away and many almost eliminated. The ergonomics may be as poor as always but the performance, which is the heart of the 911 Turbo, is far easier and safer to exploit, to the extent that the Turbo is now a far more usable supercar than some of its more exotic but more temperamental Italian rivals.

Above: The new back end has smoother, Carrera 2/4-style lines, too – apart from the wing.

Below: On the 1991-model Turbo, Porsche have tamed the rear-engined and naturally oversteering chassis' habit of brutal rear-end breakaway – so much so that the car now understeers gently until severely provoked, and lets go more controllably even then.

Above: Thanks to the 911's rearward weight bias, traction has always been a strongpoint, so the Turbo is more at home among ice and snow than most supercars. Even in its new, more civilised guise, however, with 320 bhp on tap it demands respect on slippery surfaces. On a dry road, let alone an icy one, lifting off the power abruptly will still result in lurid, tail-sliding oversteer, albeit not so uncatchably sudden as was once the case.

Driving the Turbo: *fast; less furious*

Silken the new 911 Turbo may be, but accelerating fiercely with the windows down confirms that it makes all the right noises! Snapping the throttle open is to command the launch of the car towards a far horizon in one breathtaking surge. First gear is good for 44 mph, reached in a mere 2.5 seconds, and second gear can see 76 mph. Sixty mph, the magic figure for road-testers, is reached in just 4.7 seconds, 100 mph in 11.4 seconds and 125 mph in 18 seconds. A standing quarter-mile can be accomplished without undue drama in just over 13 seconds.

In the right conditions, the determined driver will be able to see 170 mph on the speedo and he will not have to wait that long . . . Nor will he be worried about the car's hitherto fearsome behaviour. The latest revisions to the long-established design have produced a car that actually understeers at all the speeds most drivers use and has to be provoked into the oversteer that used to hang like a sword over 911 Turbo drivers. But if you still feel such performance is too much, there is the security of ABS-controlled Brembo disc brakes which bring you to a standstill from 60 mph in under three seconds and in a space of just 36 yards.

PERFORMANCE & SPECIFICATION COMPARISON	Engine	Displacement	Power	Torque (lb ft)	Max speed	0-60 mph	Length (in/mm)	Wheelbase (in/mm)	Track front/rear	Weight total (lb/kg)	Price
Porsche 911 Turbo	Flat-six, overhead-cam, turbo	3299 cc	320 bhp 5750 rpm	332 lb ft 4500 rpm	167 mph 269 km/h	4.7 sec	167.3 in 4249 mm	89.4 in 2271 mm	56.5 in 58.8 in	3216 lb 1459 kg	£74,580 (1991)
Chevrolet Corvette ZR-1	V8, quad-cam, 32-valve	5727 cc	375 bhp 5800 rpm	370 lb ft 4800 rpm	171 mph 275 km/h	5.6 sec	178.5 in 4534 mm	96.2 in 2443 mm	60.0 in 62.0 in	3519 lb 1596 kg	£58,995 (1990)
Ferrari Testarossa	Flat-12, quad-cam, 48-valve	4942 cc	390 bhp 6300 rpm	362 lb ft 4500 rpm	171 mph 275 km/h	5.2 sec	176.6 in 4485 mm	100.4 in 2550 mm	59.8 in 65.4 in	3675 lb 1667 kg	£115,500 (1991)
Honda NSX	V6, quad-cam, 24-valve	2977 cc	274 bhp 7000 rpm	210 lb ft 5300 rpm	162 mph 261 km/h	5.2 sec	173.4 in 4405 mm	99.6 in 2530 mm	59.4 in 60.2 in	3020 lb 1370 kg	£55,000 (1991)
Mercedes 500 SL	V8, quad-cam, 32-valve	4973 cc	326 bhp 5500 rpm	332 lb ft 4000 rpm	157 mph 253 km/h	5.9 sec	176.0 in 4470 mm	99.0 in 2515 mm	60.4 in 60.0 in	4167 lb 1890 kg	£70,090 (1991)

Porsche 911 Turbo Data File

Porsche's 356 model was a truly difficult act to follow. The company's reputation was founded on the four-cylinder sports car line, originally based on the Volkswagen Beetle (itself designed pre-war by Professor Porsche, assisted by his son 'Ferry'), although the VW ancestry was quickly despatched.

Dr Ferry Porsche commissioned the 356 replacement, and the earliest drawings by his son Ferdinand ('Butzi') date back to 1956. The type 7, as it was known at Zuffenhausen, would continue to offer 2+2 seating and a very sporting demeanour, but it would be quicker, quieter and more sophisticated.

Its heart would be a brand-new six-cylinder engine, air-cooled and with dry-sump lubrication. As before, the cylinders would be horizontally opposed, to keep the centre of gravity as low as possible.

The 901 was first seen at the Paris Motor Show in October 1963, but Peugeot claimed a right to the zero middle digits and the car went into production in September 1964 as the Porsche 911. Its first competition outing was at the Monte Carlo Rally in January 1965, when Herbert Linge and Peter Falk won the Grand Touring category and finished in fifth place overall.

Although the 911 was first and foremost a road car, it was homologated both as a GT car and as a Touring car (911T) and often won both categories in the same event in the 1960s. It was as much at home in rallies as on the tracks, as three Monte Carlo Rally successes show.

The significant developments in the 911's evolution were the introduction of the 911S (1966), the 2.2-litre engine (1969), the 2.4-litre engine (1971), the 2.7 Carrera RS (1972), the Carrera 3.0 and the Turbo (1974), the Turbo 3.3 (1977), the 911 Cabriolet (1982), the Carrera 3 (1983), the Carrera 4 (1988) and the Carrera 2 (1989).

Above: There's no separate air dam in the new front design (seen already on the Carrera 4 and 2); the bumper simply extends downwards into an integral spoiler/apron with air intakes.

Below: The new Carrera 2/4-style Turbo (lower drawing) looks much less fussy than the 1974 Carrera RSR that set the original trend.

Above: 911 Turbo styling changed little from the earliest 1970s cars to the last, prior to the complete updating in late 1990.

Styling

Ferdinand Alexander 'Butzi' Porsche is not rated as one of the world's top automotive stylists, but his 911 design has stood the test of time. The greatest compliment of all was paid by the Porsche company in 1988 when the 911 Carrera 4 model was introduced, a quarter of a century after the 901 made its debut at Frankfurt. Given the chance to change everything, Porsche chose to keep the style virtually unchanged. "Our customers would not have forgiven us if we made major changes," said Porsche's chairman of the time, Heinz Branitzki.

The width has increased, of course, with the fitment of modern tyres. The original 911 model ran on 4.5-in rims and 165-section tyres, and had an overall width of 63.4 inches. The

modern Turbo has 7-in wide rims at the front, 9-in at the rear, on 205- and 255-section tyres. Not surprisingly, the overall width of the 911 'flagship' model has increased to 69.8 inches.

Superficially the cars of 1964 and 1991 are very similar in appearance, although very few parts would be interchangeable. Above the waist, though, the cars are almost identical, save for the specification of the glass, and the fixing of swivelling quarter-lights. Optional for many years, the 'black look' (i.e., no chrome or brightwork) is now de rigueur.

Below: Latest and previous-pattern 911 Turbo noses together show the change in the frontal styling.

Below: Under that bulging rear arch lurks a 255/40 ZR17 tyre.

Above: The wing houses the intercooler, hence the vents.

Below: Inside the 911 Turbo, fittings and trim are of excellent quality, but control and instrument ergonomics are still poor.

Chassis

Until recently, the 911 models have had a reputation for difficult handling. As fast as Porsche's engineers wrung improvements out of the chassis, other cars came along to set new standards, often at a fraction of the cost.

The location of the six-cylinder engine, overhung behind the rear wheels, continued Porsche's pre-war philosophy and had some advantages, for instance in traction, but it was always a battle to make the car vice-free and safe for less experienced drivers. The original 911 was so tricky that the designers even resorted to putting lead in the front body recesses, to improve weight distribution.

Extending the wheelbase by 57 mm in 1968 was a significant development, while Pirelli's famous P7 tyre was developed specifically for the 911 Turbo model. It was unavailable for the first few months of Turbo production in 1975 and the early

versions, on rounded Cinturato tyres, were decidedly difficult to handle.

The original philosophy of long suspension travel and narrow tyres as a means of controlling camber change took a long time to die, and the Cinturato-equipped Turbo was probably the last really wild Porsche.

A further increase in wheelbase, with the 3.3-litre model in 1977, made a minor contribution to handling improvement, although the main purpose was to introduce a new, quieter, clutch disc centre, and to allow for the extra weight of the intercooler.

There matters rested until the current Turbo (type 964) was introduced in 1991. It is based on the Carrera 2 chassis platform, which has very different suspension, using MacPherson struts with coil springs at the front and a much more sophisticated semi-trailing-arm design at the rear.

Below: A 911 body assembly makes its way through the paint shop at the Stuttgart factory; Porsche build-quality is second to none.

Left: Stability under cornering load-reversal is enhanced by an uprated version of the Carrera 2 rear suspension, using 'toe-correcting' semi-trailing arms to give a touch of passive rear-wheel steering.

Below: Early Turbos had to have a four-speed gearbox to handle the power, but Porsche now fit a five-speed box that's more than tough enough.

Engine

With a rating of 320 bhp (235 kW) from 3299 cc, Porsche's Turbo engine is by no means highly-stressed. It is, however, a supremely practical power unit which delivers a huge chunk of power smoothly from 3,000 rpm to 6,500 rpm, guaranteeing maximum overtaking capability with the minimum of fuss.

Porsche's six-cylinder 'boxer' engine has proved to be the most versatile power unit of modern times. In the space of 27 years it has been developed from two litres and 130 bhp to 3.6 litres with double the original power, 260 bhp, in the Carrera 2 and 4 models, without the benefit of turbocharging.

It has powered an airship, and is fully certificated to power light aircraft. With turbochargers, the flat-six has yielded more than 800 bhp and won countless championships around the world, most significantly 10 class victories at Le Mans.

The technology of turbocharging was learned by Porsche's Weissach engineers in CanAm racing, with the flat-12 917-10 and 917-30 sports car

engines, and it was one inevitable step from there to the application of turbo techniques to passenger cars.

The introduction of the Porsche 911 Turbo (type 930) caused a minor sensation at the Paris Motor Show in October 1974. A single KKK turbocharger boosted the power of the three-litre engine to 260 bhp, despite a lowered compression ratio of 6.5:1, and the car was brutally fast despite the fitment of a four-speed gearbox (the torque figure of 253 lb ft at 4,000 rpm was simply too much for the 911's five-speed transmission).

Three years later, in the autumn of 1977 (for the 1978 model), the engine capacity was increased to 3.3 litres and the power to 300 bhp, while the torque figure rose to 304 lb ft. The cylinder bore was increased from 95 to 97 mm and the stroke from 70.4 to 74.4 mm, for a capacity of 3299 cc.

The addition of an intercooler to the specification, underneath the 'whale-tail' wing on the engine cover, cooled the charged air and improved thermal efficiency and the compression ratio was increased to 7.0:1.

There were no other significant changes until the current version, based on the Carrera 2 chassis, was introduced in 1991.

Left: On the 911 Turbo production line, meticulous final assembly of the light-alloy, air-cooled 3.3-litre flat-six is done by hand.

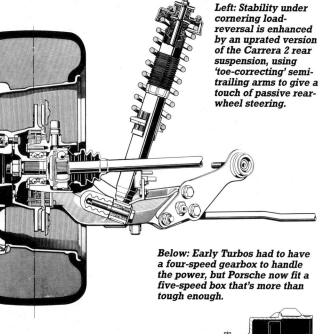

Above: For many years 911s used struts with torsion-bar front springs. Nowadays, you find conventional coil-spring MacPherson struts, with lower wishbones, a substantial anti-roll bar and negative-offset geometry. As ever, the result is firm springing and high roll stiffness.

Above: The negative-scrub-radius geometry combines with a new, power-assisted steering rack to damp out the excessive road-surface feedback that was a minor flaw of previous 911s. The power assistance enables the steering ratio to be kept high without the wide, 205/50-section front tyres now fitte, making it excessively heavy, and still gives good sensitivity.

Below: Sophistications on the latest Turbo engine even include a separate catalytic converter and silencer for the turbocharger wastegate – this means that excess gas need not be dumped into the exhaust flow upstream of the main converter, so avoiding any additional back-pressure which would cause a power loss. The single KKK turbocharger has a maximum boost of 0.7 bar, and its revised impeller geometry slightly improves response at low engine speeds. The engine, which also has a more massive flywheel to improve driveline refinement, now produces 320 bhp at 5,750 rpm and 332 lb ft of torque at 4,500 rpm.

Above: Porsche have not seen fit to turbocharge the larger-capacity, 3.6-litre flat-six now used in their Carrera 4 and Carrera 2 models. For the current Turbo they use, instead, a 'third-generation' 3.3-litre version of the familiar air-cooled unit, with revised intake passages and fuel injection, a larger charge intercooler (the box on the top) and three-way catalytic converters.

Below: Unlike the Carrera 2 and 4, the Turbo does not have a retractable rear spoiler, automatically raised as speed increases. Its big, fixed 'whale-tail' creates more drag but works effectively to minimise lift, and its base houses the intercooler.

Above: The inner mountings of the rear suspension's semi-trailing arms permit a small degree of passive rear-wheel steering under changing loads.

Porsche 928

The appearance of the bulbous, frog-eyed 928 was a shock to enthusiasts waiting to see the 911's successor in 1977 – but the V8 front-engined grand tourer has since proved a distinctive, desirable member of the Porsche family.

Above and inset: Die-hard devotees of the air-cooled, rear-engined Porsches welcomed neither the 928's front-engine/rear-gearbox layout nor its uncompromisingly different looks – but now it's just as representative as any 911 of the best the famous Stuttgart marque can offer.

hen Porsche introduced the 928, early in 1977, they weren't just introducing a car that was new from the ground up; they weren't just introducing a new and different look into the Porsche range; they were introducing a whole new philosophy.

In October 1971, Porsche's managing director, Dr Ernst Fuhrmann, gave the go-ahead for an all-new GT car, with a front-mounted, water-cooled V8 and a rear gearbox (manual or automatic) to improve weight distribution. He had rejected the idea of a mid-engined car, mainly on the grounds that it would be difficult to provide adequate occasional seating or proper luggage space; Porsche had learned with the 914 family that that hurt sales. He stopped short of commissioning a full four-seater, because Porsche built sports cars, not saloons. Nevertheless, the new model would be the biggest car that Porsche had built, and would offer 2 + 2 accommodation at least in line with that offered by the 911. It would

become Porsche Project 928.

By early November the layout of front engine and rear gearbox joined by a torque tube was confirmed and development started. Initially, the engine was to have been very over-square, with a capacity of almost exactly five litres, single camshafts, hydraulic tappets for low maintenance with good refinement, and a target of around 300 bhp. A wheelbase of 98.5 inches (some nine inches longer than a 911's) was specified, and target values for the length, width and height were fixed. It was expected that the car would use variants of double-wishbone suspension front and rear.

The torque-tube layout presented problems. Coming directly from the engine, the long propeller shaft turned at engine speed, not at the much lower gearbox output speed as it would in a more conventional layout; that created vibration and noise problems. As well as bench-testing, Porsche built their 928 torque tube and an interim rear transaxle from a 908 race car into an

otherwise standard Mercedes 350 SL, to test it in action. By mid-1973 Porsche were happy that the layout needed only detail-finishing.

Work had continued on the engine, transaxle and floorpan, each with their own problems. Major parameters for the all-aluminium engine were that it should be light and as shallow as possible, to allow a low and aerodynamically-effective nose. It must be efficient, clean, and require minimal maintenance.

A brilliant new multi-link back axle

The five-speed manual transaxle and a three-speed Daimler-Benz automatic with torque converter were finalised, and several versions of the Mercedes, Opel and Audi test-rig cars were built to test driveline elements and floorpan. Late in 1973 a virtually complete 928 lower half was

928 was unveiled at Geneva in March 1977. Popular reaction could fairly be described as 'mixed', with inevitable dissension from the air-cooled, rear-engined purists and plenty of criticism of the broad-shouldered style and open-headlamp details, but the press were impressed enough to vote the 928 their International Car of The Year.

A refined grand tourer with superb handling

It was in full production soon after its launch, selling well and generally much praised as a refined grand tourer with superb handling; but with 'only' 240 bhp it wasn't quite as quick as some people expected of a Porsche flagship and there were odd grumbles about road noise. In 1979, Porsche introduced what many thought the 928 should have been in the first place, the 928S. While the base 928 was mildly revised with higher compression, and ignition and injection changes, to be more flexible and less thirsty, the S was given a new engine of 4.7 litres and a full 300 bhp, plus appropriately better brakes.

In mid-1982 the ordinary 928 was discontinued and the S gained Bosch LH-Jetronic injection, to become more powerful again, at 310 bhp, and still faster. A four-speed Daimler-Benz automatic replaced the original three-speed for the 70 per cent of customers who took the option, 'second-generation' ABS was standardised, and the car became known as the S2. Nominally, there is no such thing as an S3, but that is how Porsche regard the heavily revised model introduced first for the US market early in 1985. It had reached a full five litres and gained twin-cam heads and four valves per cylinder, which even with emissions equipment and automatic transmission made the US car livelier.

In mid-1986, the four-valve, twin-cam heads, and the catalysts, were transferred to European models, with further improvements to produce 320 bhp for all markets. With subtly revised styling, including a new tail spoiler, plus other drag-reducing features, the car became the 928 S4, and recently the 330-bhp manual-only GT was added. Porsche intend finally to introduce a true four-seater model but the 928 isn't quite dead, because for 1992 there will be a 5.4-litre, 340-bhp version, with further slight styling changes. It will have a top speed of over 170 mph and carry the tag 928 GTS. Porsche say it will be the last 928, but then once upon a time the 928 was going to replace the 911 . . .

built into a widened Audi coupé shell for further testing, including endurance runs in Algeria, but at much the same time the project was threatened by the start of the Arab-Israeli war and the spectre of the 'energy crisis'. With Porsche sales already hit, another big-engined two-seater sports car suddenly seemed a liability. Less than two years after Project 928 started, it almost ended, as Porsche approved the continuation of a reduced development programme but held back the production go-ahead in the hope that things would improve.

When they did, contingency plans for four-seater or 911-engined 928s were scrapped, and in November 1974 the 928 in original form was given the restart, the major concession being a reduction in capacity to 4.5 litres. Having rejected other layouts (including torsion bars), Porsche had given the car a brilliant new multi-link, coil-sprung back-axle layout, in the interests of minimising lift-off oversteer by creating a small degree of controlled geometry changes, while still allowing acceptably comfortable bushing. Porsche called it the 'Weissach' axle, after the company research & development centre where it was developed.

The thoroughly refined chassis and running gear were clothed in the softly rounded body created by Tony Lapine's styling team and the

Above: As soon as it fell into the hands of press road-testers, the 928's superb balance and sure-footedness were acclaimed.

Overleaf: Its swivelling but always exposed headlamps (like those of Lamborghini's Miura a few years earlier) were a distinctive styling detail.

As well as a more powerful engine, the S4 had a larger, wing-type rear spoiler.

Driving the 928: *smooth and powerful*

The 928 is a big, wide car – and feels it. Control and instrument layout are superb, and much less haphazard than in a 911, and the 928 has a strong character of its own. The V8 sounds and feels magnificent, silky-smooth and flexible, with masses of power. The gear change can be notchy but the ratios are near-ideal, to offer (in the latest GT) around 46, 69, 96 and nearly 130 mph in the first four gears and a tested maximum of 165 mph. The 928 is heavy, but acceleration is hardly less than supercar-quick, with 0-60 mph in 5.6 seconds and 0-100 in just under 13.5, plus a superb balance between mid-range punch and long-legged cruising ability.

And, for all the comfort, this is a car which loves being driven hard on challenging roads. On 'ordinary' models, the ride is quite soft but brilliantly controlled and with little body roll, and the benefits of the Weissach axle are clearly felt in the amount of provocation it takes to make the 928 do anything wayward, even with all that power. The brakes, complete with ABS, are totally reassuring, and the aerodynamic stability, even beyond 160 mph, is outstanding. All in all, the 928 is among the most complete of supercars.

PERFORMANCE & SPECIFICATION COMPARISON	Engine	Displacement	Power	Torque (lb ft)	Max speed	0-60 mph	Length (in/mm)	Wheelbase (in/mm)	Track front/rear	Weight (lb/kg)	Price
Porsche 928 GT	V8, quad-cam, 32-valve	4957 cc	330 bhp 6200 rpm	317 lb ft 4100 rpm	165 mph 266 km/h	5.6 sec	177.9 in 4518 mm	98.1 in 2492 mm	61.1 in 60.9 in	3448 lb 1564 kg	£65,898 (1991)
BMW 850i	V12, overhead-cam	4988 cc	300 bhp 5200 rpm	332 lb ft 4100 rpm	161 mph 259 km/h	7.2 sec	188.2 in 4780 mm	105.7 in 2684 mm	61.2 in 61.4 in	4149 lb 1882 kg	£61,950 (1991)
Ferrari Mondial t	V8, quad-cam, 32-valve	3405 cc	300 bhp 7200 rpm	238 lb ft 4200 rpm	154 mph 248 km/h	5.6 sec	180.3 in 4580 mm	104.3 in 2649 mm	58.9 in 59.7 in	3560 lb 1615 kg	£69,310 (1991)
Jaguar XJR-S	V12, overhead-cam	5993 cc	318 bhp 5250 rpm	362 lb ft 3750 rpm	157 mph 253 km/h	7.0 sec	187.6 in 4765 mm	102.0 in 2591 mm	58.6 in 59.2 in	4023 lb 1825 kg	£42,400 (1991)
Mercedes 500 SL	V8, quad-cam, 32-valve	4973 cc	326 bhp 5500 rpm	332 lb ft 4000 rpm	157 mph 253 km/h	5.9 sec	176.0 in 4470 mm	99.0 in 2515 mm	60.4 in 60.0 in	4167 lb 1890 kg	£70,090 (1991)

Porsche 928 Data File

I t was in the early 1970s that Porsche started seriously to consider building cars with conventional front-mounted water-cooled engines, rather than their traditional rear-mounted air-cooled flat-six engine. Various reasons were given – noise suppression would be better, as would handling balance and accident protection. It was never Porsche's intention to use a simple front-engine installation, however. That would have biased the weight to the front of the car almost as much as the 911's engine biased it to the rear. Porsche's solution was to have the transmission mounted at the rear to equalise the weight distribution. Alfa Romeo chose a similar layout for their Alfetta/GTV series, and Porsche used it on the 924 and 944 as well.

Above: Nose styling changed slightly over the years; this is a 1987 model.

Above: To some extent the 928 was calculated to appeal to the North American market; this is an American-spec 1983 model.

Above: This handsome wheel design is from a 1991 GT.

Left: Headlamps swivel forward when in use.

Styling

Reaction to the 928's shape might have been less split had it carried anything other than a Porsche badge, and there is no doubt that the car's biggest problem in the early days was that it was so different from the 911, with which every 'true' Porsche enthusiast was inevitably besotted. Most of the criticism centred on the car's wide, stubby proportions and bulbous curves, with a share of derision, too, for the exposed headlights. But, of course, proportions were dictated by mechanical layout and accommodation needs, as fixed at the outset, and were to some extent a function of the width of the new engine. In fact, early design sketches show a longer and sharper nose and a longer rump, and for a while the flip-up headlamps had conventional covers and the bumpers were more markedly distinct from the main body,

but in the end stylist Tony Lapine had the courage to go the whole way. He knew the nose was stubby, so he used the open headlamps (and the narrow bonnet opening) deliberately to add length visually, and the integrated front and rear sections, moulded in that flexible polyurethane material, were both aesthetically pleasing and aerodynamically efficient – contributing to a Cd figure of 0.39 for early cars. That was considerably improved by the revised nose and tail of the S4 and GT, with a separate rear spoiler, deeper front air dam and better-integrated driving-light layout. The revised design also included a smoother underbody tray and an electronically-controlled flap system in the radiator opening, allowing no more airflow than the engine needs at any particular time and helping to reduce drag to 0.34 Cd.

Below: 928 interiors are noteworthy for comfort combined with excellent ergonomics, including a clear instrument display.

Above: Various sketches were produced by Tony Lapine's styling department before the shape was finalised.

Below: The 928's singularly rounded rear has always been one of its most unusual and noteworthy aspects.

Below: Later 928s, like this S4, have had significant aerodynamic improvements, including a bigger rear-deck wing.

Chassis and body

The major structure of the 928 is a conventional unitary shell, mainly formed in steel (and galvanised for corrosion resistance) but with aluminium doors, bonnet and wings to save weight. The distinctive, fully-integrated nose and tail sections are moulded from a flexible polyurethane material. Finished in a special paint, these outer covers can spring back from minor knocks but also conceal hefty metal bumper beams on shock-absorbing struts for more serious impacts. The shell sits on top of a complete drivetrain assembly with a front-engine, rear-wheel-drive layout and all-independent suspension. For optimum balance, Porsche set the wide (but very low and short) V8 at the front of the car, with the clutch assembly attached conventionally to the engine flywheel, and put the transaxle-type five-speed gearbox (or the four-speed automatic option chosen by the majority of 928

customers) at the back, largely ahead of the rear axle line. The propeller shaft runs (at engine speed) inside a large-diameter torque tube, which links engine to gearbox to form a very stiff assembly. A lot of development work went into the torque-tube design, to eliminate the unwanted vibrations that often occur with such a system, and the 928's long shaft is strong enough to need just two large bearings, one at the front and one at the rear. Steering is by servo-assisted rack and pinion, and the brakes are ventilated discs all round, with floating calipers and servo-assistance. When Porsche added ABS on the S2 in 1983, the 928 became the first model from Stuttgart to offer that feature as standard.

Below: In the Porsche works during prototype development, we can see the 928's unitary body and inner structure.

Suspension

At the front, the 928 uses a conventional system of upper and lower wishbones, with coil springs, telescopic dampers and anti-roll bar, but at the rear it uses a highly sophisticated axle assembly with some unique features. Much of the development time lavished on the 928 went into creating this 'Weissach' axle, the aim being a suspension layout which would eliminate the tendency for the car to tuck in at the front (or even to flick into oversteer) when the driver lifts sharply off the power in mid-corner. The 'tuck-in' is largely a function of the flexibility of the suspension mounting bushes, and although it can be minimised by making the bushes very rigid (or even solid, as in a racing car), that would create an unacceptably harsh ride in a road car, so Porsche needed a different solution. They approached the problem by building a degree of

track-varying ability into the rear arms, using tiny and carefully controlled toe-in changes to discourage those undesirable lift-off characteristics. During testing, dual-torsion-bar springing was tried, but the adopted layout uses coil springs and telescopic dampers, with an anti-roll bar. Basically, the rear suspension uses upper and lower transverse arms, plus additional diagonal control links with carefully angled bushes of very specific flexibility. Those cause the outer rear wheel to toe in very slightly under deceleration, removing most of the tendency towards lift-off oversteer, while the whole assembly is extremely compact and essentially foolproof.

Below: The 928's front engine and rear transaxle are linked by a rigid torque tube, which contains the propshaft.

Engine

The 928's heart has come a long way since the original 4.5-litre two-cam V8 of 1977; it's now a five-litre four-cam 32-valve engine, but the basic architecture has survived. In all versions it is a 90-degree V8 of all-alloy construction, with a five-bearing crankshaft and belt-driven camshafts. Originally, the two valves were in line, in pent-roof combustion chambers, rather than in a 'V' in hemispherical chambers as is more common in a performance engine, but it has always been important for the 928 engine to be clean and efficient as well as simply powerful. That was the main reasoning behind the current four-cam, four-valves-per-cylinder generation, introduced first for the US market and soon allowing power output to be further improved and

standardised for both catalyst and non-catalyst versions – in other words, worldwide. The heads are very compact and the camshafts are close together in narrow heads, with the exhaust cams driven by an unusually long, toothed belt. Drive to the inlet cam is provided by a short chain between the shafts, in the centre. For the S4, a substantial power increase was achieved by clever redesign of the inlet plumbing, using two linked chambers in the manifolds to set up a pulse effect in the intake air, matched to the frequency of the injection pulses, and providing a charging effect, even at low speeds. On the latest 928 GT an extra 10 bhp are added to the S4's 320 by means of further fine-tuning of the inlet system, engine management and cams.

Above: These four-valve heads are from the most recent GT, which develops another 10 bhp over the 320 bhp of the S4.

Below right: Latest 928s have a variable radiator air intake system, to lessen drag when extra cooling is not needed.

Above right: Front suspension is by means of the usual high-performance design of double wishbones.

Above: This is the 330-bhp version of the five-litre all-alloy V8 engine from the most recent 928 GT model. It gets its extra 10 bhp from slightly uprated camshafts, a modified electronic management module and a fine-tuned induction system.

Above: Earlier 4.5- and 4.7-litre engines like this had single overhead camshafts per bank and two valves per cylinder; later versions have four cams and 32 valves.

Above: Its front-engine/rear-transaxle mechanical layout gives the 928 balanced weight distribution, with centres of mass at opposite ends of the car (the reverse of the situation in a mid-engined car), producing a high polar moment of inertia and excellent stability.

Above: The 928's 'Weissach' rear suspension arrangement (named after Porsche's test centre, where it was developed) confers a small degree of passive rear-wheel steering under changes of load to cancel out excessive 'tuck-in' or sudden transition to oversteer.

Rolls-Royce
Silver Ghost

No rival could compete with the 7.5-litre Silver Ghost's smoothness, reliability and trials performance, and time after time it proved itself the world's finest motor car.

What's in a name? When it comes to early Rolls-Royces, the unofficial names are more persistent than the official designations: the 'Silver Ghost' was only one car out of 7,876 of the prosaically-titled 40/50HP chassis produced, yet that name so caught the public imagination that it was applied to the model in general. And when the new 'Continental' derivative of the London–Edinburgh chassis swept the board in the 1913 Austrian Alpine Trials, it gained the soubriquet 'Alpine Eagle'.

The 'Ghost' was a refined and dignified motor car, but it was not a sports machine. However, there were calls for added performance, and in 1909 a new long-stroke version of the original power unit raised the swept volume from 7036 cc to 7428 cc and the power output to around 60 bhp. At the same time the overdrive fourth speed which had been a feature of the early cars was dropped in favour of a three-speed gearbox because in those pre-synchro-mesh days, drivers were largely incapable of changing gear properly and therefore expected a car to 'do everything on top'.

This had an unexpected outcome: one of Rolls-Royce's rivals in the luxury car market, Napier, organised an impressive demonstration of their 65HP model by driving from London to Edinburgh using only top gear, averaging 19.4 mpg, and then recording a top speed of over 76 mph at Brooklands. In 1911, Claude Johnson, the 'power behind the throne' at Rolls-Royce, retaliated by staging a further attempt on the London–Edinburgh run with a three-speed Silver Ghost which recorded a consumption of 24.32 mpg and a top speed of 78.3 mph.

A team of cars was sent to the Alps . . .

The car was specially built for the run, with cantilever rear springing, a compression ratio of 3.5:1, against the standard 3.2:1, and a tapered bonnet. Fitted with long, flowing wings and a pretty sports tourer body, the car was one of the most handsome variants of the Silver Ghost and went into production as the London–Edinburgh model.

The London–Edinburgh was capable of an impressive turn of speed; in 1911 an otherwise-standard London–Edinburgh model fitted with a high-ratio back axle and a single-seat body achieved a speed of 101 mph at Brooklands.

However, this did not herald the large-scale entry of Rolls-Royce into motorsport, but in 1912 the well-known aviator James Radley entered his London–Edinburgh for the Austrian Alpine Trials – and on the very first day, the car ground slowly to a halt on the 1:3.5 section of the dreaded Katschberg Pass – 'the steepest pass in the Alps', climbing 2,400 feet in less than seven miles – and had to shed two passengers before it could restart.

Obviously, bottom gear was too high, taking into account the reduction in power caused by the rarefied atmosphere of the high Alps. Though pass-storming expert Charles L. Freeston said of the Alpine Trials that "nothing more strenuous has ever taken place", to Rolls-Royce the episode was "disgraceful" (though in any other car of the period, it would have passed without comment). Something would have to be done . . .

The Alps had not come into Rolls-Royce's testing programme up to that point, for the Silver Ghost line had proved perfectly capable of climbing the most testing gradients in Scotland fully laden. Having discovered their Achilles heel, Rolls-Royce set about eliminating it. A team of cars was sent to the Alps under the charge of chief tester Eric Platford to obtain the most accurate data on the length, severity and altitude of the passes, the atmospheric conditions that pre-

vailed and the severity of the hairpin bends.

The result was the evolution of a new model, the Continental, which reverted to a four-speed gearbox (though with direct drive on top) and had a radiator with a larger core and header tank, plus an extended filler cap to give additional expansion capacity for the cooling water. Ground clearance was increased, too.

And then in July 1913 Rolls-Royce entered a works team of Continentals in the Alpine Trials, with works testers E. C. Friese, E. W. Hives and Sinclair as drivers, plus a private entry from James Radley aided by a fourth Rolls-Royce tester named Ward. Of course, the cars travelled from Derby to the event by road; Radley proved a man of iron, who drove the 500 miles from Paris to Turin in one stage. Then, a couple of days before the event, he was sitting in a Viennese café with a party of competitors and officials and boasted of the capabilities of his new Rolls-Royce.

"I'll bet a thousand crowns you can't drive from here to Klagenfürt and back (it was a distance of about 400 miles) between sunrise and sunset," scoffed one of his companions.

"Done!" exclaimed Radley. "Let's stay up now and I'll start as soon as it gets light."

With three passengers, Radley drove like a demon. The group stopped for breakfast and lunch (and to let a sick passenger recover) but nevertheless, 13 hours later, the Continental was back in Vienna, where Radley, richer by a thousand crowns, ate a very satisfying dinner . . .

Nothing on the road to match their pace

The four Rolls-Royces dominated the Trials, in size as well as in overall performance. They started first, with the works cars ahead of Radley, but the impetuous Radley only recognised one place, and that was in the lead. He even gave the official pace cars a hard time "for there was nothing on the road that could match the Rolls-Royces either in pace or hill-climbing power". On the Katschberg Pass, where the year before, his London–Edinburgh had faded away, Radley roared past the pace car, climbed the 1:3.5 section at over 17 mph and, unaware that he should have waited at the summit, arrived at Innsbruck an hour ahead of the officials.

But the team's record of arriving first at every stage control was spoiled near Vienna when Sinclair's car was rammed amidships at an estimated 50 mph by a non-competing Minerva and pushed bodily into a telegraph pole, which was shifted a foot sideways by the impact. A nearside wheel was broken against the telegraph pole, the offside wing and running board were crumpled and, most seriously, the gear quadrant was damaged so badly that only third gear could be engaged. But, with the damaged wheel replaced, the car drove into Vienna; the Minerva was a write-off.

But only one Rolls-Royce (Friese's car) came through the Trials without losing a point, and won a silver medal, although two of its team-mates were docked just one point; even though the team prize went to the less spectacular Audis (whose makers celebrated the event by producing an *Alpensieger* 'Alpine victor' model), it was agreed that "there could be no question, among those who witnessed the Trials throughout, that the honours of the road fell to the Rolls-Royce team".

It was not Rolls-Royce's only triumph of 1913; shortly before the start of the Alpine Trials, the Spanish Rolls-Royce agent, Don Carlos de Salamanca, had won the Spanish Grand Prix, run under the auspices of King Alfonso XIII, by three minutes from the next car, a 60HP Lorraine-Dietrich, with another Rolls-Royce driven by Platford finishing third.

Rolls-Royce felt that to run an official team in the 1914 Alpine Trials might look like vainglorious boasting, but Radley made his third amateur entry with his Alpine Eagle and, despite a navigational error which put him 45 miles off route and let 54 cars pass him, by the time he had regained the route and arrived at the Trieste control, he had passed 52 of them!

When the results were analysed, it was found that Radley had the highest score out of the 78 competitors; that satisfying victory, coming only a few weeks before the outbreak of World War I, was a grand culmination to the competition record of the Alpine Eagle, which was to be the basis of the post-war Silver Ghost.

Above: This Silver Ghost, briefly stopped by snow in the Loibl Pass, was one of four that dominated the 1913 Alpine Trials. One journalist said that "Radley [a private entry] has certainly had an ample revenge for the misfortune of last year, a revenge which the other three Rolls-Royces have individually and collectively emphasised . . .".

Overleaf: A Rolls-Royce Alpine Eagle of 1914, the year in which the company did not field a works team but Radley, as a private entry, won the event.

Driving the Silver Ghost: *just perfection*

Drivers of the Rolls-Royce Silver Ghost spoke of its effortlessness, the sensation of being drawn along at the end of an invisible cord, and of its beautifully weighted high-geared steering which needed only one and a quarter turns from lock to lock. "One seemed to have to do little more than wish the car round even quite a sharp corner", as one contemporary account put it. And *The Autocar* of 1913 found its handling excellent, commenting that "the taking of the bends served to show how grandly the driving wheels of the Rolls-Royce hold the road . . . with no tendency to slip outwards while travelling round sharp bends".

To this potent combination, the Alpine Eagle added an extra dimension, as that great Rolls-Royce enthusiast Kent Karslake found when he drove the ex-Radley car in the 1950s, remarking: "One does not have to drive it very far before one realises that this car has real power and the life which the three-speeder lacks somewhat. As one opens the throttle of the Alpine Eagle, a delicious wiggle seems to ripple down its chassis in a manner which I have only encountered in this particular type of Rolls-Royce. One can, without the slightest difficulty, imagine it eating up the long miles of Continental roads."

PERFORMANCE & SPECIFICATION COMPARISON	Engine	Displacement	Power	Torque (lb ft)	Max speed	0-60 mph	Length (in/mm)	Wheelbase (in/mm)	Track front/rear	Weight (lb/kg)	Chassis price
Rolls-Royce Silver Ghost	Inline-six, side-valve	7428 cc	75 bhp 1800 rpm	N/A	82 mph 132 km/h	N/A	192.0 in 4877 mm	143.5 in 3645 mm	56.0 in 56.0 in	2856 lb 1295 kg	£985 (1913)
Austro-Daimler 27/80HP	Inline-four, overhead-valve	5709 cc	95 bhp 1900 rpm	N/A	70 mph 113 km/h	N/A	186.0 in 4724 mm	118.0 in 2997 mm	52.0 in 52.0 in	1675 lb 760 kg	£875 (1913)
Mercedes 45/50HP	Inline-four, side-valve	7238 cc	50 bhp 1250 rpm	N/A	55 mph 89 km/h	N/A	186.0 in 4724 mm	136.0 in 3454 mm	60.0 in 60.0 in	N/A	£775 (1913)
Napier 45HP	Inline-six, side-valve	6840 cc	45 bhp 1200 rpm	N/A	65 mph 105 km/h	N/A	192.0 in 4877 mm	134.0 in 3404 mm	56.0 in 56.0 in	N/A	£850 (1913)
Vauxhall Prince Henry	Inline-four, side-valve	3969 cc	75 bhp 2500 rpm	N/A	75 mph 121 km/h	N/A	162.0 in 4115 mm	120.0 in 3048 mm	54.0 in 54.0 in	3598 lb 1632 kg	£515 (1913)

Rolls-Royce Silver Ghost Data File

ven such an august marque as Rolls-Royce could, in the early days, be improved by motorsport. The Rolls-Royce Silver Ghost seemed the perfect touring car, but it took the Alpine Trials of 1912 to discover that the failure to test the car's hill-climbing powers outside the British Isles had left a weak spot in its design – and the Alpine Trials of 1913 to demonstrate that the problem had been solved and "the best car in the world" been made better still. Thereafter, testing under the most extreme conditions became standard practice. The result was the car that became known as the Alpine Eagle. Because Rolls-Royces were being built to operate in extreme conditions as though these were the everyday norm, they were the ideal basis for high-speed military vehicles during World War I, and the first Rolls-Royce chassis were being fitted with armoured bodywork as early as September 1914. Remarkably, Rolls-Royce armoured cars were capable of 50-60 mph even when carrying twice their designed weight in bullet-proof steel plating, and their only weak points were the tyres and hub bearings.

A 1916 report in *The Times* spoke enthusiastically of the perfect reliability of the armoured car service in the Egyptian desert, where the cars – all Rolls-Royces – moved to a timetable and engine breakdowns were unknown. "The cars have run over thousands of miles of the roughest desert, and the complete absence of engine trouble is a triumph for British workmanship."

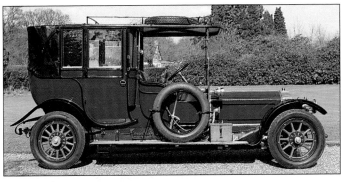

Above: Passengers in this 1911 40/50HP Ghost were enclosed, but not the chauffeur; this town car also has very high formal coachwork.

Above: A 1914 Rolls-Royce Silver Ghost, chassis number 27LB, with open coachwork typical of the period. Note the separate rear windscreen.

Styling

While the early Silver Ghosts, with their parallel-sided bonnets, could be fitted with the finest of bodywork by the leading coachbuilders, their lines were anything but flowing. It was the taper-bonneted style introduced with the London–Edinburgh chassis that really enabled Rolls-Royce to make the transition from bespoke carriage to truly integrated motor car. The sports tourer body style used on the London–Edinburgh and the Continental chassis was as near perfection as could be achieved, with a scuttle that followed the line of the bonnet hinge, low seats and a gently rounded stern. The line of the wings, too, was in direct contrast with what had gone before, the combination of straight lines and curves setting the style for the sports cars of the 1920s. And how well the uncomplicated body lines went with the austere elegance of the Rolls-Royce radiator, whose height-to-width ratio was at its optimum in those immediate pre-World War I days.

Below: The original Silver Ghost was the 13th 40/50HP model built, a car finished entirely with silver paint and fittings.

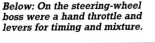

Above: The horn, handbrake and gear lever, all in brass, were mounted on the body side.

Below: Wooden-spoke artillery wheels were originally standard, before steel wheels took over.

Below: On the steering-wheel boss were a hand throttle and levers for timing and mixture.

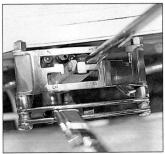

Above: Despite the four-gear gate, many owners liked to travel everywhere in fourth gear.

Below: This 1914 Rolls-Royce Alpine Eagle, chassis 31EB, has light touring bodywork.

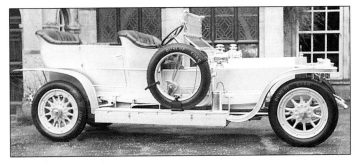

Below: The grille and bonnet sides remained in metal, but wood was used for the two-seat, boat-tail bodywork of this 1914 Silver Ghost.

Below: A 1910 'Roi de Belges' Silver Ghost, coachbuilt like the Belgian king's 1901 Panhard; the high rear seats indicated status.

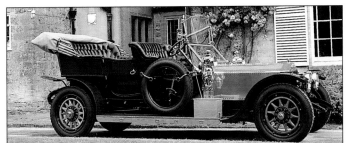

Chassis and running gear

The chassis of the Silver Ghost was basically a channel-section ladder-type frame with six cross-members; for the Continental chassis, external bracing trusses were added beneath the frame for additional strength. Front springs on all Silver Ghosts were conventional semi-elliptic leaf units, but the early cars had platform rear suspension, in which a transverse spring linked the rear ends of semi-elliptic springs. From chassis number 60581 in 1908, rear suspension was conventional semi-elliptic, but the first London–Edinburgh chassis used cantilever rear springs sliding in trunnions and attached to the underside of the back axle casing. Later L–E chassis had cantilever springs mounted over the axle, and cantilevers were standardised on all Rolls-Royces in late 1912.

Both the three-speed transmission fitted to the early London–Edinburgh chassis and the four-speed transmission introduced for the Continental and soon standardised across the range worked on Henry Royce's 'locking gate' principle. This meant that to disengage a gear, the lever had to be moved sideways out of a notch, the idea being to prevent gears from jumping out of mesh if they were not properly engaged.

Unfortunately, this made the gear change unnecessarily difficult and only the very best drivers could make a clean gear change every time.

The first Silver Ghosts all had wood-spoked artillery wheels, though double-spoked wire wheels were offered as an option from 1909, and triple-spoked wire wheels were available from 1911 and were, of course, fitted to the London–Edinburgh and Continental chassis. Beaded-edge tyres were used on the pre-war cars, but the standard fitment at the time of the L–E and Continental models was 895 × 195 tyres front and rear, usually grooved Dunlop, Michelin or Continental square-tread tyres, though other makes were available by special request from the purchaser. Like most of its contemporaries, the Silver Ghost only had rear-wheel brakes, and front-wheel brakes were not adopted until Henry Royce could find a system that came up to his high standards. That was in 1924 and he used a mechanical servo-assisted layout based on the contemporary Hispano-Suiza system.

Below: The ladder chassis of a 1910 40/50HP, revealing engine, gearbox, pedal assembly and the very long steering column.

Below: Front suspension was non-independent with a beam axle and semi-elliptic leaf springs.

Below: At the rear of the Alpine Eagle were less typical cantilever leaf springs.

Below: The chassis, finished to the highest standards, was very sturdy; it went on to support a range of body styles, including extremely heavy armoured cars.

Engine

Considering Henry Royce's lack of formal qualifications, the engine of the Silver Ghost was a remarkably competent design. Unlike most of his contemporaries, who regarded the six-cylinder engine – still a very new concept – as a four-cylinder unit with a couple of extra cylinders tacked on, Royce designed his new 40/50HP powerplant as a pair of three-cylinder blocks, with a rigid crankcase and a massive seven-bearing crankshaft which, unusually for its day, was hollow to enable pressure-lubrication of the bearings. Most cars at that period had rather basic splash-lubrication. An extra refinement added in 1908 was an extra supply of oil for the cylinder walls, controlled by a valve which opened when the throttle was more than two-thirds open. Compressions were low, even on the sports 40/50HP models, which had a compression ratio of only 3.5:1; but a 'secret weapon' on the

Continental chassis was the use of aluminium pistons at a time when cast-iron or steel was standard practice.

The engine ran on seven main bearings, the centre one being longer than the others as the engine was essentially two groups of three cylinders joined together rather than what we would recognise as a straight-six. The drive to the side-mounted camshaft was by gears rather than chain (as was the ignition drive) and the single camshafts operated all the valves directly rather than through pushrods, the valves being in line in an 'F'-head configuration. The adjustable tappets were exposed on the side of the engine blocks, so valve clearances were easily kept correct. It was a very under-stressed motor; the side-valve layout was used not because Royce could not manage an overhead-valve layout but to make the engine refined and quiet yet still powerful enough.

Below: With padded leather, semi-elliptics and a transverse leaf spring, the ride was soft.

Below: The engine was in effect two twin-plug, three-cylinder, cast-iron blocks with integral heads, supported by a long aluminium crankcase. The copper inlet manifold passed between the two blocks.

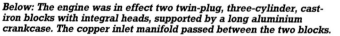

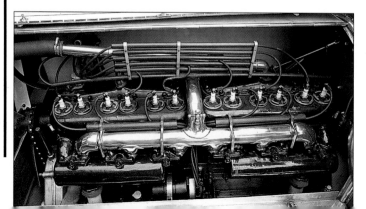

Left: This side view of the engine reveals the single two-jet Royce carburettor which supplied the side-valve engine, plus the magneto, fan and cooling-system pipes. The drive to the ignition and camshaft was by gears, because Henry Royce was opposed to chains, and only the fan had a belt drive from the crankshaft. The engine was built to extraordinary standards, with forgings designed so that grain flow should be very favourable; each connecting rod, weighing 2 lb, was machined from an 8-lb forging, and Rolls-Royce claimed that every component was filed and polished in order to detect cracks and flaws.

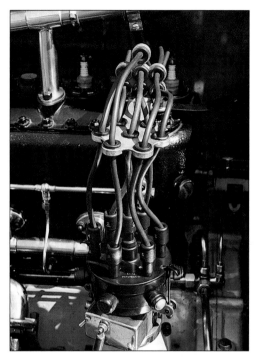

Right: Royce designed his own magneto, trembler coils and distributor. The Silver Ghost was usually started with the coils and then, in order to conserve the twin 4-volt batteries, run on the magneto. At low revs, when the magneto did not work so well, both systems could be used simultaneously. From 1919 a dynamo became standard equipment.

Below: The windscreen of the first Silver Ghost, while hardly aerodynamic, could be adjusted to give varying amounts of air and weather protection.

Below: In the days when acetylene lamps gave little useful light, it was common to supplement front lamps with others mounted on the scuttle.

Below: The classic Palladian radiator fed water into the engine through a neat copper and brass system which worked well in the hottest climes.

Above: The running boards doubled as tool and luggage lockers, and other boxes could be attached at the rear. The siting of the spare wheel and controls meant the driver entered from the passenger side.

Above: The steering column led directly to a worm-and-nut drive, and connected via long links to the front wheels. The steering was high-geared but well balanced, and did not require excessive effort.

Shelby Mustang GT350

A year after launching their smash-hit Mustang sports coupé for the masses, Ford asked ace performance specialist Carroll Shelby to give their pony car some serious muscle. He made it a classic of its kind.

You'll often find that the first model of any marque has special significance, especially if it turns out to be a success. The 1965 Shelby Mustang is no exception. Among Ford collectors today, the first Shelby version is almost revered, because it was the first true high-performance Mustang and, of course, it has the magic Shelby name. More than any other Shelby Mustang, the 1965 model is the embodiment of what its creator, Carroll Shelby, thought a high-performance street car should be. Subsequent Shelby Mustangs may have proved to be just as performance-oriented as the original, yet they all incorporated compromises – compromises made for the sake of increased sales. From Ford Motor Company's point of view, this was all well and good because it was in keeping with its primary objective of giving the Mustang a stronger performance image.

The Mustang, which was introduced in April of 1964, was a phenomenal success for Ford. Even with its success, Ford was interested in making the Mustang a car for all – and that included hard-core performance enthusiasts. However, even with the optional 271-bhp, 289-cu in V8, the Mustang wasn't much of a performance car, lacking power, and with lacklustre handling and braking. The benchmark was Chevrolet's Corvette and for those primarily interested in straight-line performance, there was Pontiac's hot new GTO.

Carroll Shelby was at the time occupied with making the AC Cobra a success on the track, which he did admirably. He was asked by Ford to make the new Mustang competitive in the SCCA (Sports Car Club of America) B Production racing class and also to produce a somewhat toned-down street version of the car to be sold through selected Ford dealers.

Although the Mustang was produced in three body styles, it was the new 2+2 fastback shape, introduced in September 1964, that was chosen as the basis for the Shelby Mustang. The plain notchback hard-top or the convertible didn't quite have the right street-racer image.

In keeping with the car's image, the name finally chosen for it was the Shelby GT350. The 350 designation didn't have anything to do with the car; it didn't have 350 cubic inches or 350 bhp, but it sure sounded strong.

The conversion was made at Shelby's 'plant', located in several empty hangars at Los Angeles International Airport. Ford shipped to Shelby partially-completed 2+2 Mustangs, all painted Wimbledon White, equipped with the biggest optional Mustang engine – the 289-cu in (4.7-litre) V8 rated at 271 bhp, coupled to the Borg-Warner aluminium-cased T-10 four-speed manual all-synchromesh transmission.

It didn't have 350 cubic inches or 350 bhp . . .

Little was done to make the Shelby outwardly distinctive from ordinary production Mustangs. All regular Mustang emblems were removed, with the exception of a Mustang horse badge located on the left side of the grille opening. The stock Mustang petrol cap was used and some cars came with a GT350 emblem on the left side of the tail-light panel. Probably the most distinctive visual characteristic of the Shelby was the wide blue racing stripes running the length of

Mustang GT. Originally developed in the late 1950s, the small-block was designed for use in Ford's intermediates which debuted in 1962. Use of this engine eventually spread to Ford's other lines. Unlike some Ford engines, the 289 was light, compact and reliable. Ford shipped to Shelby's facility Mustangs equipped with the highest-rated version, known as the High-Performance, or 'Hi-Po', 289, which produced 271 bhp at 6,000 rpm. Further modified by Shelby, it produced 306 bhp, to give 0-60 mph in under seven seconds and a top speed of over 120 mph.

Handled as well as it accelerated

Shelby made a real effort to make the Mustang handle as well as it accelerated. During the 1960s, performance in the American idiom meant straight-line acceleration as measured down the quarter-mile. Still, there were enthusiasts who could appreciate a balanced car and wanted more than just acceleration. In fact, several years later, Chevrolet introduced the Z28 Camaro, which had most of the same features.

The suspension was modified to greatly improve handling. First to go were the rather soft stock Mustang springs and dampers, which were replaced by considerably firmer springs and adjustable Konis. These were complemented by a front anti-sway bar and relocated front upper control arms. Anyone who has driven a high-powered Mustang will readily recognise that the stock Mustang rear suspension is woefully inadequate when it comes to large power in-

Above: Early Shelbys used the fastback Mustang body, mostly in this colour scheme.

puts, resulting in a bad case of wheel hop. To counteract this tendency, the Shelby used traction bars and travel-limiting tables.

In spite of the favourable press and enthusiast response, the 1965 Shelby did not sell well. In fact, the first 252 units of the 1966 model run were unsold leftover 1965s. For the majority of buyers, it was too much of a racer.

So, for 1966, the racer theme was toned down a bit. The Detroit Locker differential became an option, the loud side exhaust pipes were replaced with a conventional system, and the Konis were also relegated to the option list. The lowered suspension modification was also deleted, after the first 252 units.

To increase the Shelby's appeal, additional colours were made available, and functional rear quarter-panel side scoops and the stock side air extractor louvres were replaced with windows. 1966 was also the year that Hertz, the rental car company, bought nearly 1,000 GT350s, designated GT350H for use as rental cars. Most of these were painted black with gold stripes.

To many Shelby Mustang aficionados, the 1967 models were the last 'true' Shelby Mustangs because these were still built by Shelby. Looking racier than ever, the 1967 models were drastically restyled to emphasise the look of performance, while at the same time, creature comforts such as power-assisted brakes, steering and air conditioning were made available. By 1968 Ford had taken over the Shelby operation and by 1969 the cars were little more than restyled Mach 1 Mustangs. But in the short time that 'genuine' Shelby models existed, they created a legend

the car. These, however, were optional and most were installed at the dealer level. The blue rocker panel GT350 stripes were standard equipment on all 1965 Shelby Mustangs. The only other prominent visual cue was the glassfibre bonnet, which incorporated a functional scoop.

The engine used on the Shelby was a modified version of the Ford 289-cu in small-block V8, the same basic engine still used today in the

Above: The 1968-model Shelby GT350 had a far more aggressive look to it than the early cars although in many respects it was a tamer performer, lacking the competition-type suspension, for example. The two centre lights are non-standard.

Overleaf: This Shelby GT350 is from 1965, the first year of the car's manufacture. Those rear slats soon gave way to a side window.

Driving the GT350: *crude and quick*

The first thing you notice as you sit in the Shelby is how simple and almost quaintly old-fashioned is the interior. By today's standards the seats provide only minimal support but there's no doubt that this is a high-performance car from the moment you turn the engine on. That has the characteristic deep, throaty rumble of an American V8. The idle is fairly smooth and noise levels, even with the side pipe exhaust, are not objectionable at cruising speeds. Although the clutch pressure is reasonable, the unassisted steering and brakes make the Shelby a heavy handful to drive at low speeds; more so if radials have been fitted.

The firm suspension is also more suited to the track than the road; you feel every road imperfection and at speed over a bumpy surface the rear axle has a tendency to break loose, while the Detroit Locker limited-slip differential results in some ominous-sounding clunking, along with tyre chirping and squealing around corners.

Nevertheless the Shelby has enormous appeal; at full throttle the 289 'Hi-Po' is a delightful engine, producing acceleration which just keeps on rising effortlessly. Within 20 seconds you're past the 100-mph mark, heading to a top speed beyond 120 mph.

PERFORMANCE & SPECIFICATION COMPARISON	Engine	Displacement	Power	Torque (lb ft)	Max speed	0-60 mph	Length (in/mm)	Wheelbase (in/mm)	Track front/rear	Weight (lb/kg)	Price
Shelby Mustang GT350	V8, overhead-valve	4737 cc	306 bhp 6000 rpm	329 lb ft 4200 rpm	124 mph 200 km/h	6.8 sec	181.6 in 4613 mm	108.0 in 2743 mm	56.5 in 57.0 in	2790 lb 1266 kg	$4,943 (1966)
Chevrolet Camaro	V8, overhead-valve	5353 cc	275 bhp 4800 rpm	355 lb ft 3200 rpm	120 mph 193 km/h	9.1 sec	183.0 in 4648 mm	108.1 in 2746 mm	59.0 in 58.9 in	3240 lb 1470 kg	$3,731 (1967)
Chevrolet Corvette Sting Ray	V8, overhead-valve	5358 cc	360 bhp 6000 rpm	352 lb ft 4000 rpm	135 mph 217 km/h	6.3 sec	182.5 in 4636 mm	98.0 in 2489 mm	58.7 in 59.4 in	3050 lb 1383 kg	$4,295 (1965)
Jaguar E-type 4.2 Coupé	Inline-six, twin-cam	4235 cc	265 bhp 5400 rpm	283 lb ft 4000 rpm	150 mph 241 km/h	7.0 sec	175.3 in 4453 mm	96.0 in 2438 mm	50.0 in 50.0 in	2640 lb 1198 kg	£2,060 (1964)
Shelby Mustang GT500	V8, overhead-valve	7016 cc	355 bhp 5400 rpm	420 lb ft 3200 rpm	128 mph 206 km/h	6.5 sec	186.6 in 4740 mm	108.0 in 2743 mm	58.0 in 58.0 in	3370 lb 1529 kg	$5,043 (1967)

Shelby Mustang GT350 Data File

he Shelby was an example of just how thorough the Ford Motor Company could be when it set its mind to something. Despite the fact that the Mustang was an enormous success from the word go, Ford decided that there should be an equally successful performance and competition version to complement the ordinary models. At the time, Carroll Shelby was showing just how much could be achieved by the rather crude AC Cobra, and as that was powered by the same Ford V8 engines that would find their way under the new Mustang's bonnet, who better to approach for a competition Mustang programme than the dynamic Texan? Shelby's task was twofold: to give the car credibility it had to be competitive on the racetrack – in particular, Ford had its eye on the SCCA B Production class – and yet it had to be tractable enough to be saleable as a road car. Shelby achieved both aims, and within a very short time.

Above: The first Shelby Mustangs were fitted with a bonnet-mounted scoop; the whole bonnet was made in glassfibre rather than steel.

Styling

The Shelby needed little major attention to the styling, as the original fastback Mustang on which it was based was such an obviously right design from the start. Nevertheless the Shelby had to look different from standard and that was achieved by the use of a distinctive colour scheme as well as various body modifications. To begin with, all Shelbys were Wimbledon White with blue side stripes and the GT350 logo, and dealers often added the optional wide blue racing stripes.

The bonnet was different. For one thing, it was made of glassfibre (which must have helped weight distribution);

that was because a bonnet scoop had been added, and for a low-production-volume car it was easier to use a new glassfibre panel than a new metal pressing. Apart from these differences you have to look hard to tell a standard Mustang from a Shelby, although the removal of the running Mustang badge from the centre of the grille (it was replaced by a smaller version on the driver's side of the grille) is a help. Overall the Shelby was remarkably free of the masses of chrome that had distinguished American cars of the 1950s; it was testimony to the design that it needed little dressing-up to look good.

Above: Interiors changed every year; this 1966 car has a central speedo flanked by gauges. Note the rev-counter above the steering wheel.

Below: Rear lights were the same as those on standard Mustangs.

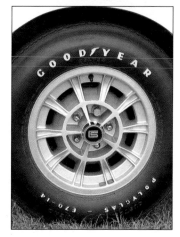

Above: This snake emblem was found on the fuel filler cap.

Left and below: Alloy wheels were a popular option. The rear scoop was functional on the 1966 models.

Above: This 1965-model Shelby GT350 is in stock factory colours; the large blue stripes (as on the cutaway, far right) were a dealer option.

Below: Two GT350Hs: the 'H' stood for Hertz, the car rental company, who bought 936 1966 Shelbys. Some people hired and raced the cars!

The later Shelbys

The Shelby Mustang line continued until 1970, by which time Ford had been in charge of the programme for two years.

In 1967, although the 350 was continued, another model was added to the line, the GT500. This used a modified version of Ford's Police Interceptor 428-cu in (seven-litre) V8, rated at 355 bhp. The 1967 models no longer had the stiffer and rather more sophisticated suspension of the first GT350, and so had a softer ride.

In 1968 Ford added a convertible version to the range, while the 289 engine was replaced by the 302 and the 428 Cobra Jet engine supplanted the Police unit, producing the GT500KR (King of the Road).

By 1969 the larger, flatter-looking Mach 1 Mustang had appeared and the Shelby version was very little different. The GT350 was now powered by Ford's new Windsor 351 V8; the GT500 continued with the Cobra Jet engine.

There was only a 1970 Shelby, as Ford marketed the unsold 789 1969 cars (somewhat updated) as 1970 models. A Shelby Mustang was again marketed in the 1990s, but that was a version of the latest five-litre GT model.

Below: The 1970 GT500 was a fine example of how later Shelby Mustangs changed as the stock Mustang line evolved.

Chassis and suspension

The standard Mustang unitary-construction body was deemed to have sufficient strength without major chassis stiffening, except in the engine compartment. Here the damper towers were braced to the firewall while a 'Monte Carlo bar' connected both damper towers across the engine. That bar was named after the device used in the successful Monte Carlo rallying Ford Falcons.

An attempt was made to improve the weight distribution (at least on the first 324 cars) by moving the battery to the boot.

Not surprisingly, the suspension was modified compared with the standard Mustang, with stiffer springs all round

and expensive adjustable Koni dampers. A 0.94-in-diameter front anti-roll bar was added, while the front control arms were relocated, lowered an inch. More attention was needed at the rear, where the standard Mustang had very poor axle location. That was remedied by adding traction bars, which required a novel modification; they ran forward from the top of the axle and their front mountings were actually housed within the car.

Special Pitman and idler arms were fitted to the steering, which was also given a quicker ratio, while 11.3-in-diameter disc brakes were fitted, along with larger rear drums.

Right: The standard Mustang double-wishbone front suspension configuration was retained for the Shelby, but with uprated springs and Koni dampers. The Konis were later dropped on the grounds of cost.

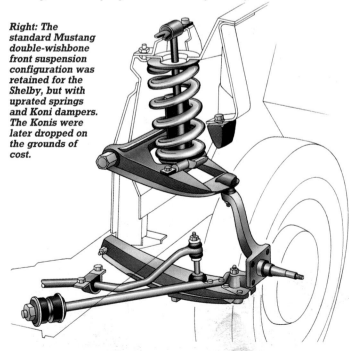

Engine

There was never any question of which engine would make the Shelby really go. Unlike Rootes, who used the 260-cu in Ford V8 in their Tiger before switching to the 289, Shelby always used the slightly bigger 289, which had far more tuning potential.

It was a standard American V8, although utilising Ford's new lightweight iron-casting technique to give an excellent power-to-weight ratio. The Shelby started with the Hi-Po version of the engine as the base to work on. This version had stronger connecting rods, mechanical (rather than hydraulic) valve-lifters, a dual-point distributor and a high compression ratio of 10.5:1, which was enough to give 271 bhp, but Shelby took that one stage further. An alloy high-rise intake manifold was fitted to improve the breathing for the new Holley 715CFM four-barrel carburettor

while tubular Tri-Y exhaust manifolds were used to speed the exhaust gases out of the engine to a straight-through exhaust system. These modifications upped power and torque, to 306 bhp at 6,000 rpm and 329 lb ft at 4,200 rpm respectively. A larger, alloy, sump pan was also fitted to increase oil capacity to 6.5 quarts and alloy was used for the valve covers too, but this time only for show.

For those wanting even more power, there were further dealer-fitted options – the Cobra kits, which included multiple carburettors rather than the single four-barrel, and ported cylinder heads with improved gasflow.

Below: These twin Holley carburettors were fitted to the GT350R race version of the Shelby.

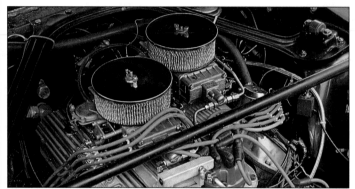

Below right: Front strut braces had proved helpful on Ford's rally Falcons, so the Shelby had a 'Monte Carlo bar' arrangement.

Above: With a single 715-CFM four-barrel Holley carburettor, the standard Shelby High-Performance 289-cu in V8 engine produced 306 bhp at 6,000 rpm, along with 329 lb ft of torque at 4,200 rpm. Compare that with the 101 bhp of the first six-cylinder Mustang.

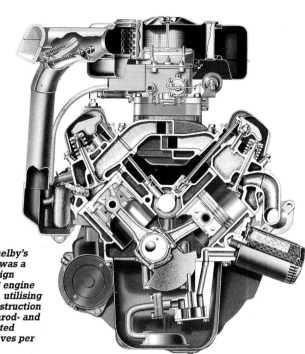

Right: The Shelby's 289-cu in V8 was a standard-design American V8 engine of the period, utilising cast-iron construction and two pushrod- and rocker-operated overhead valves per cylinder.

Left: A close look at the rear suspension shows the control arm running forward from the axle. These arms (one on each side) were added to limit unwanted axle movement. They were removed on later models.

Right: In 1965 Shelby built 37 'R' (for race) models, with 350-bhp versions of the 289 and stripped interiors. All of them were track-tested at Willow Springs Raceway.

TVR Griffith

The Griffith is the pinnacle of modern TVR road car production. It's a combination of a tubular steel chassis, a glassfibre body styled by TVR themselves and a 280-bhp 4.3-litre V8 engine giving 160-mph performance.

Above: The Griffith is one of the very few convertibles that looks as good with the top up as with it down. With the hood up, the aerodynamics are improved, helping the powerful TVR reach the 160-mph mark while remaining stable at very high speeds.

 hen *Autocar & Motor* first road-tested the Griffith, in June 1992, their findings must have been music not only to the ears of TVR but also to all those enthusiasts who had so desperately wanted the new car to be right. "With the Griffith", the magazine wrote, "TVR might just have rewritten the rulebook on sports cars for all time, just as Jaguar did with the E-type more than 30 years ago. The car's list of tangible assets – thundering performance, fabulous looks, a £27,000 price tag and its build quality (a first for the small Blackpool-based company) – reads even more like a fairy tale than *Alice in Wonderland* ever did.

It was the sort of reception that any major-league car company, let alone tiny TVR, would have died for, and the fact that production didn't begin until some 18 months after the appetite-whetting unveiling showed that TVR wanted the Griffith to live up to expectations.

The longish gap from introduction to production also reflected something of modern TVR design philosophy. The marque has had a turbulent history, with highlights in many classic models and troughs in several near-terminal collapses. In 1981, though, the company was taken over by Yorkshire businessman and unashamed car fanatic Peter Wheeler, and 12 years on, it is stronger than it has ever been.

Wheeler made it work, gradually sorting out the design and infamous build-quality problems. He ended the usual reliance on American sales, settled for realistic and sustainable production targets, and started building new products based solely on the notion that the public would like the same sort of cars that Wheeler likes him-self – which means fast, uncomplicated, traditional sports cars.

The Griffith is one such, and when TVR first showed it, at the NEC in September 1990, they were doing something they have since made a speciality of – using a show car to gauge reaction in place of conventional market research. But the response to the Griffith was something even TVR themselves could hardly have dreamed of. The car was one of the major stars of the show, even faced with competition like the world debut of the open-topped Aston Virage Volante and the latest sighting of the amazing Jaguar XJ220.

There was no better compliment than the fact that enthusiasts immediately began likening the Griffith's curvaceous lines and simple, powerful character to those of a modern-day Cobra. Within hours of removing the covers from the Griffith, TVR had literally dozens of prospective buyers offering deposits for the car, and away the company went to turn the show car into production reality.

The basics were simple enough, and archetypally TVR. A jig-built tubular chassis carried all-independent suspension and disc brakes, a further developed version of the ubiquitous but still brilliant all-aluminium Rover V8 engine pro-

Left: To some extent the Griffith is a milder version of the Tuscan racer, whose enormous performance needs handling with great care.

![TVR logo]

Above: There has been a powerful V8 Griffith in TVR's line-up before, in the early 1960s. It was a model intended primarily for the North American market.

vided ample power, and TVR clothed the whole package in a simple glassfibre shell.

Making the recipe work, however, took a little time. At the showtime unveiling, the Griffith was little more than a rebodied TVR V8 (itself a newcomer), but it didn't take TVR long to work out that the extra power planned for the new car could justify some chassis development under the sleek new clothes. In the end, the Griffith kept the V8S's 90-in wheelbase and the normal tubular backbone layout, but in a form closer to that of the mighty Tuscan racer than that of the relatively mild-mannered V8S road car. The rear suspension was taken from the Tuscan virtually in its entirety, save for gentler springs and dampers and rubber rather than metal bushing; and a lot of attention was paid to platform stiffness, via careful triangulation and judicious sheet-metal gussetting. At the front, more of the V8S remained, with appropriate fine-tuning to suit the different requirements of the new car, not just in terms of handling but also of accommodating a very different exhaust system. Most noticeably, both front and rear tracks were a little wider than on the S, and the split-rim wheels were a new and substantially larger design.

Once again, power was to come from a re-worked version of the Rover V8 engine – or rather a choice of versions, from a 'basic' 240-bhp four-litre, to a slightly more powerful 250-bhp four-litre with gas-flowed heads, to the mighty 280-bhp 4.3-litre version that most testers were given to play with. Peter Wheeler, in spite of his love of big, gutsy engines, did stop just short of offering the race-bred 4.5-litre unit from the Tuscan, because although its 320 bhp sounded

attractive, it was considered to be on the outer limits of refinement, even for a TVR enthusiast.

And refinement was to be part of the Griffith, in spite of its emphasis on performance. As shown at the Birmingham launch, it had an interior based on that of the existing six-cylinder S3C, which was fairly neat but unmistakably a product of the industry's parts bins and a lot of fairly basic hand-crafting. When TVR began to see the Griffith order book filling, though, and when they looked at the way it was apparently attracting buyers who might normally have gone for more more illustrious marques, they totally re-designed the interior too, to produce an elegant and fully-trimmed cockpit.

Nothing for the money comes close

And then they clothed the car in that stunningly curvaceous body, with its distinctive scalloped doors and adornment-free lines. By the time it went into production, there weren't even any external door locks – the remote locking key worked by pointing its invisible beam at a sensor in the dashboard. Even the rear number plate was back-lit to avoid the untidiness of a tacked-on light unit.

The reworking took until late spring of 1992 and then the Griffith went on sale to generally rave reviews and full order books, the one misgiving that most testers had being about high-speed nervousness on poor surfaces. Within a couple of months, TVR were promising to rectify that during a break in production to catch up with orders for other models, which had taken a back seat to the flood of Griffith orders. More radically still, at the 1992 NEC Show they unveiled a completely new, all-TVR, V8 engine, with even more power than the most potent of Rover-based V8s and destined, naturally, for the next Griffith. It should be the last step in laying aside the image of a kit-car builder once and for all, and with the Griffith the motoring magazines were already mentioning the model's name in the same breath as some very unlikely competitors.

Let *Autocar & Motor* have the last word. They bemoaned the damping problems on poor surfaces, but of the original car they concluded: "The Griffith is so close to being a world-beater that it hurts . . . Already it possesses an armoury so full of crushing assets that nothing for the money seems close."

Left: The bonnet is lowered at the front, both for styling effect and to allow a good flow of air through the inclined radiator.

Top: There's no superfluous bodywork on the Griffith; the smooth glassfibre skin is drawn tightly over a typical TVR tubular backbone chassis to form a compact and light car with an excellent power-to-weight ratio.

Above: At the front of the Griffith is TVR's version of the ubiquitous Rover V8 engine, enlarged and modified to produce from 240 to 280 bhp depending on displacement and tune. Whatever version is chosen, the performance is shattering.

Driving the Griffith: *simply sensational*

On the road, the Griffith is as sensational as it looks, with performance that would shame supercars at many times the price. The driving position is low, but the visibility is fine. The Griffith feels small, but the performance is huge; with big-bore exhausts and the familiar V8 thunder it *sounds* like a TVR and goes like a rocket. It is slippery enough for a maximum of around 160 mph, powerful enough for a 0-60 mph time of less than five seconds and 0-100 mph in less than 11½, with the flexibility and gearing to give 50-70 mph in less than three seconds in third gear. Those are impressive figures by any standards and matched by superbly

strong brakes dealing with only just over a ton of car, including driver and fuel. The steering is heavy at low speed but becomes lighter on the move, when the ride is also better than the uncompromising looks might suggest. Although the chassis is stiff enough for scuttle-shake to be non-existent, the Griffith initially suffered problems with high-speed handling balance. On good surfaces it has incredible grip and surprisingly mild, flat-cornering manners, but at high speed on a less friendly surface the car could become unsettled and nervous – a damping problem with the rear suspension which TVR were quick to accept and confront.

PERFORMANCE & SPECIFICATION COMPARISON	Engine	Displacement	Power	Torque (lb ft)	Max speed	0-60 mph	Length (in/mm)	Wheelbase (in/mm)	Track front/rear	Weight (lb/kg)	Price
TVR Griffith	V8, overhead-valve	4280 cc	280 bhp 5500 rpm	305 lb ft 4000 rpm	161 mph 259 km/h	4.7 sec	156.1 in 3965 mm	90.0 in 2286 mm	58.0 in 58.4 in	2304 lb 1045 kg	£27,206 (1993)
Caterham Super Seven HPC	Inline-four, twin-cam, 16-valve	1998 cc	175 bhp 6000 rpm	155 lb ft 4800 rpm	126 mph 203 km/h	5.2 sec	133.5 in 3391 mm	87.8 in 2230 mm	48.8 in 52.2 in	1384 lb 628 kg	£18,255 (1993)
Lotus Elan SE	Inline-four, twin-cam, 16-valve	1588 cc	165 bhp 6600 rpm	148 lb ft 4200 rpm	136 mph 219 km/h	6.5 sec	149.7 in 3802 mm	88.6 in 2250 mm	58.5 in 58.5 in	2253 lb 1022 kg	£22,720 (1993)
Morgan Plus 8	V8, overhead-valve	3946 cc	190 bhp 4750 rpm	235 lb ft 2600 rpm	121 mph 195 km/h	6.1 sec	156.0 in 3962 mm	98.0 in 2489 mm	54.0 in 54.0 in	2059 lb 934 kg	£24,821 (1993)
Porsche 968 Cabriolet	Inline-four, twin-cam	2990 cc	240 bhp 6200 rpm	225 lb ft 4100 rpm	153 mph 246 km/h	6.1 sec	170.1 in 4320 mm	94.5 in 2400 mm	58.0 in 57.1 in	3131 lb 1420 kg	£38,724 (1993)

TVR Griffith Data File

When TVR first started in 1947, there was little to suggest that by 1992 the Blackpool-based company would have overtaken Lotus as the main British builder of low-volume, very high-performance sports cars. They have done so by realising that the market required a combination of outright performance with style and high standards of build quality. TVR offered high performance early on, with cars like the original V8 Griffith of 1963 and the Tuscan that followed, and in that respect TVR have gone back to their roots in producing the current V8 Griffith. As far as quality is concerned, however, the modern cars represent a quantum leap forward.

Right: Single halogen headlights are housed behind clear plastic covers.

Below: The sunken recess to the left of the rear light unit is purely a styling feature.

Above: There is not a straight or angular line in sight on the TVR Griffith, but its smooth, sinuous exterior hides enormous power.

Styling

In finest TVR tradition, the Griffith was styled in-house and its shell is built in simple moulds, from hand-laid, hand-finished glassfibre mat. By common consent it is produced to the highest standards the company has ever achieved, from tight and even shut lines to superb paint and trim. Also by common consent it is one of the most stunning designs for many years. It was styled by boss Peter Wheeler and engineer John Ravenscroft – almost as a sculpture, carved in full size from blocks of foam. It is long-nosed, short-tailed and softly curvy, but with proportions that ooze power; at its launch, everybody was recalling the AC Cobra. It could hardly be smoother or simpler, from covered headlamps, past the steeply-raked windscreen, to a tall, rounded tail. There are no separate bumpers, no tack-on door handles, not even external door locks to spoil the purity of line. The only obvious styling tricks are the under-bonnet air outlets created by recessing the leading edges of the doors, and the mildly 'countersunk' bonnet. Those features conveniently remove some of the shut-line problems familiar to glassfibre car builders, but the viewer doesn't need to know that, and the overall look is incredibly dramatic. And, of course, it is all topped off by one of TVR's simply folded and easily stowed convertible tops, with a removable rigid centre panel (which stows in the boot) and a rear window which drops almost out of sight behind the cockpit.

Below: The Griffith runs on low-profile tyres mounted on five-spoke alloy rims.

Below: A script badge is used rather than the mythical beast found on the original model.

Left: The door handles are flush-mounted push-buttons designed to minimise drag.

Above and right: The original Griffith of 1963 was powered by a 4.7-litre Ford V8. Although decades apart, it and the new car share some of the same design features. They are named after the American Jack Griffith, who pioneered the V8 conversion.

Below: Inspiration for the Griffith came from TVR's almost untameable V8 Tuscan racer; this attitude on the track was not untypical.

Above: Arranged on the wooden dashboard are instruments to monitor every engine function.

Left: The ultra-rounded design philosophy of the exterior is carried on in the interior.

Below: The Griffith's convertible top is delightfully simple, the rear section being held up by two struts, one of which can be seen here.

Chassis and running gear

Under the voluptuous glassfibre skin (which is bolted as a fully-finished unit onto precisely-located mountings and which contributes to the overall stiffness of the car), the Griffith would be familiar to any TVR enthusiast. The separate chassis, with the same 90-in wheelbase as the V8S, is based on a massive central backbone, jig-built in steel tubing and protected against corrosion by a tough plastic coating. It is similar to the chassis of the Tuscan racer (rather than the V8S on which the original show car was based), and it provides a suitably stiff base for all-round independent suspension. That also reflects TVR's interest in racing, with unequal-length wishbones and concentric coil spring/damper units at each corner and an anti-roll bar at the front. The front engine and gearbox (a five-speed Rover manual unit, with the change reworked by TVR) drive through a standard Quaife limited-slip differential at the rear, and sit far enough back in the chassis to give nearly 50/50 weight distribution. The five-spoke wheels are in cast alloy, split-rimmed and odd-sized at 7J × 15 in front and 7.5J × 16 in rear. They carry 215/50 ZR15 and 225/50 ZR16 Bridgestone RE71 Expedia tyres respectively, which give four big footprints. The brake system features ventilated front and solid rear discs, which operate with the help of a servo. There's no such assistance, though, for the high-geared rack-and-pinion steering, which only requires 2½ turns between locks.

Left: *The front suspension system features very wide-based wishbones. Front discs are ventilated for efficiency.*

Below: *The chassis is typical TVR in being a multi-tube backbone construction.*

Right: *The rear hub-carrier is actually fabricated, although it looks cast.*

Left: *The final drive unit is held in a very substantial cradle; the triangulated frame above it provides the location for the top rear wishbones, coil springs and telescopic dampers.*

The AJP8 engine

At the 1992 NEC Motor Show TVR dropped another bombshell: by 1993 the Griffith would be available with TVR's own V8, to give even more performance and still greater individuality. The all-new engine had been taken from concept to reality in only eight months, by Al Melling – a British engineer with a low profile but a fine pedigree, including previous work on both Formula 1 and Group C engines. The AJP8 was introduced in 4.2-litre form, with a single-plane steel crankshaft, single chain-driven overhead camshafts and two valves per cylinder, the latter aimed at keeping production costs low but with a new combustion-chamber design and a 12.3:1 compression ratio to produce ample power. TVR claimed 363 bhp at 7,000 rpm and 348 lb ft of torque at 4,500 rpm for the road, or 470 bhp and more for racing – and they intend both to sell and to lease the compact and ultra-light AJP8 engines to racing customers.

Left: *The AJP8 engine will be used in future models and is notable for its light weight, compact dimensions and power output of 363 bhp.*

Engine

The heart of the Griffith is yet another version of the incredibly versatile and successful, all-aluminium Rover V8 engine – the rights to which Rover bought from General Motors way back in the 1960s. This one is based on the 3.9-litre version currently used in the Range Rover, but comprehensively upgraded by TVR's engine-building subsidiary, TVR Power. For the Griffith, the 3.9-litre unit is bored and stroked to 94 mm × 77 mm, which gives a capacity of 4280 cc. The alloy block has additional stiffening webs welded on and the main bearing locations are strengthened by additional bolting to cope with the extra capacity and power. The flywheel is lightened and balanced, the two-valves-per-cylinder heads are gas-flowed and the ports are polished, while the single central camshaft is treated to a high-performance re-profiling. Big-bore tubular exhaust manifolds are used, and with the engine sitting so far back in the Griffith's chassis the four separate pipes from each cylinder bank run forward into massive single pipes before they are routed backwards under the chassis. The engine isn't particularly sophisticated, but it is very potent; with a 10.0:1 compression ratio and specially-remapped Lucas electronic engine management, it produces claimed maxima of 280 bhp at 5,500 rpm and an even more impressive 305 lb ft of torque at 4,000 rpm, but with a spread of torque which starts way down the rev range and stays usefully above 250 lb ft all the way from 2,000 rpm to almost 6,000 rpm, beyond the power-peak engine speed.

Above: *Cooling is assisted by a pair of electric fans, thermostatically controlled.*

Above: *The twin-rear-wishbone suspension is clearly visible in the cutaway. The concentric coil spring/damper unit is mounted ahead of the driveshaft to provide clearance.*

Above: *Chassis members extend to the sides of the car at floor level to help give side-impact protection for the occupants.*

Above: To allow the V8 to be mounted low down and as far back in the engine bay as possible, the tubular exhaust manifolds were routed to a common pipe at the front of the power unit, with the exhaust then flowing into twin pipes.

Below: The tall alloy cylinder in the centre of the engine bay ahead of the V8 is the coolant header tank.

Above: Despite its larger displacement, the engine used in the Griffith is still recognisably the old Rover V8 unit with its distinctive belt ancillary drives and long water pump (mounted below the alternator). Note that the exhaust manifold ports are still square, just as they were on the original design.

Left: Like most production pushrod overhead-valve V8 engines, the Rover V8 (from which the TVR unit was developed) is an American design. Unusually for an American engine, however, it is all-alloy rather than the traditional cast-iron. Original displacement was 3.5 litres and its power output, at a fraction over 150 bhp, is far removed from the Griffith's 280 bhp.

Below: The Griffith's nose projects well forward past the front chassis cross-members, onto which is mounted the anti-roll bar.

Venturi 260

The French Venturi 260 is a recent addition to the ranks of European supercars. Built by MVS, and developed by racing drivers, the mid-engined Venturi produces 260 bhp to give a top speed near 170 mph and startling acceleration.

Above: In appearance, the Venturi is perhaps the most understated of all modern supercars. In many ways, it could be mistaken for an English specialist car, which probably explains why 100 cars – almost half the production run – are destined to come to this country.

hen the prototype of the MVS Venturi was displayed at the Paris Motor Show in 1984, it was impossible to predict if it could be more than just another speculative 'show special'. Few thought that, only two years later, the first production car would be on display in the same hall.

The quality of construction of that first show car was impressive, and the people behind it had impeccable credentials, but France, at least since the end of World War II, has had scant reputation as a producer of high-performance road cars, and it is far harder to raise the capital to set up a production line than it is to create one well-finished prototype and then relapse into obscurity.

MVS stands, rather prosaically, for *Manufacture des Voitures de Sport*, the word 'manufacture' translating as 'hand-built'. The men behind the creation of MVS were Gérard Godfroy and Claude Poiraud. The basic car shape, as shown in the full-scale model at the Paris Motor Show, was created by Godfroy, a designer formerly employed by Heuliez (a specialist design house, also in western France) and Peugeot, with the engineering conceived by Poiraud, who later became chairman and factory manager.

That first car was called the Ventury, but the

last letter was later changed to 'i', to return to the aerodynamic term on which the name had been based originally.

The speculative venture of Godfroy and Poiraud paid off: they attracted backing from financiers Hervé Boulan and Hervé Lejeune, and MVS was created. This in turn captured the attention of Jean Rondeau, a successful French racing driver who had won the Le Mans 24 Hours in 1980 in a car bearing his own name. Thus was born a new contender in the supercar market.

Rondeau offered technical assistance in developing the chassis and handling of the Ventury, as well as workshop facilities at his Le Mans-based factory.

Tested by racing drivers Bianchi and Beltoise

By December 1985, the first car was undergoing trials, powered by a turbocharged four-cylinder engine (taken from the Peugeot 505). Top speed was claimed to be 155 mph, with 0-60 mph in seven seconds.

By May 1986, when the first cars were ready for sale, the four-cylinder engine had been re-

placed by a 200-bhp version of the PRV (Peugeot-Renault-Volvo) V6 turbo, which formed the basis of the considerably modified engines still used in Venturis today.

The original suspension, by MacPherson struts, was discarded and replaced with the more complex system used today. That was following tests by racing drivers Mauro Bianchi and Jean-Pierre Beltoise, Jean Rondeau having died in a road accident when his Porsche 911 was hit by a train on a level crossing.

Production began at Cholet in western France (about 30 miles from Nantes) in June 1987, and continued there until early in 1991 when a new, purpose-built 59,000-sq ft factory was opened at Coueron, downstream of Nantes on the River Loire. The research and development department continues to be controlled by Claude Poiraud at Le Mans, some 120 miles north-east of Coueron.

A change of ownership of MVS occurred in June 1989, when Primwest France took a 90 per cent share in the company. Primwest was already involved in the motor industry through its president, Xavier de la Chapelle, who also owns Automobiles de la Chapelle (producing BMW-engined replicas of the Bugatti Type 55 and an enormous 'people carrier' with a choice of Jaguar

V12 or Mercedes V8 engines). At this time, MVS's working capital was doubled.

The takeover coincided with the introduction of the cabriolet, with its 'Transcoupé' modular roof system and retractable roll-over bar/ heated rear window arrangement.

In May 1991, there was a substantial injection of extra finance, increasing the company's total capital to £18.5 million, when the industrial group Omnium Europe took a 10 per cent stake.

The new Coueron factory is part of a 9.8-acre site which will have its own 1.2-mile test track. Late in 1991, 70 people were employed there, but the intention is to double that when the target production figure (500 units a year on a single shift) is reached.

At the 1991 French Grand Prix, MVS announced a sponsorship deal with Gérard Larrousse's Formula 1 team, and in January 1992, MVS bought the entire outfit to become a fully-fledged Grand Prix entrant. If nothing else, this should give the Venturi a high profile appropriate to a modern supercar.

Although the basis of the Venturi's engines is the same as that of those fitted to Alpines (the PRV V6), in the MVS the power unit is mounted ahead of the rear axle line, whereas the Alpine is truly rear-engined.

A hint of Lotus influence

With 260 bhp, the more expensive '260' version of the Venturi uses the most powerful roadgoing version of the PRV engine yet produced (though staggering outputs were achieved several years ago by the WM-Peugeot Le Mans cars: they became renowned for heading the Porsches, Lancias and the rest for 10 laps or so before 'grenading' spectacularly; it didn't matter – 10 minutes of prime TV had been captured).

MVS claims a maximum speed of 168 mph for the 260, with 0-62 mph (100 km/h) in 5.3 seconds, and a standing quarter-mile in 24.6 seconds – all very impressive figures if correct (and they are probably not far off). The lesser 210 is no slouch, either, with 0-62 mph in a claimed 6.9 seconds, on the way to a maximum speed of 152 mph and a standing quarter-mile in 26.8 seconds.

In appearance, the MVS Venturi is perhaps the most discreet and understated of all modern high-performance cars. If a hint of Lotus (or possibly Ferrari) influence can be found in its clean lines, it is no more than that; the car has its own distinct shape and character, though it is a character without strongly national 'cues'. All those involved in the design and manufacture of the Venturi are French, and almost all the components are sourced from France, but its country of origin is not immediately obvious to the eye, unlike many French designs.

Indeed, in many ways the Venturi could easily be mistaken for an English specialist car, which goes some way towards explaining why no fewer than 100 of MVS's currently planned annual production total of 250 cars are right-hand-drive versions destined to be distributed in Britain by the importer, Raptor (UK) Ltd.

In Britain, the starting price tag on a new Venturi (the 210 coupé) is £45,443, rising to £55,371 for the 210 cabriolet. The more expensive 260 cabriolet costs over £59,000.

Above: The basic shape of the Venturi was created by Gérard Godfroy, a designer formerly employed by Heuliez and Peugeot. French racer Jean Rondeau offered technical assistance in developing the chassis and handling. From behind the wheel, this racing pedigree shines through.

Overleaf: The performance claims for the 260 cabriolet are a top speed of 168 mph and 0-62 mph in 5.3 seconds. On the road, these figures seem only mildly optimistic.

Driving the Venturi: *plastic perfection*

An unfortunate quality of most modern high-performance cars is their sheer width, so MVS has done well to keep the Venturi relatively narrow: at 66.9 inches wide, it's six inches narrower than the Lotus Esprit, which makes it more nimble.

The Venturi is probably the world's best-built plastic-bodied car, and no other mid-engined car offers more space for two people.

It has safe yet satisfying overall handling, including tenacious grip, predictable and progressive breakaway, clean steering responses and powerful brakes, combined with more than acceptable ride quality.

The 260 is clearly not short of power, and the claimed performance figures seem only mildly optimistic, though there may perhaps not be quite as much torque quite as low in the range as the manufacturer hopes. While much worthwhile tuning is evident, this is not the sweetest engine in the world, and the gear change is only adequate.

MVS provides useable performance in a surprisingly practical package. The image, so vital in this sector of the market, is being constructed. The only question is whether buyers are yet ready to pay Porsche 911 prices for a plastic-bodied sports car, however good.

PERFORMANCE & SPECIFICATION COMPARISON	Engine	Displacement	Power	Torque (lb ft)	Max speed	0-60 mph	Length (in/mm)	Wheelbase (in/mm)	Track front/rear	Weight (lb/kg)	Price
MVS Venturi 260	V6, overhead-cam, turbo	2849 cc	260 bhp 5500 rpm	318 lb ft 2000 rpm	168 mph 270 km/h	5.1 sec	161.0 in 4089 mm	94.5 in 2400 mm	57.5 in 57.9 in	2866 lb 1300 kg	£59,825 (1992)
Ferrari 348 tb	V8, quad-cam, 32-valve	3405 cc	300 bhp 7000 rpm	224 lb ft 4000 rpm	163 mph 262 km/h	5.6 sec	166.5 in 4229 mm	96.5 in 2450 mm	59.0 in 62.2 in	3300 lb 1497 kg	£76,534 (1992)
Honda NSX	V6, quad-cam, 24-valve	2977 cc	274 bhp 7000 rpm	210 lb ft 5300 rpm	162 mph 261 km/h	5.2 sec	173.4 in 4405 mm	99.6 in 2530 mm	59.4 in 60.2 in	3020 lb 1370 kg	£55,000 (1992)
Lotus Esprit Turbo SE	Inline-four, twin-cam, turbo	2174 cc	264 bhp 6500 rpm	261 lb ft 3900 rpm	161 mph 259 km/h	4.9 sec	171.0 in 4343 mm	96.0 in 2438 mm	60.0 in 61.2 in	2650 lb 1202 kg	£48,260 (1992)
Renault GTA Turbo	V6, overhead-cam, turbo	2458 cc	200 bhp 5500 rpm	214 lb ft 2250 rpm	149 mph 240 km/h	6.3 sec	173.8 in 4415 mm	92.1 in 2339 mm	59.2 in 57.2 in	2328 lb 1056 kg	£31,720 (1992)

MVS Venturi Data File

 was founded in 1985 by Gérard Godfroy and Claude Poiraud, who still run the company. Having raised finance by displaying a full-scale model of their proposed car at the 1984 Paris Motor Show, they returned to Paris with the first Venturi production car in 1986. Two years later, the cabriolet was introduced at the same show. At the Geneva Show in March 1990, the 2.85-litre version made its debut, still based on the PRV V6 which has been used in the Venturi from the beginning (the two-litre, four-cylinder turbo from the Peugeot 505 was dropped before production began).

Up to now, the MVS Venturi has been little known outside a small circle of enthusiasts. However, with considerable capital behind it, and having launched itself into the heady world of Formula 1 motor racing, MVS could be on the brink of much wider fame and recognition.

Above: There are hints of Lotus in the Venturi's styling, and, like the Lotus, it features a glassfibre body.

Above: The plastic front bumper houses recessed driving lamps. The main headlamps are pop-up.

Styling

Designed by Gérard Godfroy, the Venturi is available in two body styles: a coupé and a cabriolet. The aerodynamic term 'Venturi' was chosen as a name to underline the design team's commitment to aerodynamic integrity, although this does not indicate a pursuit of the least resistance to airflow at the expense of all other considerations.

The final shape of the Venturi was arrived at after extensive testing at the St Cyr University's wind tunnel, under the direction of aerodynamicist Robert Choulet, who had been responsible for the aerodynamics of Jean Rondeau's successful Le Mans cars.

The Venturi has a 0.31 Cd factor, and the CdA (efficiency multiplied by frontal area) is 0.496. Neither of these figures sets any records these days, but the Cd is comfortably below the generally agreed critical point, and Godfroy and Choulet set out to provide a satisfactory compromise between sheer aerodynamic efficiency and stability.

The point is that, once the Cd factor is below 0.35, the law of diminishing returns sets in; the benefit will be only marginal improvements in performance and economy. It isn't merely that the lower Cd you achieve, the more it costs, but any gains in smooth passage through the air must be offset against losses in stability, and in particular, a car's resistance to cross-winds.

Right: A well-integrated wrap-around rear apron contributes greatly to the car's smooth, rounded lines. Note the large-bore tail pipe.

Below: The solid roof is in two pieces. Half or all of it can be removed and stored in the boot. The rear window folds away flush with the bodywork.

Right: The window and roll-over bar are operated electrically.

Below: In right-hand-drive form, the Venturi costs from £45,443 to £55,371.

Below: Connolly leather and wood door cappings are optional in the opulent interior. Note the removed roof panels in the front boot.

Body and chassis

A unique approach is to be found in the body/chassis design of the Venturi. It is true that the steel chassis contains a backbone similar to the type pioneered by Lotus, and since followed by that other French specialist manufacturer, Alpine. But in this case the chassis outriggers and body mounting points extend further, and the 'tub' is completed by filling in all the spaces with steel panels.

The chassis assembly is extensively rust-proofed, with a catophoretic dip, before the body (treated with an anti-chip compound) is bonded to it, and then the body and chassis together form a monocoque. In the coupé, the roll-over hoop is integrated with the roof, but a pop-up system (similar to that found in the Mercedes-Benz SL) is used in the cabriolet.

It is a complex manufacturing process, but produces an exceptionally rigid shell, likely to give better torsional and beam stiffness than is found in many plastic-bodied cars. The proportion of plastics here, in any case, is considerably lower. The engine is inside a tubular subframe which is bolted to the chassis and to which the rear suspension is attached.

MVS's confidence in its product is reflected in a four-year warranty against corrosion, two years against paint defects, and 12 months for all mechanical components.

Below: The one-piece body, made from a variety of composite materials, is bonded to the chassis for extra stiffness.

Suspension and brakes

The Venturi's front end is suspended conventionally, which means by upper and lower wishbones, coil spring/damper units and an anti-roll bar.

At the rear, a more complex five-link system was chosen. This consists of one upper arm located by a single tie-bar and two parallel lower rods with an adjustable tie-bar. Again there are coil spring/dampers and an anti-roll bar. Compliant bushing is used in the rear suspension in order to provide a small degree of passive rear-wheel steering.

Large (11-in diameter) ventilated disc brakes are fitted to each corner. The dual-circuit system is servo-assisted, and the mechanical parking brake acts upon the rear discs. A Wabco anti-lock system is fitted.

Above: The Venturi could be driven without its external body panels.

Below: The front-wishbone suspension uses coil spring/damper units.

Engine

Two versions of the turbocharged V6 are available to Venturi buyers, designated 210 and 260, the numbers referring to the horsepower. The engines are given a modified Renault designation: the 210 is the Z7U-730, and its more powerful version is Z7W. Both are extensively modified in detail by MVS's engineers.

This 90-degree V6 is all-aluminium (both the cylinder block and heads) and has four main bearings and removable wet liners. There is one chain-driven camshaft for each bank, and only two valves per cylinder, operated via rockers.

In both engines, the turbocharger is a water-cooled Garrett T3, with an air-to-air intercooler, and both are fitted with a three-way exhaust catalyst, so they run on unleaded fuel (minimum 95 RON, which means our 'premium' four-star grade).

The 260 is based on the biggest engine that Renault fits to the Alpine and its large saloon, the 25. But Renault, unlike MVS, does not turbocharge this longer-stroke (73-mm) variant, in which the capacity (with unchanged bore) is extended to 2849 cc, so does not get near to the 260's power output (still produced at 5,500 rpm) or torque, claimed to be a thumping 318 lb ft at only 2,000 rpm.

MVS fits new pistons, re-profiled camshafts, stronger valve springs and, of course (because in most Renault applications, the engine is mounted over the front axle), an entirely new exhaust system.

The compression ratio is raised slightly, to 8.2:1, and boost pressure goes up to 0.95 bar. AEI Renix numerical engine management is fitted, controlling both fuel injection and ignition.

Above: Two versions of the turbocharged V6 engine are available, with 210 and 260 bhp. Access to the narrow engine bay is restricted.

Above: Large, 11-in diameter, ventilated disc brakes are fitted to each corner. The dual-circuit system is servo-assisted and an Wabco anti-lock system is fitted as standard equipment. Front tyre size is 205/55 ZR16.

Right: A complex five-link system is used for the rear suspension. It consists of one upper arm located by a single tie-bar and two parallel lower rods per side.

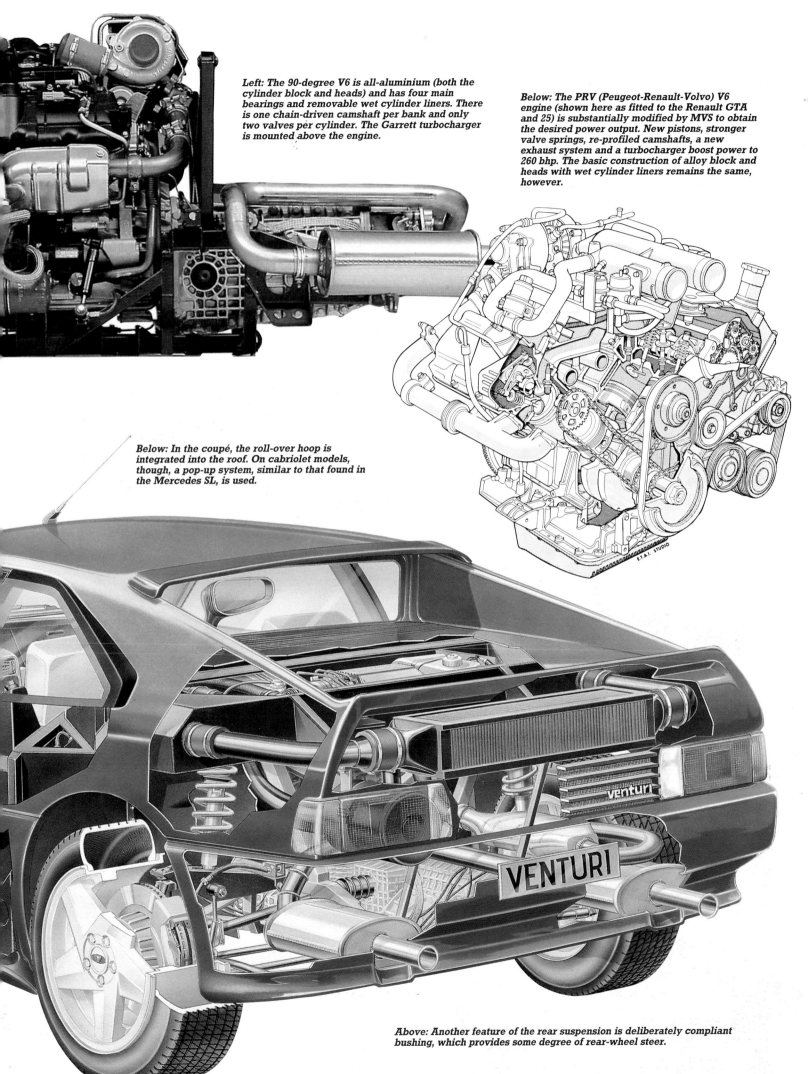

Left: The 90-degree V6 is all-aluminium (both the cylinder block and heads) and has four main bearings and removable wet cylinder liners. There is one chain-driven camshaft per bank and only two valves per cylinder. The Garrett turbocharger is mounted above the engine.

Below: The PRV (Peugeot-Renault-Volvo) V6 engine (shown here as fitted to the Renault GTA and 25) is substantially modified by MVS to obtain the desired power output. New pistons, stronger valve springs, re-profiled camshafts, a new exhaust system and a turbocharger boost power to 260 bhp. The basic construction of alloy block and heads with wet cylinder liners remains the same, however.

Below: In the coupé, the roll-over hoop is integrated into the roof. On cabriolet models, though, a pop-up system, similar to that found in the Mercedes SL, is used.

Above: Another feature of the rear suspension is deliberately compliant bushing, which provides some degree of rear-wheel steer.